Confessions

of a

REAL ESTATE ENTREPRENEUR

Confessions

of a

REAL ESTATE ENTREPRENEUR

What It Takes to Win in High-Stakes Commercial Real Estate

James A. Randel

McGraw-Hill

New York Chicago San Francisco Lisbon London
Madrid Mexico City Milan New Delhi San Juan
Seoul Singapore Sydney Toronto

2 3 4 5 6 7 8 9 0 FGR/FGR 0 9 8 7 6

ISBN 0-07-146793-9

This publication is designed to provide accurate and authoritative information in regard to the subject matter covered. It is sold with the understanding that neither the author nor the publisher is engaged in rendering legal, accounting, futures/securities trading, or other professional service. If legal advice or other expert assistance is required, the services of a competent professional person should be sought.

—From a Declaration of Principles jointly adopted by a Committee of the American Bar Association and a Committee of Publishers

McGraw-Hill books are available at special quantity discounts to use as premiums and sales promotions, or for use in corporate training programs. For more information, please write to the Director of Special Sales, Professional Publishing, McGraw-Hill, Two Penn Plaza, New York, NY 10121-2298. Or contact your local bookstore.

Library of Congress Cataloging-in-Publication Data

Randel, James A.
    Confessions of a real estate entrepreneur : what it takes to win in high-stakes commercial real estate / by James A. Randel.
        p.   cm.
    Includes index.
    ISBN 0-07-146793-9 (alk. paper)
    1. Commercial real estate. 2. Real estate investment. 3. Commercial real estate—United States. 4. Real estate investment—United States. I. Title.
HD1393.55.R36 2006
332.63'24—dc22
                                                                                2005030874

Contents

Knowledge is power.

SIR FRANCIS BACON (1561–1626)

Power is the faculty or capacity to act, the strength and potency to accomplish something. It is the vital energy to make choices and decisions. It also includes the capacity to overcome deeply embedded habits and to cultivate higher, more effective ones.

GEORGE BERNARD SHAW (1856–1950)

1

Introduction: Learning to Add Value

I graduated law school in 1974 and immediately started buying real estate (a two-family house in Los Angeles). I had no money and as "necessity is the mother of invention," I had to be very inventive. In the next 10 years I bought and sold 50 or so investment properties.

I also became an active real estate attorney and real estate broker. My assumption was that if real estate was involved, I should be able to figure out how to make money buying, selling, brokering, or lawyering it. I soon began to think of myself as a real estate entrepreneur, someone who took risks in an effort to turn time, information, and some capital into much, much more capital.

In 1985, I wrote a book titled *The Real Estate Game (And How to Win It)*. That book advocated real estate as an investment but was limited to what I had learned up to that point in my life. In the 20 years since writing *The Real Estate Game,* I have continued to buy and sell. Only the deals got bigger and bigger. And I learned a lot about maximizing one's success with real estate entrepreneuring.

One of the points of *The Real Estate Game* was that you could use real estate to obtain wealth, simply by buying and holding. And that still is true. Notwithstanding a relatively low rate of inflation over the last five years, real estate appreciation has continued to clip along at double-digit numbers.

Over the last 20 years I have observed that whereas buying and holding is certainly a valid (fairly safe) strategy for making money with real estate, there are other—and I dare say better—ways for doing that. These are the strategies employed by the super-successful real estate players. These are techniques used by entrepreneurs who are not satisfied with a "reasonable" return on their investment. The Dow Jones may go up in a year by 10 percent, and equity investors are generally pleased with that. On the other hand, the real estate entrepreneurs I know would be quite disappointed with a 10 percent return on their equity. These people are looking for multiples many, many times a 10 percent return.

Now before we start down our path of learning, let me make one important point: real estate, as with most entrepreneurial endeavors, has a risk-reward quotient. If you are looking for risk-free ways to make a ton of money in real estate, toss this book. I have never seen such things. Certainly, risk can be quantified and minimized, but life in the real estate world is pretty simple: the greater the risk, the greater the potential reward.

In that regard, I am NOT A FAN of the real estate promoters who write books about making money in real estate with no or little cash invested. Or who hold seminars claiming to make their attendees instant millionaires. Sorry, guys, I just don't buy it.

Real estate investing is not some magic potion to riches. Yes, it's a means for making a lot of money. *But* it's no risk-free, lazy man's way to wealth. It's hard work. And there is definitely risk involved. But with information, diligence, determination, and calculated risk, there is *plenty* of opportunity to make A LOT of money.

One last disclaimer: I tell many stories in the pages to follow. All of them are actual deals that I was involved with (sometimes with names or numbers changed a little bit so as not to offend anyone) or are compilations of several similar deals in which I participated. Some of these deals make me look very smart. My intent is not chest-pounding. The point of these stories is to show you what can be done if you are a knowledgeable real estate entrepreneur. But as you will discover, I have also made my share of mistakes. And frankly, one of the reasons for writing this book 20 years after my last venture into publishing is that I wish I'd had a road map to follow that would have helped me avoid some of the real stupid stuff I have done. I hope that this book can be that kind of road map for you.

So, you in? Okay, then let's get going.

The General Premise

My belief is that in order to maximize your success in real estate investing you need to ADD VALUE to either the process by which you acquire property and/or the property itself.

Introduction: Learning to Add Value

The techniques that I write about in ensuing chapters are all about ADDING VALUE; in other words, finding some way to TIP A DEAL IN YOUR FAVOR. There are techniques for creative acquisition, for finding hidden wealth in a property, for using other people's money to generate disproportionate returns, for using information to create outsized commissions, and so on. Hopefully, you noticed the quotation at the beginning of this book ("Knowledge is power"). I am a great believer in that statement. With knowledge, you have the power to catapult your existing net worth to a level you may have only dreamed about. My goal is to impart some of that knowledge to you . . . to get you familiar with the types of techniques that I have seen work time and again. To give you a good foundation in the basics of real estate investing so you can exercise your own creative muscles to find new, exciting, and lucrative ways to do deals. There is no one right way.

By the way, real estate entrepreneuring is gender neutral. Most of the time in this book I use the word "he" instead of "he or she" just to save space. And speaking of words, please note that at times I address real estate entrepreneurs as "players." I am using the terms synonymously.

The next chapter is a story—a true story—about friends of mine who made almost $3 million in two years on an investment of $100,000. I was their attorney, so I did not share in the upside, but that deal widened my eyes to the wondrous possibilities open to the creative and intelligent real estate entrepreneur. As such, I thought it would be a good starting point for you, as it was for me.

2

Possibilities

I want to start my book with a story. A true story. It helped open my eyes to the possibilities of success with real estate once you know the principles of intelligent real estate entrepreneuring. In the storytelling, I may use terms that are not yet familiar to you; don't worry about that. We will learn about these concepts. For now just enjoy the "rags to riches" result.

Years ago two friends of mine were interested in buying a building in Shelton, Connecticut. I was their attorney. The building was 66,000 square feet, commonly called "flex" space, meaning that its style and configuration made it flexible, that is, usable for office, assemblage, light industrial, or Research and Development (R&D).

My two friends had done their homework, learning about the Shelton market and especially about flex buildings like the one they were interested in. They knew what type of companies would be interested in that type of space. They knew what rents the market was commanding. This homework had taken them no more than two weeks; they just talked to everyone in the business who would speak with them.

Although my friends have since both gone on to great things in the real estate world (making lots of money), at the time they did not have a lot of money. They were, however, both very entrepreneurial.

The owner of the building ("Owner") was prepared to sell for $5.5 million. There was a tenant ("Tenant") in the building occupying the entire 66,000 square feet. The Tenant was paying a rent of $660,000 (triple net, i.e., plus all expenses of ownership). The problem was, the Tenant was not a good credit risk and could go out of business at any time. And without the Tenant paying rent, the deal was problematic.

To complicate things, the Tenant also had a $1 million mortgage on the property. This mortgage was the result of a transaction between the Tenant and the Owner years earlier. It was "assumable" (see Chapter 3) and contained some very important language, known as a "subordination clause," which read something like this:

> Tenant agrees to subordinate the lien of its mortgage to a subsequent lien if the amount of the said subsequent lien does not exceed 70 percent of the fair market value of the Property.

We'll learn all about subordination clauses later in the book. For now just understand that this clause allowed the Owner (or Purchaser) to get a new mortgage, which would be in first position—with the Tenant's mortgage moving to second position. As you'll see in Chapter 3, these distinctions are important to lenders.

My friends found a lender willing to loan them $4.5 million to buy the property. Still, they needed $1 million. Unfortunately, they did not have $1 million. So they took another look at the Tenant's mortgage. Could they buy, leaving that mortgage in place (assuming the debt), thereby needing only $4.5 million to close? And since they had an offer for a $4.5 million first mortgage . . . well, keep reading.

My friends realized that this deal had NO CASH possibilities. If they could convince a lender to make a $4.5 million first mortgage loan, and leave the Tenant's mortgage in place, they could buy this property with no money. First my friends had to speak with the prospective $4.5 million lender, and here is how that discussion went:

FRIEND: As you know, there is an existing $1 million assumable mortgage on the property and we can subordinate that lien to your loan. So, you will be in first position.

LENDER: Yes, well that's good, but if I'm doing my math correctly that means you buy with no cash in the deal. We want to see some of your skin in the game.

FRIEND: Well, we actually do have skin in the game. First of all we will have plus or minus $100,000 in closing costs. That's real money. But second and perhaps more important, don't punish us because we have created a great deal. We're buying this property for $5.5 million but if you capitalize the $660,000 of annual net income the Tenant is paying, the property is worth conservatively $6.6 million, and the extra $1.1 million over the purchase price is really our equity, albeit sweat equity.

LENDER: That does make sense to me.

Note: Perhaps the lender had not done as much due diligence on the Tenant as it should have. One of the reasons that my friends were able to get the deal for $5.5 million was because of the dubious creditworthiness of the Tenant. And without the $660,000 per year of rent flowing in, the property was worth well below $5.5 million.

Anyway, the $4.5 million lender agreed to make the loan. **Step #1.** Now my friends had to remind the Tenant of its obligation to subordinate its mortgage to the lien of a new lender. But the Tenant was not without bargaining power because of the cap in the subordination clause: to a lien not in excess of 70 percent of market value. Fortunately, here again the creativity and persuasiveness of my friends prevailed.

Here's how that meeting went:

TENANT: Why should I subordinate to a new first mortgage of $4.5 million? That puts my mortgage in a much worse position than it is now. If you get into trouble with the building, I have a $4.5 million lien ahead of me. That's the reason for the 70 percent cap in the subordination language, and the new $4.5 million loan is well beyond 70 percent of the market value of the property.

FRIEND: Well, no, it really isn't. True, we are paying $5.5 million for the deal, but candidly, we got a good deal and we believe that the true market value of the building is $6.6 million. The reason we're getting the deal is that some people are worried about your company continuing to pay rent, and we've done our homework and concluded that you will not default on your lease. Am I right?

TENANT: Well, of course you're right. We are not going to default. We've been in business for 20 years and I'm sick of hearing about our shaky financial position.

FRIEND: Right. That's why the true market value of this building is $6.6 million or more and why the $4.5 million does not really exceed the 70 percent threshold.

TENANT: Hmmm . . . (thinking)

FRIEND: But I am going to make your decision even easier. Here is what we're willing to do: Under your Lease Agreement you are paying rent of $55,000 per month. The debt service on our new mortgage is $30,000 per month. The debt service on your mortgage—which as you know is being amortized very quickly—is $20,000 per month. Instead of paying us rent every month of $55,000, we'll agree that you pay the first mortgage and your mortgage instead, and then just $5,000 per month to us. That way you don't have to worry about our ever defaulting on the mortgage ahead of you . . . or on your mortgage, for that matter.

TENANT: Okay, that seems fair. I agree. **Step #2.**

Let's review what my friends have done so far. They were now able to buy a $5.5 million property with none of their own cash although they did have closing costs of about $100,000 (some portion of which went to me as the attorney—as you'll see, I wish I had a piece of the deal instead). As soon as they closed the purchase, they began to troll for opportunities to add value.

And, as things can happen, opportunity found them. A month or two after closing, we hear that the Tenant has decided to sublease its space and, in fact, has found a subtenant willing to take over the Lease. What's more, this subtenant is willing to pay the Tenant more rent than the Tenant is paying my friends.

As you will recall, the Tenant is paying my friends $660,000 per year in rent. There are about 9.5 years to go on the Lease Agreement. The rent is flat, that is, no increases over the remaining term. But the subtenant is willing to pay the Tenant $660,000 per year for the first 4.5 years of the sublease and then $850,000 per year for the next five years. Because the Lease Agreement does not have a clause requiring the Tenant to share the excess $190,000 a year (beginning in year six) with the Owner, none of that extra money goes to my friends. Still, it is a good thing to have additional revenue coming to the property, and my friends, being appreciative of the Tenant's willingness to subordinate its $1 million lien to the new $4.5 million mortgage (above), consent to the sublease.

The Tenant vacates and the subtenant moves in—and now things get interesting. It turns out that the subtenant is positioning itself to be bought (which is why it wanted much larger space, i.e., the 66,000 square feet, than it had been occupying), and one of the suitors is a AAA credit Fortune 100 company. This company decides it wants to buy the subtenant BUT wants to create a new entity to own the subtenant, so that the Fortune 100 company's credit is not exposed to the subtenant's obligations. My friends are against that. What they want is a AAA credit behind the subtenant's obligations. They know that is a good thing because as long as the subtenant is meeting its obligation to the Tenant, then the Tenant will meet its obligation to them. Having the AAA credit on the hook keeps the financial structure of this arrangement intact.

The Sublease and Assignment clause in the Lease reads as follows:

Tenant, or any Subtenant or assignee, may not sublease or assign this Lease, without the consent of the Landlord, which consent shall not be unreasonably withheld. In addition, should Tenant, Subtenant, or an assignee transfer a majority of its ownership interest, that act shall be considered an assignment hereunder, which shall require the Landlord's consent.

Possibilities

The Fortune 100 company takes the position that my friends would be unreasonable in withholding consent to an "assignment," that is, the purchase of the subtenant by the new entity they are forming. But again my friends' creativity and preparation carry the day:

FRIEND: Listen, the whole point of a Landlord consent clause is to give the Landlord some assurance that the assignment will not impact his property. We know the owner of the subtenant. He is a local man with lots of ties to the community. We know that he will meet his obligations under the Sublease if for no other reason than to keep his word to his employees, friends, and neighbors who have worked for him for many years. But once your new entity takes over, there is none of that local protection. In six months, a person in California could decide to collapse the new entity and stop paying the rent due under the Sublease. That will not work for us and we are not giving our consent.

FORTUNE 100 COMPANY: You are being patently unreasonable.

FRIEND: Maybe so . . . but you are talking about a multimillion-dollar acquisition that you want to get done, and fighting us in court will take a year or more. All we are asking you to do is give us a solid commitment to keeping your contractual obligations under the Sublease.

That point was hard to argue with, and the Fortune 100 company caved and guaranteed the Sublease. **Step #3.** The next day my friends and I meet to brainstorm:

FRIEND #1: Let's recap what we have. We have a good building in a good location with a flat rent for 9.5 years of $660,000 per year. But we also have a Sublease that increases the rent in 4.5 years to $850,000. And that Sublease rent is guaranteed by a AAA credit. We should be able to do something with this.

FRIEND #2: How about this? Suppose we go to the Tenant and offer to buy him out. We owe him about $950,000 on his mortgage. Suppose we offer him that amount plus something for the $190,000 in extra rent he will be receiving from the subtenant for five years beginning 4.5 years from now?

ME: Yes, good idea, but that additional rent is worth almost another million dollars: five times $190,000 per year.

FRIEND #2 (SMILING): Randel, that's why you're the lawyer. You still do not understand present valuing.

ME: Huh?

FRIEND #1: Well, money in the future is not worth the same as money in the present. The fact is, the right to receive $190,000 4.5 years from now is worth much less than $190,000. And that decrease to present value is even more dramatic for the subsequent years.

FRIEND #2: We can find someone to help us do the math, but I would guess that the right to receive $190,000 a year in years six, seven, eight, nine, and ten of the Sublease is only worth about $350,000 today. *But*—and here's the cool part—the lending world won't be thinking about present value, they'll just look at the face rent increases and capitalize that.

ME: Huh?

FRIEND #1: Don't they teach you anything in law school? The lending world will look at our rent stream and lend us against some multiple of that. That's what is meant by capitalizing rental income. It's the same thing that a buyer will do. And since we now have a AAA credit behind that rent obligation, a lender will know that in years six to ten, our rent will assuredly be $850,000 per year, which fact will be significant to the amount they will lend us today.

ME: Oh, I get it.

And that's just what happened:

1. My friends went to the Tenant and offered to buy him out of his mortgage and leasehold position for $1.3 million. My friends showed the Tenant the math on the present valuation, the Tenant saw that the math was correct and agreed to my friends' offer. **Step #4.**
2. My friends found a lender who was willing to make them a $6 million loan if they controlled the leasehold. In other words, if my friends could show that they would be receiving rent for 4.5 years of $660,000 per year and then five additional years of $850,000 per year (backed by a AAA credit), the lender was very comfortable with a $6 million loan.
3. My friends closed the $6 million loan, paid off the first lender ($4.5 million), paid off the Tenant's mortgage and bought its leasehold position ($1.3 million), paid all their closing costs, and put about $50,000 in their pocket. **Step #5.**

Good, but still not the end of the story, for the real play results from the ADDED VALUE my friends created in this property. Here is what they now own: A 66,000-square-foot building leased to a AAA credit tenant with a 9.5 year lease and a rent flow of $660,000 per year for 4.5 years and then $850,000 per year for the ensuing five years. At a cap rate of 8 percent (lower than market at the time, but justified by the big bump in rents in years six through ten), the building was worth plus or minus $8,250,000, and in fact my friends sold the property for just that price to a happy, institutional buyer. (Later in the book I will speak at length about how entrepreneurs make fortunes doing their thing, adding value, and then selling to nonentrepreneurial, institutional buyers.) **Step #6.**

As you can see, my friends did quite well for themselves: They invested $100,000 (closing costs) to buy a $5.5 million property. Two years later they sold it for $8,250,000, almost a $3 million profit and an obscene return on their $100,000 investment (how does 1,500 percent per year sound?). How did they do this? Was it luck? NO . . . NO . . . NO. And that's the point!

These guys were smart real estate entrepreneurs. They are both still my friends, and neither one would mind me saying that he's no "brain surgeon." They are just creative guys who understand all the concepts and principles of the real estate game.

They are also risk takers. As one of them said to me recently: "We really had no idea where we were going with the deal when we first got into it. All we knew was that it was a good, well-located building in a decent market and we believed that once we owned it we would find opportunities to add value." In other words, these entrepreneurs knew what a lot of entrepreneurs know: confidence comes from knowledge, knowledge of a market and knowledge of the tools to add value. The path to success is not always clear at first. What my friends relied upon was their instinct that good real estate will sooner or later present opportunities for reward.

Conclusion

This story may sound a bit complicated, but that's because some of the concepts and approaches may be new to you. My goal is that by the end of this book you'll be comfortable and familiar with everything my friends did with this deal (and with the many other stories you'll read). I believe that once you have the tools, you can build anything. My job is to help give you the tools. That's why the next chapter is on the basics: instruction in the concepts you need to understand so you can create your own hugely profitable deals.

Some of you will be able to read Chapter 3 quickly, just to refresh your understanding of points, concepts, and terms you are already familiar with. For others, the next 35 or so pages may be difficult sledding, but stay the course. The rewards will be well worth the effort.

3

The Basics

There are books and books to read on the basic principles of real estate ownership and investment. It is not my intent to write a book that addresses all of these principles since my assumption is that you already know something about real estate investing. However, some space is warranted because, I believe, many people *think* they understand the basics but in reality have only a partial understanding. But just before speaking to the terms and concepts you must fully understand, let's restate our premise:

The purpose of this book is to teach you to add value while investing in real estate either by using the process of buying/selling more effectively than others or by taking some action(s) that quickly (and hopefully dramatically) increases the market value of the properties you acquire.

Okay, let's get going. Please treat the next 35 or so pages as either an introduction or a refresher (just fly through it). Note that terms commonly used by real estate investors appear in bold when they're introduced. You should be particularly sure that you have a good understanding of these terms since they represent the most important concepts in the real estate game.

Ownership

Individuals

It is important to understand that there are many different ways to own a piece of real estate. The simplest and most common is to own as an individual. You buy a piece of real estate and you put title in your name: John Doe. The next simplest is ownership by two people. You and your wife buy a house and put the title in both of your names: Jane and John Doe.

But Jane and John Doe need to identify something about their ownership. What if something happens to one of them? What if John gets hit by a bus (euphemism for "dies")? Does his interest in the real estate go to Jane or does it go to his children by a former wife? That depends on how you take title.

If Jane and John take title "in joint ownership, with rights of survivorship," then should one of them get hit by a bus, the other *automatically* becomes the sole owner of the property. Every State has laws that provide for this type of ownership; upon the death of one owner, the deceased's ownership interest instantaneously vests in the other.

If, on the other hand, Jane and John take title as "tenants in common" and John gets hit by a bus, his interest in the property goes into his estate, where presumably his Last Will and Testament describes how his assets are to be distributed. (If he has no Will, then the laws of the State where he resides will dictate.) In this case, if John's Will says that he wants all of his assets to go to his children by a prior marriage, then Jane Doe owns a 50 percent interest in the property with John's children (who collectively also have a 50 percent interest).

The next most common way to own investment real estate is in an entity form, which is how most real estate players take title to property. The commonly used entities are partnerships (of which there are different types), corporations, and limited liability companies (LLC). As you will see in later chapters, the type of entity you use to purchase and how you set it up can be very important to earning huge returns on your investment. For the moment, however, let's just be sure you understand each vehicle.

Partnerships

Let's say Molly Smith and John Doe want to create an entity to own a piece of property. So, they shake hands and form a partnership, SD Associates, with the intent that title to this property will be taken in the Partnership name. But why would they take title in a partnership name when they could have taken title in their names as individuals? (They could hold title as "Molly Smith and John Doe, tenants in common," which means that each has an undivided 50 percent interest in the property.)

The Basics

Well, if Molly and John are real estate players, they may want to bring others into their partnership, leveraging their skills to make money off the capital of more passive investors, a technique we will explain in detail later in the book. But for now here is a simple example: Molly just happens to have a rich uncle, Charlie, who has mentioned to her on many occasions that he wants to invest in real estate. So Molly and John create the partnership and make Uncle Charlie a partner. Molly and John will locate the property, put together the financing, oversee the closing, and then operate the property (presumably successfully). Uncle Charlie has no time to be looking at or operating real estate; he just wants the economic benefits of ownership and he has agreed to invest 95 percent of the **equity** (the money needed in excess of debt to consummate the purchase).

So Molly and John prepare a Partnership Agreement defining how the property will be owned, who will do what for the Partnership, *and* who will make what money from the cash flow and sale of the property. Finally, Molly and John may need to check with the laws of the State in which the property is located to see if they need to make any additional filings. Some municipalities and States have what are called "trade name" laws. Basically, these rules say that if individuals are going to buy property in an entity form, like a partnership, they need to make some filing at the local or State level identifying the entity and the name of its principals.

General versus Limited Partnerships. Now let's say that although Molly's Uncle Charlie has no problem putting in 95 percent of the equity required to purchase the property, he is not willing to sign for any loans procured by the Partnership. This may mean that Molly and John have to form a **Limited Partnership**—where *only* the General Partner(s) is liable for the debts of the Partnership—as opposed to a **General Partnership**—where *all* the partners are liable for these debts.

Let's use an example to clarify:

Molly and John have identified a small office building they can buy for $500,000. They have gone to a local bank to get a loan, and the loan officer indicates that the bank will make a loan for 70 percent of the purchase price, or $350,000. Therefore, the equity required to purchase is $150,000 (assume no closing costs). Uncle Charlie has indicated that he will put up 95 percent of the $150,000, so Molly and John only have to dip into their pockets for $7,500 (5 percent of $150,000). Now here's the rub: the banker says that he wants all owners to sign for the $350,000 loan, meaning that each owner of the property has to stand behind the loan with his or her personal assets. In the vernacular of the real estate world, each signatory would have **personal recourse** for the debt. Unfortunately for Molly and John, that idea is a nonstarter for Uncle Charlie. He has already told them that he will not sign the loan.

Fortunately, Molly and John are familiar with Limited Partnerships, and so they push back in conversation with the banker:

MOLLY: But Mr. Banker, we are forming a limited partnership to own this property, with John and me acting as the General Partners. As you well know, our limited partner will have no active role in this type of partnership. He is just a passive investor and would not anticipate signing for your loan.

BANKER: Yes, that is true, but I am going to have to see your Partnership Agreement to be sure that all active partners are signing for the loan.

MOLLY: No problem. We have a standard Limited Partnership Agreement whereby John and I are the General Partners and we are the only ones with day-to-day control over the partnership.

Here's the point: In a General Partnership, all the partners are responsible for the debts and liabilities of the partnership. Not just debt knowingly incurred, like the loan to purchase the property, but also liabilities that may arise if the partnership is sued. That's why most rich people investing in a real estate partnership prefer the limited partnership vehicle. Their investment may be at risk, but there is no potential liability to them beyond the amount of this investment. In the Limited Partnership Agreement only the operators of the partnership (called the General Partners) have the ability to act for the partnership, and by law in every State, responsibility for the debts and liabilities of the partnership are limited to the General Partners.

Corporations and Limited Liability Companies (LLC)

There are two main reasons for owning property in a corporate or LLC form. The first reason is to insulate the individuals who own the entity from liability that may accrue to the entity. For example, let's say that you own a multi-unit residential property and one day there is a fire and one of your tenants is injured. Presumably you have insurance to cover this liability, but maybe for some reason your insurance carrier disclaims coverage. Since you do not want your personal assets at risk, you feel better when owning in a corporate form because the presumption (usually true) is that only the *corporate* assets are at risk in a lawsuit against the property's owner. Since the corporate assets would normally be limited to the equity in the property owned, you know exactly what your downside could be in an uninsured loss.

Second, for the same reason that Molly Smith and John Doe decided to create a partnership to own property with Uncle Charlie, investors form corporations specifically to provide a vehicle for several different individual owners who may

The Basics

have different roles, responsibilities, and risks as to the property. As we saw with Molly, John, and Uncle Charlie, a partnership vehicle can provide for differing ownership positions within the partnership entity—same thing with a corporate entity. Instead of a Partnership Agreement, the document defining each individual's position is called a Stockholder Agreement.

Today, the entity of choice for most real estate investors is the LLC or Limited Liability Company. The LLC is a creation of the legislatures of every State. It is intended to provide the same protections to individual owners as does a corporation, but with the tax treatment of a partnership.

As we saw above, a corporation protects its individual owners from liabilities. That is not the case, however, with a General Partnership. If Molly Smith, John Doe, and Uncle Charlie buy an office building in the name SD Associates, and there is a lawsuit against SD Associates, then all three of its owners are responsible for the ultimate judgment, if any (and a creditor does not need to split its judgment into thirds; the creditor can seek 100 percent of the amount due from the rich partner). Contrast the corporation: if there is a judgment against the corporation, only its assets are at risk. None of the individual owners can be pursued for the liabilities of the corporation.

The reason not everyone likes investing in the traditional corporate form is about income taxes. In a partnership, income (and loss) generally *flows through* to the individuals, that is, the partnership is not taxed on this income. So if a partnership owner of real estate has annual cash flow of $50,000, for example, and there are two (50-50) partners in the partnership, then each reports on his or her tax return income of $25,000. Contrast the corporation: since the income tax laws treat the corporation as an entity separate and distinct from its owners, it must pay income taxes on the property's cash flow. *And* (here's the rub) when the corporation distributes money to its shareholders they *also must pay* income taxes; hence the ugly phrase "double taxation." So, in our example above, if cash flow to the corporate owner is $50,000 and the corporate tax rate is 10 percent, then the net income after taxes is $45,000, *and* when that comes out to the shareholders (let's say there are two and they own the corporation 50-50), each will show a dividend or some other type of distribution for $22,500 on their individual income tax return *and* that will then be taxed too.

There is a corporate form that does answer the double taxation issue. It is called a Subchapter S corporation, but it can be cumbersome in certain situations. So, state legislators came up with a new idea: in order to make life easier for investors, they created an entity that is a "partnership" for Federal Income Tax purposes but provides corporate protection to the individual owners . . . the Limited Liability Company. LLCs now exist in all 50 States and address the needs of the real estate player: simplicity in formation and operation, protection from individual liability, no double taxation. And today the LLC is the vehicle of choice for most real estate investors.

Last point: The terminology with an LLC is a bit different from a corporation. The owners of the LLC are **Members** and the ownership interests are **Membership Units**. The agreement defining the rights among the Members is called an **Operating Agreement**, and the person running the LLC on a day-to-day basis is called the **Manager** (he may or may not be a Member).

Deeds

The document that conveys ownership in a piece of real estate is called a **Deed**. The individual who conveys the ownership is called the **Grantor**. The recipient of ownership is the **Grantee**. The Deed contains a legal description of the property being conveyed. It is signed by the Grantor (but not the Grantee) and must usually be witnessed and/or notarized, the exact requirements of execution depending upon the State where the Deed is signed. There are three main types of Deeds.

The **Warrantee Deed** conveys the Grantor's warranty that the ownership he is conveying to the Grantee is exactly as indicated in the legal description of the Deed. The Grantor warrants or stands behind the integrity of the title, and if there is a problem, the Grantee has a lawsuit (for breach of warranty) against the Grantor.

The **Quitclaim Deed** is at the opposite end of the spectrum, for the Grantor makes absolutely no representation with this form of deed. In fact, one way to think of the Quitclaim Deed is to consider the Grantor handing it to the Grantee while saying, "Here, I cannot make any representations to you but whatever I own, I am conveying to you."

The **Bargain and Sale Deed** is between the Warrantee and Quitclaim Deeds in terms of the type of warranty the Grantor makes. This Deed essentially warrants the integrity of the Grantor's title only from the point that the Grantor took title. Where a Warrantee Deed is an absolute guaranty, the Bargain and Sale Deed only says, "Look, I warrant to you, Mr. Grantee, that the title is good from the date I took ownership . . . before that, I do not know."

That's enough about Deeds, because the fact is that something called **Title Insurance** has supplanted the importance of the type of Deed you get. A number of national title insurance companies will search the title of a property you're interested in buying and give you a title policy indicating who the owner is, its legal description, and what the encumbrances to the title may be. The title insurance company (regulated by the State in which it is doing business, and therefore creditworthy) will stand behind its title policy, so if there is a problem after the closing (e.g., you bought from Mr. Jones and after the closing Mr. Smith shows up and claims to have ownership interests in the property), the title company is responsible. With the title insurance policy as your security blanket, should a

The Basics

problem arise after closing, it's not that important whether you get a Quitclaim Deed or a Warrantee Deed from the Grantor.

Mortgages

A real estate player has to have a good understanding of the use of debt in buying and operating a real estate property. There are many types of debt, and knowing how to access and use debt is crucial.

The Mortgage Deed (or Deed of Trust)

It never ceases to amaze me how many people do not understand what a mortgage is. So, let's spend a few moments on this topic.

> I'm happy to report that Molly Smith and John Doe have found a property to purchase, and good old Uncle Charlie is putting up 95 percent of the equity they need. It's an office building with a $500,000 purchase price, and they have a lender willing to loan them $350,000. Molly and John have formed an LLC (SD Ventures, LLC), the Members of which are Molly, John, and Uncle Charlie. The bank's loan will come in the form of a Mortgage. This means that the Borrower (SD Ventures, LLC) will sign a Promissory Note obligating itself to repay the $350,000 loan, *and* will also sign a Mortgage Deed such that the property is **encumbered** by a **lien** owned by the bank.

Okay, that was a lot of language; let's take it apart. This is what happens. At the closing (the event at which the Purchaser gives the Seller the funds necessary to consummate the purchase of the property, and the Seller gives the Purchaser a Deed of ownership), a representative of SD Ventures, LLC will sign a Promissory Note obligating SD Ventures, LLC to repay the loan. This individual will also sign a Mortgage Deed that is recorded and prevents SD Ventures, LLC from transferring the property without paying off the loan.

Essentially, a Mortgage Deed says: "Hey, world, SD Ventures, LLC has borrowed $350,000 from me, and if anyone is interested in buying this property, just be aware that I have rights to the first $350,000 of value in the property, and I'm not going anywhere until I'm paid off." A good way to think about a Mortgage Deed is to remember that it is, in fact, a DEED, a document conveying rights from the **Mortgagor** (Grantor)—in this case SD Ventures, LLC—to the **Mortgagee** (Grantee), that is, the bank. In other words, the Mortgagee (the bank) has received a Deed to SD Ventures, LLC's property that conveys certain ownershiplike rights to it: specifically, the right to **foreclose** on the property (initiate a legal action to obtain title) should SD Ventures, LLC not do everything it is supposed to do under the Mortgage Deed. That is why real estate players say that the property is **encumbered** (think "burdened") with a mortgage . . . or, similarly, that there is a **lien** (again, think "burden") on the property.

Since a Mortgage Deed is usually at least 10 pages long, it has a lot more to say. In fact, it speaks to the Mortgagor's obligations under the Promissory Note and to what the Mortgagor can and cannot do with its property. For example, the bank does not want SD Ventures, LLC to make significant alterations to the office building without its consent. It does want SD Ventures, LLC to insure the property and pay all real estate taxes . . . and so on. The Mortgage Deed will probably also say that SD Ventures, LLC is not allowed to obtain any further debt against the property without the bank's consent.

An important component of the acquisition and financing process is **recording**. Every town, city, or county in the United States has a Clerk's Office in which records are kept with respect to every real estate transaction in the area. So when SD Ventures, LLC closes on the office building purchase, the Deed to it from the Seller will be filed (recorded) in the Clerk's records. Similarly, immediately after the recording of the Deed conveying ownership to SD Ventures, LLC the Mortgage Deed (conveying rights back to the bank) will be recorded. This puts the world on notice of the bank's rights. Anyone who wants to purchase the property from SD Ventures, LLC would go to the Clerk's Office first to be sure that SD Ventures, LLC was indeed the owner. He would then see that the bank has a Mortgage on the property, and would therefore know that in order to get a good title, he had to pay off the bank's loan (or assume it). And anyone who purchased from SD Ventures, LLC without paying off the Mortgage would take title *subject to* the bank's $350,000 lien. In other words, the bank's claim to the first $350,000 of value in the property would take precedence (i.e., the Mortgage is **superior**) to the purchaser's rights.

So, what do you think happens when a loan is paid off? Yes, correct, a Release of Mortgage is recorded in the Clerk's records telling the world that the Mortgage Deed recorded on January ___, 2006 in Volume ___ at Page ___ of the Smithtown Land Records is no longer encumbering the property since the loan which was secured by that Mortgage Deed has been repaid.

Subordinate or Secondary Financing

As I have indicated, every good real estate player knows how to use debt to his or her advantage. And the beginning player must be particularly adept at obtaining "other people's money" to purchase, since the beginning player does not usually have a lot of his own funds.

One way to buy property using a lot of other people's money is to use subordinate or secondary debt—loans that sit in position behind (are **inferior** to) another mortgage.

The Basics

Let's go back to Molly Smith and John Doe.

SD Ventures, LLC obtained a $350,000 loan from a bank to purchase an office building. IMMEDIATELY after the Deed (by which it obtained ownership) was recorded, the bank recorded the Mortgage Deed. This put the bank in **first position,** and the bank's Mortgage is accordingly called a **First Mortgage.** Now let's assume that Molly and John were not able to convince Molly's Uncle Charlie to invest in this building. So in order to buy, they somehow have to come up with $150,000, and unfortunately they only have $50,000 available to them. Fortunately, John has an uncle, Doug, who has a lot of money (but not an entrepreneurial bone in his body). Doug thinks like a lender. He wants to earn money on his money and cares only about **yield** (i.e., the return on his money). John asks Doug whether he would consider loaning him and Molly $100,000 to help them buy the office building. Doug says yes, "so long as the return on my investment is competitive and I am protected with a mortgage on your property."

But how is Doug going to get a mortgage on the property when the bank also wants a mortgage? Well, there can be lots and lots of mortgages against the same property. This is where the concept of **priority** comes into play. Doug can put a mortgage on the property and obtain a Mortgage Deed from SD Ventures, LLC just like the bank, but since, as noted, the bank will only make its loan if it is in first position, Doug's loan is going to have to be **subordinate** to the bank's loan. In other words, Doug will have a **Second Mortgage** on the property. What does all this mean?

Well, it goes back to **recordation** and a concept similar to an accounting term you may have heard: "First in, first out." Remember that the recording of the bank's Mortgage Deed occurred IMMEDIATELY after the Deed was recorded to SD Ventures, LLC. (Clerks have a policy of recording documents one minute apart; for example, a Warrantee Deed into a buyer might be recorded at 9 a.m., and then a first Mortgage Deed at 9:01 a.m., a second Mortgage Deed at 9:02 a.m., and so on.) There is great significance to the timing of the recording of mortgages. Once SD Ventures, LLC obtains title, the bank wants to be sure that its Mortgage Deed is the next document filed (recorded). This ensures that its Mortgage is in first position, which essentially means that in the event of any problems, the bank has a claim to the first $350,000 of value in the property before anyone else has any rights at all.

Uncle Doug will want to record his mortgage as well. But since the bank demands that it be in first position, Doug's mortgage will have to come *after* the recording of the bank's mortgage. Again, the sequence is critical because Doug can exercise his rights under the mortgage from SD Ventures, LLC to him only *after* the bank has exercised its rights. Let's use an example.

Say that SD Ventures, LLC gets into trouble with the property because it's unable to lease the office building. With no rents coming in, it cannot meet its payments under the Promissory Note to the bank. The bank loses patience after about 90 days and starts a **foreclosure action** to obtain title to the property. Let's assume that there is a foreclosure auction and the office building is sold for $400,000. (Often, auctions do not yield the highest price possible, which is why, from a Purchaser's point of view, there are sometimes good deals to be had at auctions.) After sales expenses of the auction, the net proceeds from the auction sale are $375,000. Who gets what?

Well, the proceeds are distributed according to the priorities of the liens on the property. The First Mortgage has the first lien, so the bank would get all of its loan back ($350,000) plus (as often happens) any back interest and late fees. Let's assume in this case that those charges come to $5,000. That means there is only $20,000 left for any subsequent lien holders (lienees); in our example, Uncle Doug. Of course he is not happy. All but $20,000 of his $100,000 loan (even though secured with a Second Mortgage on the property) is lost.

But the news is not necessarily all bad for Uncle Doug. If Molly and John have guaranteed the Promissory Note from SD Ventures, LLC to Uncle Doug, and if he chooses to, he can sue them on the Guaranty for the shortfall of $80,000 (often called a "deficiency"). Then, of course, they need to have the assets to pay any judgment he obtains.

One last point: Remember that Uncle Doug, a yield investor, was very focused on the return on his money. When he agreed to make the loan to Molly and John, he noted to them that being in a second position on the property put him at greater risk than the first lender (and, as you can see above, he was right). Therefore, he noted, he would need a *higher* interest rate than the bank was getting. And so, although Molly and John were only paying the bank an interest rate of 7 percent, they had to agree to pay Doug a rate of 12 percent. This is often the case. The lower the priority of the loan (a Second Mortgage has a lower priority than a First Mortgage), the higher the interest rate, because the greater the risk incurred by the subordinate lender.

Subordination

Subordination is an important concept to understand if you're going to be aggressively financing your purchases . . . or if you're going to get into development.

The Basics

Subordination is when a mortgagee agrees to lower the priority of his mortgage to that of a mortgage to be placed on a property at a later date. A common example is when a developer purchases a piece of land from a property owner and the owner takes back a First Mortgage (often called a "purchase money mortgage"). Since the developer knows that he will eventually need to put a construction mortgage on this property (and that the construction lender will only make the loan if it is in first position), the developer negotiates with the seller to include in the first mortgage document a **Subordination Clause**. That clause says:

> Mortgagee agrees that it will subordinate the lien of the herein Mortgage to the lien of a mortgage to be hereafter placed on the Property by Mortgagor.

Let's look at an example.

John Doe locates a piece of land he would like to buy. The owner of the property, Albert Einstein, is asking $500,000 all cash or, alternatively, $550,000 if the buyer wants him to take back a first mortgage, and in this situation, Albert is willing to take back a first mortgage in an amount of $450,000. John decides he would rather pay the higher price and get the seller financing, so he elects to purchase the property for $550,000. But John is pretty smart, and he asks Albert for a subordination clause in Albert's first Mortgage Deed. Here is how the conversation might go:

JOHN: Albert, as you know, in order to build an office building on this property I am going to need construction financing.

ALBERT: Yes, I know that . . . I am not stupid.

JOHN: Well, then you also know that I can only obtain construction financing if the construction lender is in first position.

ALBERT: Well, I had not thought about that . . . but yes, I guess that's true.

JOHN: So I need to ask that your Mortgage Deed include a standard Subordination Clause, whereby you agree to put the lien of your Mortgage behind that of the construction lender.

ALBERT: Well, that is going to raise my risk a bit . . . so I will only do that if you pay me another half point in interest.

JOHN: Yes, okay, we have a deal.

And so John buys the land and Albert takes back a $450,000 first mortgage. Then, at some point in the future, John obtains a commitment for a construction loan of $1 million from the Smithtown Bank for the purpose of funding the construction of an office building on the land. At the time that the construction lender is ready to record its mortgage (and before it will advance any money), it will require that John obtain a Subordination Agreement from Albert. So John presents Albert with a Subordination Agreement that says:

> I, Albert Einstein, the mortgagee under a Mortgage Deed dated November 10, 2005, and recorded in the Smithtown Land Records at Volume 100, page 50, hereby agree that the lien of said mortgage is subordinated to a Mortgage Deed to be recorded immediately after this Subordination Agreement from John Doe to the Smithtown Bank in an amount of $1 million and which lien is secured by the Property indicated on Exhibit A hereto.

What has happened is that the lien of Albert's purchase money mortgage is now *behind* the lien of Smithtown Bank's mortgage lien of $1 million. Smithtown Bank is now in the first position and Albert Einstein is in the second position. And should this deal ever get into trouble and there is a liquidation of the property, Smithtown Bank will get its $1 million (or whatever the balance of the loan may be at the time), plus interest and fees, *before* Albert Einstein gets anything.

As you might be thinking, subordination can be a useful tool for the creative real estate player who does not have a lot of capital and is looking to use as much "other people's money" as possible in buying properties. See Chapter 15 for ideas in this regard, but to get your thinking started now, consider this: where might Albert Einstein have done a better job in his negotiation with John Doe? Here's a clue: if John was able to get a first mortgage of $1.5 million, how would Albert feel about being in second position behind that amount of debt?

Recourse versus Nonrecourse Loans

You will recall from our initial discussions relative to partnerships, corporations, and LLCs that one of the issues a real estate player must be aware of is the liability of the individual owners of the entity. As we discussed earlier in this chapter, Molly Smith and John Doe were able to convince Uncle Charlie to make an investment in the partnership they established only after they settled on a Limited Partnership (versus a General Partnership) so Charlie would not be personally liable (none of his assets exposed) for the debts of the Partnership. Eventually Molly and John formed SD Ventures, LLC to buy the office building because the LLC format (like a corporation) gives all its Members protection from the liabilities of the entity.

As is traditional with entities purchasing property, the LLC is actually the borrower and signatory on the Promissory Note. This is fine with Uncle Charlie since the LLC signs the Note, not him, and the LLC (as we have discussed) is legally considered a separate entity in terms of liability. BUT the bank making the loan

The Basics

to SD Ventures, LLC is not satisfied with just the LLC signing the Promissory Note. The bank is well aware of the separation in the law between an entity (the LLC) and its owners, and it wants more than just the assets of the LLC (usually just the property in question) at risk. It wants the neck of the owners (or some of them) in the noose as well—it wants their "skin in the game." It figures people tend to stay focused when their personal assets are at risk, and the bank wants Molly and John very focused. And so the bank asks for personal **Guarantees** from Molly and John; it asks them to guarantee the loan to the LLC (so their assets stand behind the loan), just in case the real estate investment does not work out as planned.

The Guarantee will say: "I, John Doe, promise to stand behind the loan evidenced by a Promissory Note dated _____ to SD Ventures, LLC." It is essentially an insurance policy to the lender. If there is a problem in collecting payments under the Promissory Note to SD Ventures, LLC, the lender can sue John Doe under the Guarantee.

Anytime there is a personal signature involved with loan documents, the loan is considered **recourse**, such that if the lender does not get paid by the entity that signed the Note, it has recourse against some individual or entity that presumably has a lot of assets (usually one or more of the owners of the entity). Recourse protection for the lender means: (1) if it chose to, it could initiate a lawsuit for payment of the Note directly against a **Guarantor** instead of the entity signing the Note/Mortgage Deed, and (2) it could start a lawsuit against the entity, foreclose the property, and then, as to any shortfall, the **deficiency,** sue the Guarantor for that amount. In either case, the point is that the Guarantor is theoretically at risk for the whole amount of the debt. (A worst case scenario: a building burns down, the land is worth very little and if the entity owner of the property neglected to get adequate insurance coverage, the lender to the entity recovers very little on foreclosure, leaving the Guarantor liable for the entire amount of debt.)

In our example, Molly and John were only able to entice Uncle Charlie to make an investment in SD Ventures, LLC by assuring him that he would not be asked to sign a Guarantee. So Uncle Charlie's personal assets are not at risk. Yes, he can lose his investment in SD Ventures, LLC if everything goes wrong, but that is his maximum exposure.

Whether a loan is recourse or **nonrecourse** depends upon a lot of factors. If a lender can get recourse, it will always want it. And, depending on the type of deal, the risk to the lender, and the type of lender, some lenders will not do a deal without having some type of guarantee (or recourse) from a "deep pocket" (someone with assets). Conversely, there are commercial real estate players who will not do a deal if there is recourse. Their attitude is that they will risk their investment in the property, but no more than that.

Confessions of a Real Estate Entrepreneur

My attitude is that you cannot be a successful real estate player if you never borrow recourse. Unless you already have a lot of money and don't care about creating additional wealth, if you're playing the real estate game, there are times when you have to put yourself (your assets) at risk. Yes, there are plenty of loans with no recourse (e.g., pension fund and insurance companies rarely ask for recourse), but these lenders are usually looking for larger transactions, and while you're working your way to a position to do this level of deal, you'll probably have to consider recourse loans.

Finally, under the heading that most everything is negotiable, if confronted with a lender who wants recourse protection (since almost everyone buys in an entity form, this means a Guarantee of the Promissory Note), you can try to limit the guarantee. For example, I have often tried to put a limit on the amount or the duration of the Guarantee when negotiating with a lender (e.g., that it goes away X years after the Promissory Note is signed). I cannot say that I am always successful in this regard, but occasionally, if the lender really wanted the loan, I was able to limit the extent or duration of the Guarantee.

Assumable Loans

Since one of the goals of the creative real estate investor is to find the best and least expensive way to finance the acquisition of a property, we need to have an understanding of assumability, or the buying of real estate that is encumbered with an existing mortgage (or mortgages), and leaving that mortgage in place.

There will be times when a property you're interested in purchasing is encumbered with an existing mortgage that the seller does not want to pay off, perhaps because there is a prepayment penalty or because the rate on the existing loan is so low that the seller can lever off it (we'll get to Wrap Mortgages in a moment). The Seller may suggest that the deal can still be made by you, the Purchaser, taking subject to (assuming) the existing mortgage. This means that you step into the Seller's shoes in terms of his relationship with the lender. You essentially become the borrower in his stead. Assumption is more common with nonrecourse loans, where the creditworthiness of the Borrower is not a factor.

Not all loans are assumable. Lenders do not like a low interest rate loan to be assumed if they can help it. When rates increase dramatically, lenders would rather have their money back so they can loan it out at higher rates. So, if you are considering assuming an existing mortgage, you need to review the language in the Mortgage Deed to see what kind of approval the lender has over an assumption (see "due on sale" clauses in "Wrap Mortgages," below).

At times a Seller and Purchaser will get creative if the Purchaser would like to assume the Seller's mortgage, but the Seller's Mortgage Deed has language that precludes an assumption. Hence the invention of something called the Wrap Mortgage.

The Basics

Wrap Mortgages. A Wrap Mortgage is a form of seller financing. Instead of the seller telling its lender that a purchaser of the property will be assuming its mortgage (and perhaps giving the lender the opportunity to call the loan), the seller simply leaves the existing mortgage alone and takes back a second mortgage that "wraps" or includes the amount of the first mortgage. Here's an example:

> Seller owns a property that he wishes to sell for $5 million. There is an existing first mortgage to ABC Bank. This loan has a principal balance of $2 million. The interest rate on this loan is 5 percent, and the going rate today is 8 percent. The Seller suggests to a prospective Purchaser that he will "take back" a mortgage on sale in an amount of $4.5 million at an interest rate of 6.5 percent. He does this to make his property more attractive to a Purchaser and to provide a cash flow to himself (the 1.5 percent spread on $2 million). The Purchaser is interested in this offer because he would rather pay interest at 6.5 percent than 8 percent.
>
> The Seller will likely not even inform ABC Bank what he is doing, and he continues to make the loan payments to ABC Bank. For simplicity purposes, putting aside amortization, Purchaser pays Seller 6.5 percent per year on the $4.5 million "Wrap" Mortgage (annual interest of $292,500), and the Seller turns around and pays ABC Bank $100,000 ($2 million times 5 percent). The Seller has made his property more salable by providing undermarket financing. The Purchaser is happy because he did not have to procure an institutional loan and he is paying an undermarket interest rate. Only the lender is unhappy (assuming the lender is even aware of what happened) because it has $2 million out there earning interest of 5 percent when—if it had that money back—it could presumably earn 8 percent.

Lenders responded to Sellers offering Wrap Mortgages by writing Mortgage Deeds with "due on sale" clauses, such as: "This Mortgage is due upon a transfer of the Property encumbered hereby." These clauses theoretically prevent a Seller from conveying title to his property, taking back the financing, and leaving an existing mortgage in place. But as you might expect, creative Sellers and Purchasers have found ways to beat this clause too. One example is an installment contract where the Seller continues to hold title (i.e., no recorded Deed) while the Purchaser makes monthly "contract" payments and operates with all the rights of the owner of the property.

The point is, there are many ways to "skin a cat," and real estate investors are particularly creative when it comes to financing. Books have been written on creative real estate financing and you may want to look at one or two. I believe that by the end of this book you'll know enough to notch up your game.

Real Estate Contracts

To be a successful real estate player, you need to have a good understanding of contract law in general and real estate contract law in particular. A contract is any agreement between two parties where each is obligated in some way to the other. A **Real Estate Contract** (sometimes called a Purchase and Sale Agreement, or P&S) is a specific example: one party agrees to sell and another agrees to buy a particular piece of real estate.

The Law of Contracts

Let's start with general contract law: rules that apply to all contracts. This stuff is important. I've seen situations where clever real estate entrepreneurs have created good deals for themselves by having a better understanding of contract law than the other party.

In order for two people to be bound to each other, there must be mutual promises and something called **consideration.** Consideration is something of value that each party promises to do or give to the other. If each party has not committed to give something of value to the other, there is no enforceable Contract. Here's a typical law school question: Mr. Jones and Mr. Smith have the following conversation. Is there a Contract?

JONES: I promise to clean your house tomorrow.

SMITH: Okay.

Well no, there is no Contract, because there is no consideration promised by Mr. Smith to Mr. Jones. He never said that he would pay Jones for the cleaning, or do anything for Jones. So, there's no mutual consideration; Jones is not legally bound to clean Smith's house, and Smith could not sue Jones if Jones never showed up.

Now, how about a slightly different scenario:

JONES: Tomorrow, I promise to clean the house I am renting to you. (Here Smith is Jones's tenant.)

SMITH: Okay. I'll have my family out of there by 9 a.m.

Is there any consideration extended from Mr. Smith to Mr. Jones? Well, Mr. Smith and his wife have five young kids, so it's a real hassle for them to all be out of the house by 9 a.m. But that may not be enough as the test is whether there is something of value being offered to Mr. Jones. What if Mr. Jones could care less whether the kids are there or not? Then perhaps there is no consideration. What if, on the other hand, Mr. Jones is offering to clean the house because Mr. Smith's lease is up in a few days and Mr. Jones wants the house ready for occupancy by a new tenant the day that Mr. Smith's lease expires? In other words, Jones wants to be able to clean the house in advance of the new tenant's lease starting *and* that is much eas-

The Basics

ier for him to do if there's no one in the house when the cleaning crew shows up. Well, then it would appear that Mr. Smith's promise to get everyone out (to facilitate the cleaning) does have value to Mr. Jones, and thereby constitutes consideration.

Is there consideration from Jones to Smith? Does Smith care if Jones cleans the house? Well, presumably he would like living in a clean house. But he and his family are about to move out. So what does Smith care if Jones cleans the house? Perhaps the agreement is part of a larger conversation whereby Smith is actually obligated to clean the house when his lease is up, but in order to induce Smith to be out of the house on the exact last day of the lease, Jones has promised to do what Smith is actually obligated to do. So Jones has extended something of value to Smith, taking on a responsibility that is actually Smith's.

Law school professors are great at coming up with hundreds of these situations where you need to analyze the value of promise that each party makes to the other. If there is not something of value being offered from each party, then there is no consideration and hence no enforceable contract.

For our purposes as real estate investors, when we want to bind another party to a deal, it's imperative that we always make sure there is mutual consideration. Here's an example of a matter I was involved with years ago:

An individual was selling a building in my town. He and I had sketched out on a piece of paper our understanding. It looked something like this:

Seller promises to sell 123 Main Street, Westport, Connecticut, to Randel for $1 million. Closing will be on July 1, 2000. Randel's obligation hereunder is subject to his reasonable satisfaction with the building and other inspections he wishes to do. Randel has 30 days to conduct these inspections. If for any reason he is not reasonably satisfied with these inspections, he may cancel this Contract.

The day after we both signed this piece of paper, the Seller changed his mind (someone came along with more money). He refused to honor our agreement and would not even let me come to the property to do my building inspection. I got a lawyer and so did he. We went to court.

His lawyer's position was that there was no consideration from me to the Seller. There had been no down payment (he refused to take one, although I tried). So no money had changed hands at that point. And, the lawyer argued, although I had made a promise to purchase (i.e., the promise to pay $1 million on July 1, 2000), it had no value because the inspection contingency I had put in the writing gave me an out if I wanted one—so I had made no commitment at all to the Seller and hence promised nothing of value.

Confessions of a Real Estate Entrepreneur

My lawyer argued that I had offered consideration, $1 million on or before July 1, 2000. The fact that I had the right to do a building inspection was standard operating practice, and in fact I did not have total freedom to change my mind. I could only terminate the deal if I was not **reasonably** satisfied. In other words, my lawyer argued, I had made a promise to pay $1 million by a certain date so long as there were no problems with the property that would dissuade any **reasonable** purchaser. Therefore, I did not have an unrestricted ability to just void my commitment to purchase; hence I had made a promise of value to the Seller.

The judge never issued a final ruling but indicated that she was leaning in my favor, and that persuaded the Seller to settle with me, paying me money to cancel the Contract (so he could sell to the other interested purchaser). It was not my first choice, but the money was significant enough to reimburse me for my troubles and pay legal fees. And, had I not added the word "reasonably" to our piece of paper, I might well have lost, since without some limit on my ability to cancel the deal, my promise to pay $1 million was meaningless; I could have changed my mind the next day for **any reason** I wanted. In that case the Seller would not have received anything of value from me, therefore, no consideration.

The point: There are times, even in larger deals, when two parties will attempt to reach an agreement before the lawyers get involved. So you need to understand when a contract is a contract *in the eyes of the law*, and the issue that very often trips people up is the requirement of mutual consideration.

The Statute of Frauds

Real Estate Contracts not only need mutual consideration to be enforceable, they also need to comply with a law (each State has one) called the **Statute of Frauds**. This law says that in order to be enforceable, a contract for the purchase and sale of real estate must contain certain critical elements *and* must be in writing, signed by each of the parties to be bound thereby.

In other words, if you promise to sell me your house and I promise to buy it and we do not put our understanding in writing, too bad for whichever one of us wants to enforce the agreement. Without a *written* promise, there is no enforceable contract. Contrast the situation where I promise to sell you my car and you promise to buy it. If you change your mind and don't come up with the money, I can sue you for breach of contract. But over the years the law has said that since each piece of real estate is a unique asset, there can be no enforceable obligation to sell or to buy without putting the understanding in writing.

So, when dealing with real estate, you *must* put your agreement in writing, or any attempted suit by you (whether you are the seller or buyer) will be summarily thrown out of Court. What are the critical elements of the deal that the

30

The Basics

Statute of Frauds says must be in the writing? Well, the statutes in each State vary a bit, but your writing better have:

- The description of the Property (does not necessarily have to be the legal description so long as a fact finder can determine exactly which property the parties were addressing)
- The names of the Seller (owner of the property) and Purchaser
- The sales price
- The date when title is to transfer
- The signatures of each party

Without *at least* these points, your writing will not pass muster with the Statute of Frauds. What follows are two stories that illustrate the importance of complying with the Statute of Frauds. One has a happy ending, one does not.

Happy Ending

Years ago I was negotiating to buy a 100,000-square-foot warehouse in Monroe, Connecticut. It was owned by a large corporation. I exchanged correspondence with the vice president of this corporation with respect to a prospective sale, and the letters (in my mind) constituted a Contract that contained all the elements of the Statute of Frauds (note that the letters were signed by him). However, after the exchange of letters, some higher-up in the corporation decided that the company should not sell the property, and so the vice president had to call me and take the position that there was no contract between us.

I had no choice but to bring an action for **specific performance,** which is a request to a Court to order the Seller to sell to the Purchaser according to the terms of the Sales Contract. The corporation contested, claiming that the letters exchanged between the vice president and myself did not meet the threshold requirements of Connecticut's Statute of Frauds. So again I went off to Court.

My lawyer took the position that the Statute of Frauds can be met by the exchange of more than one piece of paper (the letters), so long as each letter is signed by the party to be bound by the promises therein and so long as all the critical elements of the Statute of Frauds are identified in the letters.

The attorney for the corporation insisted that there had to be ONE writing, signed by both parties, which includes all the elements of the Statute of Frauds. He disputed the position that several letters—no one of which was signed by both parties or had all the elements of the Statute of Frauds—could be enforceable.

Confessions of a Real Estate Entrepreneur

Although this was a pretty interesting legal issue, I did not feel good about my chances. Fortunately, however, I had a very clever attorney, and during his pretrial discovery he came across an internal corporate memo that read something like this:

MEMO

To: VP (guy I had been dealing with)
From: EVP (higher-up)

I understand your commitment to Randel and that he may have acted in reliance. On the other hand, our real estate department has changed its position and is not willing to lose that location for distribution purposes. Accordingly, we are no longer willing to sell.

My lawyer argued that this MEMO proved that the intention of the corporation had been to sell to me and that it then changed its mind for reasons having nothing to do with the deal. The corporation's lawyer recommended to its client that it settle and the corporation paid my partner and me $400,000 going away money.

Whereas it would have been nice to know how the Court would have decided on the Statute of Frauds issue, $400,000 was more than enough for me to lose interest in the legal stuff.

Unhappy Ending

Just six months ago I was negotiating to purchase an apartment building and an adjoining development parcel in Miami Beach, Florida. The asking price was $2,250,000, and the seller and I settled on $2,125,000. In Miami the real estate brokers usually prepare the Sales Contract for properties like this, using a standard form prepared by the Florida Association of Realtors. So, my broker prepares the Contract.

I ask my broker to confirm that the person claiming to be owner of the property (the Seller) is, in fact, the owner. He goes to the Web site for Dade County and confirms that a Mr. Harry Carey (I would like to use his real name since he tricked me, but the lawyers say "No") is indicated on the Tax Assessor's information page as the owner of the property in question. Mr. Carey had hired a broker to list his property for sale, and the broker's information sheet also indicated that Mr. Carey was the owner.

I sign the Contract, put down a deposit, and Mr. Carey signs the Contract as well. All changes are initialed by both of us and we exchange originally signed Contracts. I begin my due diligence and then get a call from Mr. Carey's broker:

The Basics

BROKER: Unfortunately, Mr. Carey's plans have changed and he is no longer willing to sell you the property.

ME: That's crazy! We have a signed Contract and I intend to enforce it.

BROKER: I am afraid that you don't have a valid Contract. To my dismay [she too had been duped] I have just learned that the property is actually owned NOT ONLY by Mr. Carey BUT ALSO by his brother. And, since his brother did not sign the Sales Contract, you have not complied with the Statute of Frauds in that you do not have all owners of the party listed as sellers.

ME (to myself, once I confirmed that she was correct, i.e., that in fact the property was owned by Carey AND his brother jointly): HOW COULD I BE SO FRIGGING STUPID?

Mr. Carey had me. Maybe I could have sued him for some kind of misrepresentation—holding himself out as the sole owner of the property—but I did not think I could win a breach of contract action (what I wanted was specific performance) since the writing I had did not include ALL the provisions of the Statute of Frauds—it was missing a critical element: the name of *all* owners of the property.

Needless to say, this was a painful lesson to me. Here I am, supposedly the Big Shot Real Estate Expert, making a rookie mistake. The fact is, I was not as familiar as I should have been with procedures in Miami Beach, and I assumed that if the Tax Assessor's information sheet indicated the name of only one owner to the property, then in fact *there was only one owner*. WRONG!

What I should have done, and of course have done in any deal I have negotiated since, is checked with the City Clerk's Office and found the Deed transferring title to Mr. Carey. (It is available online.) I then would have seen that the owners were actually Harry and Barry Carey, and I would have known that I did not have an enforceable Contract unless both Harry and Barry signed.

Here's the point: There will be times when, as a Seller or Purchaser, you will perhaps change your mind and/or have to contend with the other party changing his or her mind. If you are going to be a savvy real estate investor and make good decisions when this happens, you need to understand when an agreement for the sale of real estate is enforceable and when it isn't.

Elements of the Real Estate Contract

Ninety-nine percent of the time you are not going to be litigating and fighting with other parties. The standard Real Estate Contract is pretty straightforward and basically says that one party agrees to sell and the other party agrees to buy. What can complicate things—and in fact present opportunities for the clever

Confessions of a Real Estate Entrepreneur

real estate investor—are the terms and conditions of the Seller's obligation to sell and the Purchaser's obligation to buy.

Let's quickly review the basic clauses within most Real Estate Contracts.

Legal Description.   The Contract will describe the real estate that the Seller intends to convey to the Purchaser. This is usually in a schedule to the Contract. It is important for the real estate player to understand exactly what he is buying and hence spend time reviewing the legal description.

Every area of the country has its own system for identifying individual properties. In my State, most properties are described by their **metes and bounds** and usually with reference to a recorded map.

Here is a typical metes and bounds description:

ALL THAT CERTAIN piece or parcel of land with improvements thereon and bounded as follows:

NORTHERLY: 145 feet by Parcel 206 on Map 3113
EASTERLY: 250 feet by Sturges Highway
SOUTHERLY: 145 feet by land now or formerly owned by Jones
WESTERLY: 250 feet by land of the Aspetuck Land Trust

Note that the legal description does not speak to the specific improvements on the land. The legal description almost always refers to land "with improvements thereon." So don't expect the legal description to tell you whether there is an office building, apartment complex, or strip shopping center on the property.

Whereas the metes and bounds description does at least give you the dimensions of the perimeters of a property (e.g., from the above we know that the property is 36,250 square feet), when I am buying and look at a description, I always try to find reference to some type of filed map. Here is what that language might look like:

Said premises are also shown on recorded Map #3113 entitled "Map Prepared for Joe Jones, Sturges Highway, Westport, Connecticut," which map was prepared by Leo Leonard Surveyor, is dated June 1, 1985, and is recorded in the Westport Town Clerk's Office.

A filed map is generally more helpful than a metes and bounds description as it is usually easier to get a sense of the property when viewing a diagram. But even recorded maps don't always tell you all you'll want to know. Generally what you want is a **survey**.

A survey shows you the footprint of all **improvements** (buildings, driveways, parking areas, fences, etc.) on the property. A survey will also show you if there

34

The Basics

are **encroachments** onto or off of the property you are purchasing. An encroachment is an improvement owned by one person but protruding into another's property. Encroachments are not uncommon; as an example, it's not rare to discover that fences and walls people think are entirely on their property extend into a neighboring property. Usually this is not a big deal, but sometimes surveys can expose encroachments that can be a real problem; for example, when some portion of the parking area of the property you are buying is actually on the neighbor's property. If the neighbor wants, he might be able to erect a fence on the property line and prevent you from using that portion of the parking area. A survey is a good thing to obtain when you're buying.

Understanding **encumbrances** is also very important. An encumbrance is some limitation on the use and enjoyment of your property. The legal description in the Contract usually identifies all of the encumbrances on the property being conveyed.

There are many types of encumbrances. A mortgage is considered an encumbrance since its existence limits or burdens the use and enjoyment of one's property. But a mortgage would not normally be shown in the legal description of a Contract since most of the time the seller's mortgage(s) is (are) paid off at the time of the transfer of title (closing). An exception would be the situation when a purchaser is assuming the seller's mortgage.

As a Purchaser, the encumbrances I am interested in are those that could have an impact on my prospective use of the property. Let's review one common encumbrance, an **easement**. This is a written agreement between two parties whereby the owner of a property gives another person (or entity) rights to the use of the property. A typical easement might be a right of passage over property.

For example, let's say that you own a strip shopping center fronting on Main Street and I own adjoining land with a restaurant on it that has some but not much Main Street frontage. I would like my customers to be able to access my property through your property since your driveway is at a stoplight and you have better frontage than I do. So I approach you and ask if I can buy an easement through your driveway and the parking lot in front of your center into my property, essentially a right of passage over those areas of your land. You think about it and decide that the additional car traffic generated by customers coming into and out of my restaurant will cause problems for your tenants and that may hurt the rent you are able to charge for your center. So you tell me to buzz off.

I up my offer. In return for allowing me this easement of passage over your property, I offer you a right of passage over my property to a side street that borders my property but not yours. This right of passage over my property will give your tenants' customers an additional way to exit your property and will improve the flow of traffic in and out of your property. You check with your tenants.

They like the idea, so we write up an **Easement Agreement** (in this example it includes what are often called **cross-easements**) whereby we exchange rights of passage over our respective properties. Usually this type of document would have a survey attached, showing exactly the areas of the respective rights of passage we have given each other.

Now fast forward 10 years. I am thinking about selling my restaurant site. A prospective Purchaser comes to me and offers me a lot of money. But he is not interested in operating or leasing to a restaurant. His goal is to knock down the restaurant and build a McDonald's. We shake hands and I produce a Contract including, of course, a legal description. This description must show as an encumbrance the Easement Agreement that I entered with you 10 years ago. And, unfortunately, the attached survey reveals to my Purchaser that your right of passage over my property is right smack in the area of the land where he wants to build a McDonald's. Therefore, he either passes on the purchase or convinces you to release the easement over my parcel.

An easement is just one type of possible encumbrance. The point is, as a prospective Purchaser you must review all encumbrances noted in the legal description to the Contract to be sure that none of them will interfere with the intended use of the property you are purchasing.

Due Diligence Clauses.   Nobody buys a piece of commercial property without doing some amount of homework first. That homework is often called **Due Diligence**. The clause in the Contract that speaks to a Purchaser's right to conduct this Due Diligence is an important one. By the way, there are times when a Seller will say: "Do your homework first. If you're happy with the results of your homework, then I'll draw up a Contract." As a Purchaser, I do not like that approach. If I'm going to undertake research on a particular property—including perhaps an engineering inspection, environmental study, zoning review, market analysis, survey, title search, and so on—I want to know that I have the property tied up. I do not want to spend all that time and money doing careful due diligence if the Seller might change his mind and not sell (or sell to some higher bidder who comes along). Therefore, when I am a Purchaser, I always want a Contract executed before I begin my Due Diligence, and, of course, I want a Due Diligence clause in the Contract.

Here's how the typical Due Diligence clause reads:

In the 30 days following the execution of this Contract, the Purchaser shall have the opportunity to conduct whatever inspections and tests relative to the Property that it wishes. The Seller agrees to grant the Purchaser access to the Property for these purposes. If, at the end of said 30-day period, the Purchaser does not want to purchase the Property, then Purchaser shall give written notice to the Seller of Purchaser's decision and the herein Contract shall be terminated, the Purchaser's Deposit returned, and the rights and obligations of the parties to each other shall thereafter cease. If, however, the Purchaser does not give written notice to the Seller of a decision not to purchase, then Purchaser shall be deemed to have waived the right to terminate this Contract.

In other words, the Purchaser has the property tied up (the Seller is committed to the transaction) and then has the opportunity to conduct whatever homework it wishes. Although a Seller is in limbo while the Due Diligence is under way (Seller does not know if there is a deal or not), Due Diligence Clauses are typical in most larger transactions, and in fact do serve a purpose for the Seller. As a Seller, I want the Contract to be very clear that I gave the Purchaser every opportunity to do whatever studies it wants. I don't want a Purchaser coming to me after a closing and saying, "Hey, you didn't tell me about this or that." So, when I'm a Seller, I add language to the Due Diligence Clause as follows:

If, at the expiration of the Due Diligence Period, the Purchaser determines that it wishes to purchase the Property, then that decision is an acknowledgment by Purchaser that it was provided unlimited access to the Property, to all books and records in the Seller's possession relative to the Property, and that Purchaser conducted any and all investigations, studies, and tests that it wished to perform. The decision to go forward is an acknowledgment by the Purchaser that it is satisfied in all respects with the condition of the Property and with all matters relative thereto and that it is not relying upon any representation or information from the Seller in making its decision to purchase the Property.

In other words, if I am a Seller, I want the Purchaser signing off on the fact that it had an unfettered opportunity to examine and investigate the property, because if things do not work out with the investment the way the Purchaser hoped, I do not want the Purchaser coming back to me and whining about this or that.

Financing Contingencies. Sometimes a Purchaser will try to condition its obligation to buy on its ability to get a mortgage of X with Y terms. A typical mortgage contingency might read as follows:

Purchaser's obligation to buy is contingent upon Purchaser's ability to obtain a mortgage in the amount of $2 million at an interest rate not higher than 6 percent, fixed for five years, and at an amortization schedule not shorter than 20 years. The Purchaser will use best efforts to obtain such a mortgage. If the Purchaser is not able to obtain such a mortgage and gives written notice to Seller by _____ (date) of that fact, then Purchaser may terminate the herein Contract and the Purchaser's Deposit shall be returned to Purchaser and the rights and obligations of the parties hereto to each other shall cease.

So the Seller is obligated to sell to Purchaser, and Purchaser is obligated to purchase from Seller, *if* Purchaser can get the stipulated mortgage. If not, it can notify the Seller, pull the plug on the deal, and get the initial deposit on Contract returned. Later in this book I am going to speak to contingencies in Contracts and how the clever real estate player can use them to his or her advantage. For the moment, I want to say this about financing contingencies: as a Purchaser, don't expect to rely on them as you grow in the real estate game.

As deals get larger and Sellers more sophisticated, Sellers expect that a Purchaser can get a mortgage and do not agree to condition the obligation to buy on the Purchaser's ability to obtain financing. Generally, a Seller will figure that a prospective Purchaser does not need financing to close, or if it does, will either have a line of credit (a relationship with a lender whereby Purchaser knows in advance what kind of loan it can get), or Purchaser will finalize its financing during the Due Diligence Period under the Contract. In fact, if I were a Seller of a larger deal and a prospective Purchaser said to me that it needed to put a mortgage contingency in our Contract, I would think that Purchaser might not be strong enough to close the transaction and would therefore not want to go to Contract and tie up my property with this type of Purchaser.

Default. The Seller and Purchaser of a Contract should always have a clear understanding of what happens if one of the parties is in **default** of the Contract. "Default" means a **breach** (not doing something one is obligated to do, or doing something one should not be doing) of the Contract that is **material,** and thereby entitles the other party to certain legal rights and remedies. Note that the event that leads to default must be material—meaning more than insignificant.

For example, there may be language that during the Due Diligence Period the Seller will allow the Purchaser access to the Property. Let's say that the parties are fighting over the Purchaser's ability to access the Property on a Sunday morning when neither the Seller nor any of his employees are available to meet the Purchaser or Purchaser's inspectors at the Property. Although the Seller's unwillingness to provide access to the Property on a Sunday is some kind of misdeed (the Seller should have put language in the Contract like: "provide access to the Purchaser at reasonable times"), I doubt that any Court would consider that action (or inaction) significant enough to constitute a default . . . it is just not important enough to get agitated about; that is, it does not rise to the level of "material."

A default is a big deal because it means the nondefaulting party can now go into Court and bring a lawsuit against the defaulting party. And if the Court does its job (when entering litigation *never* assume that the Court will see things the way you do . . . or even that the Court will see things the way most people do—litigation is unpredictable), then the nondefaulting party will get some kind of order or reward from the Court.

Of course, your analysis of the default provisions in a Contract depends upon whether you are a Seller or a Purchaser. Since a premise of this book is learning to buy real estate in such a way as to **add value**, most of the time I am thinking about Contracts from the Purchaser's point of view; that is, it is usually the prospective buyer who is using the language in a Contract to lever his position in the deal.

When I am the Purchaser, I'm always very aware of what the default provisions of the Contract say and how I might take advantage of them . . . or at least avoid being hurt by them. Specifically, I am always trying to figure out how to craft a default provision in a way to convert a traditional Contract, with a standard default clause, into something more akin to an Option Agreement. As we will learn later, an Option gives one the opportunity to run with another person's property in an attempt to accomplish something of value with that property, AND with a limited downside if the effort is not successful.

The point to understand relative to the default provision of the Contract is that if you are a clever real estate player, you may be able to negotiate this clause to give you a form of Option on the property. Here is an example:

I'm negotiating to buy an office building from a Seller. The price of the office building is $5 million. It is 50,000 square feet (sf) and 50 percent vacant. The price I am paying is fair and takes into account the 25,000 sf of vacant space. But being an aggressive real estate player, I am not interested in fair prices . . . I want deals where I can make a lot of money, and if I pay a fair price, that may mean there is no super and quick upside to the property.

Now, being a diligent real estate entrepreneur, I know (and in this example, the Seller doesn't) that there is a large tenant, call it "Big Tenant" in the market to occupy a lot of space, and as it happens the vacant 25,000 sf in the building I am negotiating to buy is perfect for Big Tenant. If I can convince Big Tenant to take the vacant space, I will immediately boost the property's value in a big way. But Big Tenant is looking at a lot of other buildings too, and I'm just not sure I can convince it to come to "my" building (the property I want to tie up). Though I do like this property, I do not think it has enough pop given the vacancy and so have concluded that if I can get Big Tenant to commit to this building, great, I buy; and if not, then I pass.

I considered asking Seller for an option to buy the property, but he would be put off by that proposal. Seller wants to know whether I'm committed to the purchase or not. Whether I'm in or out. I say that I'm in. And now I have to figure out a way to tie the property up, go after Big Tenant, and still limit my downside on the deal (create a way to get out) if I'm unable to persuade Big Tenant to come to this building.

Here's where the clever real estate player has to be very cognizant of the default provision in the Contract and attempt to use it to his advantage. I say to the Seller, "Yes, I'm in . . . I'm ready to go to Contract." So the Seller instructs his attorney to draw up a Contract. Let's say the Contract provides for closing 90 days after execution (when both parties have signed the Contract). Okay, I now have 90 days to try to convince Big Tenant to lease the building. What happens, however, if at the end of that period I am unsuccessful with Big Tenant and so do not want to close the deal?

Remember our strategy: to attempt to use the default language in the Contract to create a virtual Option. So I need to pay a lot of attention to the wording of the default clause.

There are a couple of different types of clauses lawyers use to address Purchaser defaults. The most common default clause in larger real estate transactions is a **liquidated** or **stipulated** damages clause. The liquidated damages clause says something like: "In the event that the Purchaser is in default of this Contract, then the parties have agreed in advance that the Seller's sole remedy is to retain the Purchaser's deposit on Contract and the rights and obligations of the parties to each other shall thereafter cease and terminate."

Usually a deposit on Contract—the amount that the Purchaser puts down until closing—is some percentage of the sales price. In smaller deals, the deposit can be as much as 10 percent. In larger deals it will fall to 5 percent or less. In our $5 million deal, the deposit is $250,000, and that's a lot of change for me to drop in the event I decide not to proceed with the deal (if I cannot convince Big Tenant to come to the building). So I have to come up with some other language in the Contract for addressing the Seller's rights in the event of my default . . . something that will protect me from dropping $250,000 should I decide not to close. Here are some suggestions:

- Try to negotiate a clause that limits the Seller's rights to retain *some portion* of the Deposit in the event of Purchaser's default. Say to the Seller,

The Basics

"Look, I'm willing to put up $250,000 on Contract to show you my good faith and ability to proceed, but just in case something happens to me and I am unable to close, I want to limit my downside to $100,000." (Will the Seller read this comment as you're backing off from a commitment to buy? Maybe.)

- Try to negotiate a clause that defines the Seller's rights in the event of your default as its actual damages: "In the event of the Purchaser's default, then Seller shall be entitled to Seller's damages incurred as a result thereof, up to the amount of the Deposit herewith." Now, if you're only going to tie up the property for a short period of time and do not see a risk that property values will drop during that period, what are the Seller's damages by reason of your failure to close? In my judgment, so long as the price in the Contract is fair and will most likely be attainable from other potential purchasers should you default, the Seller's damages are not much. Therefore, the fact that the Deposit is $250,000 is not relevant if you're convinced that the Seller's damages, should you not close, will be nowhere near the amount of the Deposit.
- Try to negotiate a clause that ties the Seller's damages to the time between the execution of Contract and the point where you either close or give notice to him that you will not close. As indicated, the period between execution of the Contract in our example and closing is 90 days. You might try this position with the Seller:

> I am prepared to put down $250,000 on Contract and have that be at risk should I not close. But I do want to provide for an out, at much less money, should I give you notice within 30 days after execution of Contract that I cannot close. We are moving quickly here and I think I have all my ducks in a row, but just in case something comes out of the woodwork and I cannot move forward on this transaction, I would like to limit my damages to $50,000 if I terminate within 30 days of execution of Contract.

Maybe the Seller goes for this or some variation. Okay, so what have you accomplished? Well, you still have 90 days to close. But you only have 30 days to figure out and make a calculated judgment as to whether you can persuade Big Tenant to lease 25,000 sf from you once you own the property. And, if at the end of 30 days you feel great about your ability to do that, well then you do not terminate the Contract. If, on the other hand, you think the odds of convincing Big Tenant to come to the property are slim, then you terminate the Contract, lose $50,000, and go on to fight another day.

There is no one way to accomplish what I am suggesting here: tying up the property with a limited downside, which you negotiate via the default clause in the Contract. There are many ways to accomplish the same thing. The key is to have a strategy in mind and to go forward looking for openings to implement your strategy.

We're almost done with the basics. You are already starting to get the idea. Entrepreneurial, knowledgeable real estate players can use information and experience to create opportunities for themselves to add value to their position in the purchase/sale process, or to the property itself. Just one more stop before we jump into a discussion of specific techniques for adding value. How about a little side trip down Ethics Street.

A Walk on Ethics Street

Welcome to Ethics Street. As you will learn later in this book, I am a huge believer in playing the real estate game straight up . . . meaning fair and square. **I do not believe that those who are tricky, cut corners, don't honor their word, or are just plain liars have any chance at long-term success in the real estate game.**

So what about the above example where we are trying to add value to a property by using the Contract process to determine Big Tenant's interest in the deal? We know that the Seller does not know about Big Tenant. We also know that we will not be closing the purchase if Big Tenant cannot be convinced to lease the building we're trying to buy.

First, I believe that each person needs to answer those questions as he or she sees fit. For myself, I believe there are times when a real estate player must use an information imbalance to be successful. Here, our real estate player knew about Big Tenant and knew that the Seller did not. I have no trouble at all using that information imbalance in an effort to buy something at a price lower than its potential eventual value (i.e., should Big Tenant lease the building). To me, part of business is knowledge and information, and if one person has more than the other, I do not believe it is incumbent on the more knowledgeable individual to educate the less informed one. That is all part of business, and certainly an information advantage is a key element to being a successful real estate player.

What about the fact that I have not told Seller that if Big Tenant does not show a high level of interest in leasing the building, I have no intention of closing on the purchase? Perhaps if the Seller knew that he would not go to Contract with me. Staying with the premise that each person has to answer these questions for himself and herself, I cannot tell you how candid to be with the Seller in this situation. My sense is that many real estate players would not feel obligated to give the Seller in our example much insight into his/her intentions. In my mind, those of us in the real estate game who have been there for a while are all sophisticated and perhaps wealthy. The real estate owner wanting to sell a $5 million building does not have to take the Purchaser's $5 million. If he agrees to language in a Contract that limits the Purchaser's downside in the event of a default, then should not Purchaser be guilt-free about taking advantage of his superior negotiating skills?

As with everything in life, one must tailor his or her conduct to the specific situation at hand. If the Seller is a rich, sophisticated real estate player and consents to language in the Contract limiting the Purchaser's downside, perhaps that is okay. There are, however, other scenarios that are not so clear.

What if the Seller is the son or daughter of a successful real estate player who just inherited the property? Perhaps the son or daughter is not very knowledgeable. And what if this son or daughter likes and trusts the Purchaser (you) as a person and believes that you, among several other purchaser candidates, are the right person to get the building? What if there's a chance that your passing on the deal, should you not get the requisite level of interest from Big Tenant, would actually harm the Seller's ability to sell the building to another purchaser?

My point is that there is not always a black-and-white answer to questions of ethics. I find that I struggle a lot with these issues. On the one hand, I want to be a very successful real estate player, and the measure of success is, of course, good deals = money. Sometimes, making a good deal means getting the better of another person: a competing purchaser, for example, or a seller who is perhaps not as sophisticated as you are. For the moment (we will address integrity in the final chapter) all I can say is that you should always be aware of the ethical issues raised by your conduct. I think you'll find that once you make a certain amount of money (perhaps different for each person), doing additional deals has a lot to do with your ego and self-image, and if you make a deal on the back of someone else's lack of knowledge or sophistication, the joy of the "kill" may not be what you anticipate.

Leases

As we will see in many of the examples that follow this chapter, a real estate entrepreneur must have a good understanding of leasing. Often the entrepreneur is the developer and/or owner of property that is or will be leased to tenants. Sometimes a real estate entrepreneur must act as the tenant; he may determine that he cannot acquire an ownership interest in a piece of real estate and must instead exercise control over the property using a long-term lease agreement. In any event, all good real estate players are quite knowledgeable about leasing.

The Lease Agreement

A Lease Agreement is just a form of Contract whereby Party #1, "Landlord," allows Party #2, "Tenant," the right to occupy or control Landlord's real estate. Tenant, in turn, agrees to pay money (Rent) to Landlord for this right. Following are the most important business paragraphs in a Lease Agreement.

What Is the Length of the Commitment the Parties Make to Each Other? The stipulated length of the Lease Agreement is called the **Lease Term**. Often, a tenant will have rights to extend the Lease Term. Sometimes a tenant will have a kick-out or termination clause that allows it to cancel the Lease Agreement earlier than the stipulated Lease Termination Date. Tenants who are uncertain they will need the rented space for the entire Lease Term may want a kick-out clause. But why would a landlord agree to this kind of clause? Well, we landlords do what we have to in order to make a deal, and if a prospective tenant will not sign a Lease without such a clause, we may agree to an early termination. But we will also extract something in return: most termination clauses can only be exercised by a tenant upon the payment of a termination fee such that the tenant will have to pay for the right (at the time he terminates, if he does) to end the Lease early.

What Is the Exact Area That a Tenant Will Be Leasing? This too is an important question and requires discussing what may be new concepts to you: **usable square feet** and **rentable square feet**. But let's back up for just one minute. Are you clear about square feet (everybody abbreviates to SF or sf)? Obviously a square foot is the area on your floor that measures one foot by one foot. Get comfortable with this measure because many standard real estate concepts are tied to square footage: the area being rented, the sales price of a building, the buildable area of a piece of land, and so on.

Okay, back to usable and rentable square feet. Most multi-tenant buildings will have areas that are occupied exclusively by particular tenants and other areas that are common, that is, shared by all tenants. Examples of common area include lobbies, hallways, stairwells, and restrooms. As with all the other square feet in his building, a landlord wants to obtain rent for these areas. So landlords invented something called **rentable square feet,** which is simply the square footage that a tenant *pays for,* not necessarily the square footage the tenant has exclusive control over.

The square footage over which a tenant has exclusive use and control is called **usable square footage.** This is the area within the four walls of the space the tenant occupies in a building. The square footage of this area *plus* a proportionate share of the common areas is the rentable square footage. So, for example, let's consider a 10,000 sf multi-tenant office building with 8,000 sf of usable area—area within demised (walled-in) spaces over which tenants will have exclusive control—and 2,000 sf of common area (hallways, restrooms, lobby, etc.). Since the owner of this building wants to rent all 10,000 sf of his building to the tenants, he will assign each of them a pro rata amount of the 2,000 sf of common area. In order to do that, the landlord must allocate a certain percentage of the common area to each tenant.

Here's how it's done: each tenant will pay the same percentage of the common area that its usable space is to the total usable space. Okay, that's a mouthful. Let's use an example:

Tenant has 1,500 sf of usable sf, which is 18.75 percent of the total usable sf (1,500 sf/8,000 sf). Therefore, the landlord will add 18.75 percent of the common area (the 2,000 sf) to this tenant's usable sf to get this tenant's rentable sf:

$$1,500 \text{ usable sf} + 375 \text{ sf of common area } (2,000 \text{ sf} \times 0.1875)$$
$$= 1,875 \text{ of rentable sf}$$

And the landlord will do that for each space it rents (or wishes to rent).

Another way to get from usable to rentable sf is to employ what is sometimes called an **Add-On Factor**. In our example, the Add-On Factor is 1.25. The Add-On Factor is 1 plus the percentage of common area to usable sf (2,000/8,000), or 1.25. So the tenant in our example above will have his usable sf (1,500) multiplied by 1.25 to yield his rentable sf:

$$1,500 \times 1.25 = 1,875 \text{ sf}$$

Of course, there are limits on what a landlord can add to the usable square footage to derive the rentable square footage. There are standards in the business as to what is an acceptable Add-On Factor or **Loss Factor**. The Loss Factor is just another way of looking at the Add-On Factor; it is the percentage of the rentable square footage attributable to common area. In the case above, where a tenant is paying rent on 1,875 sf, the Loss Factor is 20 percent (375/1,875). That is about the limit of what a landlord can get from tenants. If a landlord has a building with more common area than say 20 percent of the building's total sf, the landlord may have to eat some of it, that is, not charge tenants for it, because tenants have a limit as to how much common area they will pay for.

Rents

The biggest issue between landlords and tenants is of course how much rent the tenant pays to the landlord. Rents are figured by the square foot. To determine annual rent, one multiplies rentable square footage by the rent per square foot.

For example, if a tenant will be renting 5,250 rentable square feet at a rent of $22 per sf, the tenant will be paying the landlord $115,500 in annual rent, usually payable monthly . . . in our case in the amount of $9,625 per month.

Needless to say, rents are a hotly negotiated item. Related issues are:

Is the Rent Flat during the Lease Term? Landlords will want rental increases over the Lease Term. Tenants will not. The rental increases (if agreed to by the tenant) can be a stipulated amount, for example, $1,000 per year; or a stipulated square footage increase, such as $1 per sf per year; or tied to the Consumer Price Index (CPI) (rents increase in line with increases in CPI); or just a percentage increase every year, such as 3 percent per year. And rents can go up every year or every two years or never. Rents can even go down, and I have negotiated Leases where the rent will be say $X per year for the first three years and then go down to 90 percent of $X in years four and five. In other words, how to deal with rent payments is only limited by the creativity of the parties.

When Does the Rental Obligation Begin? One way landlords and tenants can break a logjam over the exact rent per square foot that the landlord wants, but the tenant is not willing to pay, is **free rent**. This is simply the nonpayment of rent by a tenant during a stipulated period between a Lease Commencement Date (when the Lease begins) and a Rent Commencement Date (when the tenant's obligation to pay rent begins). As an example, parties may agree on a 10-year lease term that commences on January 1, 2006. But the obligation of the tenant to pay rent may not commence until July 1, 2006. The nonpayment of rent during the first six months of the Lease Term is called free rent. Why would a landlord agree to this? Well, as always, perhaps it's what is needed to induce the tenant to agree to terms. But it can also be a way to get a tenant to pay a higher rent per square foot (sometimes called face rent) than it otherwise might. Here's an example of how free rent can be used to achieve what the landlord wants—a specific amount of total rent at the highest face rent possible.

Let's say that we are the Landlord and we're negotiating a five-year Lease for 5,000 square feet. Our goal is to achieve $550,000 of total rent during the Lease Term and we are asking for a rent schedule that looks like this:

Year one:	$20/sf × 5,000 sf =	$100,000
Year two:	$21/sf × 5,000 sf =	$105,000
Year three:	$22/sf × 5,000 sf =	$110,000
Year four:	$23/sf × 5,000 sf =	$115,000
Year five:	$24/sf × 5,000 sf =	$120,000
	Total rent =	$550,000

Unfortunately the Tenant we are negotiating with is not willing to pay us $100,000 in the first year of the Lease Term. It is a start-up company and wants to preserve as much of its cash as possible for the first year of its operation.

So the Landlord offers the Tenant a deal with no rent due (free rent) in the first nine months of the Lease Term. This is very attractive to the Tenant. In return the Tenant agrees to pay $22 per sf for the remaining three months of year one, $24/sf for year two, $26/sf for year three, $26/sf for year four, and $28/sf in year five. Let's see what happens to the Landlord's total rent revenue.

Year one:	$22/sf × 5,000 sf/12 × 3 =	$ 27,500
Year two:	$24/sf × 5,000 =	$120,000
Year three:	$26/sf × 5,000 =	$130,000
Year four:	$26/sf × 5,000 =	$130,000
Year five:	$28/sf × 5,000 =	$140,000
	Total rent =	$ 547,500

As you can see, the Landlord has not hurt itself by offering the Tenant nine months free rent. And there may be a bigger reason that the Landlord is willing to do this. As you'll learn later, the value of a property is tied to its net operating income. Investors look at a future income stream in determining what they will pay for a property. Though the Landlord took a hit on the first nine months of the Lease (collecting nothing from this Tenant), Landlord (1) boosted his rent/sf beginning in month 10 above what it would otherwise have been, and (2) established a higher rent/sf as the "market value rent" for the property. Since this point illustrates something important about valuing real estate, I will elaborate.

Trading Free Rent and Increasing Fit-Up Concessions to Boost Value.
Real estate players understand how the lender and investment community will value their property, and I discuss that at length in later chapters. For the moment I just want to illustrate how free rent and other concessions can be used by a property owner to his advantage. In our example above, the Landlord offered the Tenant nine months of free rent, and in return the Tenant paid a

higher rent/sf than it otherwise would have, albeit beginning 10 months after the Lease commenced. Coincidentally, let's say that the Landlord made a deal with another prospective Tenant in the building; it offered this Tenant a lot of **fit-up money** (up-front dollars to modify the space to the Tenant's needs) in return for a higher rent per square foot than the Tenant would otherwise have been willing to pay. Like the Tenant being offered nine months of free rent, this Tenant also happily took the Landlord's offer. These Tenants accepted the Landlord's offers figuring they could meet their rental obligations in later years, and because what they needed at the time of the Lease signing was free rent or fit-up money.

Now fast forward three years and assume that the Landlord has the building on the market for sale. Where some other buildings in this area are renting at $23/sf, Landlord has Leases (with the two Tenants we discussed) showing a rental value of $26/sf. If a Purchaser is savvy, it will go back, review the history of the Leases, and see that the Landlord offered one Tenant a lot of free rent and another a lot of fit-up money. The Purchaser might therefore conclude that the Landlord "bought" rents a bit higher than market. But (1) not all Purchasers do that, and (2) sometimes the free rent, fit-up, and other concessions can be disguised (not even addressed in the Lease Agreement) so that it is hard to identify what happened. Now certainly there was a cost to the Landlord to obtaining the higher rent roll (the free rent and the fit-up money), but like any smart real estate entrepreneur, the Landlord did the math and figured out that the multiples received on the net operating income on sale outweigh the money expended to obtain a higher rent roll.

Gross versus Net Rent. It is important for you to understand that there are rents and then there are rents. The distinguishing factor is what, in addition to the stated rent, the Tenant is obligated to pay. A **net rent**, sometimes called **triple net**, means that in addition to the stated **Base Rent**, the tenant will pay all operating costs, real estate taxes, and utilities attributable to the property. In a single-tenant building, this calculation is not difficult. In a multi-tenant building, each of the tenants pays their proportionate share (**pro rata share**) of the operating expenses and real estate taxes; they also pay for their utilities, usually at some agreed-upon price/sf or, if available, by direct metering (measuring actual consumption).

A truly **gross rent** means that the tenant pays one check for everything. Most gross rents, however, are "plus utilities," meaning that the tenant pays for the utilities consumed in its space in addition to the Base Rent. Most gross rent deals also have what are called in the industry **operating expense** and **real estate tax stops**. The concept is that the landlord's obligation for operating expenses and real estate taxes STOPS after the first year, and that the tenant pays for increases in these expenditures beginning in the second year of the Lease. The

The Basics

terminology is that the initial lease year is the **Base Year,** and the tenant pays for all increases in operating expenses and real estate taxes over the Base Year amounts. Again, in a single-tenant building, this is easy to administer. In a multi-tenant building, each tenant pays its pro rata share of the operating expense and real estate taxes over the Base Year (and often these are different Base Years, i.e., the calendar year in which the tenant signed the Lease).

The stated rent in a Lease Agreement is usually called the Base Rent. All other charges that a tenant owes to a landlord, including triple net charges or operating expense and tax increases over Base Year, are generally called **Additional Rent**.

It's important for you to learn how rents in your particular area are calculated. In my area almost all office rentals are gross plus utilities, and all retail rentals are triple net. That may or may not be the case in your area, and types of rents can even vary from building to building (e.g., some of the office building landlords in my market accept gross rents and others want triple net rents).

Conclusion: Enough for Now

Okay, okay, enough of the basics for the moment. I could go on and on, but as I have indicated, there are already lots of books on this subject and, as you will discover, I will continually be supplementing the information in this chapter as we work our way into specific techniques of advanced real estate entrepreneuring. So let's get started and roll up our sleeves, for in the next chapter we are going to learn how to add value to the process of purchasing a property by first obtaining control over it and then using time to our advantage.

4

Options

An Option Agreement is a form of Real Estate Contract. There is an obligation on the part of the Seller to sell. And although the Purchaser is theoretically also obligated to buy, if it does not, the Seller's sole remedy is to keep the Purchaser's Deposit, called the Option Payment, and the deal is terminated. In other words, the Seller has no suit for damages against the Purchaser for breach of Contract should the Purchaser elect not to consummate the purchase. One way to think about an Option Agreement is to consider it as payment to a property owner for the right to tie up his property for a defined period of time.

The Option Payment is usually less than the standard deposit given by a Purchaser. And the time between execution of the Option Agreement and closing is usually considerably longer than the time between execution of the standard Real Estate Contract and closing.

As we discussed in the previous chapter, most Real Estate Contracts provide for the Purchaser to forfeit the deposit if he does not close, and since most Real Estate Contracts contain stipulated or liquidated damages clauses, the Seller cannot sue the Purchaser for damages. But in most Real Estate Contracts the deposit is large enough to deter a rational Purchaser from forfeiting, that is, not closing. The Option Agreement, on the other hand, contemplates the situation where a Purchaser may well elect not to close and thus the deposit (Option Payment) is less than the typical Real Estate Contract deposit.

The typical deposit on Contract varies according to the size of the deal, but it is usually at least 5 percent of the sales price. So if you're buying a $5 million property, plan on putting down at least $250,000 and expect to lose those funds should you not close. On the other hand, an Option Payment for a deal of that size might be $50,000 to $100,000.

As for the duration between execution and closing, the typical Real Estate Contract might provide for three or four months. The Option Agreement, on the other hand, may call for a year or two before closing. Option Agreements are usually employed when there is some higher-than-normal risk with a deal, for example, the Purchaser would not buy unless he can make something happen with the property (and the Seller recognizes the risk). The most common example is the development deal. The following situation, for instance, calls for tying up property with an Option Agreement:

You have a relationship with a retailer, Mr. Retailer, who would like to open a store in your community. He needs 40,000 square feet and would prefer a "build-to-suit" situation, meaning a new store that you build for him. He explains the kind of location that works for him. With the amount of parking and loading areas he requires, most of his stores are on about four acres of land.

So you get in your car and start driving the general vicinity of your community that could work for him. And you're fortunate. You come upon a piece of undeveloped land, which appears to be four or five acres, at the outskirts of a dense residential area. You get Mr. Retailer into your car, show him the parcel, and—good news—he likes it.

Now you need to find the owner of the land, figure out whether it's for sale and at what price. So you go to the City Hall—usually the Tax Assessor's Office is a good place to start—or easier still, you go on the Internet if you live in an area where your Assessor has put owner's information online. In any event, you find out that this piece of land is owned by Mr. Isaac Newton. You also learn that the parcel in question is actually five acres and that it's zoned for residential purposes only—housing. Not what you had hoped.

Still, as a persevering and creative real estate player, you decide to call Mr. Newton. The conversation goes something like this:

You: Hello Mr. Newton, my name is Joe Entrepreneur and I have learned from the Tax Assessor's Office that you are the owner of the five acres of land on the corner of Main and Broad Streets.

Options

NEWTON: Yes, that's correct.

YOU: Well, I am a real estate investor and I'm looking for land in that general area and was wondering if you would be interested in selling the land.

NEWTON: Well, I have thought about it at times . . . What type of money are you willing to pay?

YOU: Well, I am not prepared to give you a number at this time, although with a little homework I will get back to you on that. My interest, however, is not residential development, and that's all your property is zoned for. My preliminary analysis is that your property would be worth *a lot more money* if it were zoned commercial.

NEWTON: Yes, I'm sure that is true, but at my age I do not have an interest in trying to get it rezoned. As you know, it's very close to the big residential area in town and it's very possible that the neighbors will organize to fight any attempted rezoning.

YOU: Yes, I do know that, and I want to tell you that I am *young and energetic* and *strong enough to take on a fight*, and I have the capital to make this deal happen, and so perhaps you would consider giving me an option on your property.

NEWTON: What do you mean by an option?

YOU: Well in *higher-risk* transactions like this, developers *usually* get an agreement from the landowner, which agreement gives them the time to try to get property rezoned. If they're successful, they pay a price to the landowner that reflects the increased value in the property by reason of the rezoning. And if they're not successful, they don't close and the landowner hasn't lost anything in the meantime.

NEWTON: Yes, I've heard about such agreements, but how long do you plan on needing to attempt a rezoning?

YOU: Well, I've done some preliminary homework and I would say that the time needed to get a public hearing and a favorable decision is at least six months, and then there is the chance of an appeal from the neighborhood. Fighting the appeal can take at least another 18 months.

NEWTON: Well, if you're talking about tying my property up for two years, I would not be interested . . . I am too old for that. I may not even be around in two years.

YOU: Would you consider one year?

NEWTON: I thought you just said that the appeals could take you 18 months to get rid of.

Confessions of a Real Estate Entrepreneur

You: Yes, I did say that. But maybe, *if I get lucky,* I can prevent an appeal from being filed, and then I can close within one year instead of two.

Newton: What kind of down payment are you going to give me?

You: Well, with an option, the down payment is not that large because the Purchaser has so many other costs to incur and *the risk is so large.* Here, not only do I have a lot of risk, but I'm going to have to hire lawyers, zoning consultants, surveyors, environmental people, and so on. I would guess that I'll spend at least $75,000 trying to get this property rezoned.

Newton: So, what kind of down payment are you going to give me?

You: Well, my numbers are very preliminary, but here's what I can probably do: I will give you $25,000 on signing of the Option Agreement. If I can get your property rezoned, I'll pay you $3 million for it . . . a lot more than it's worth as a residential piece. If I don't get the rezone, I'll walk from the deal and you will keep my $25,000 and I'll also give to you all the benefits of my homework, the new survey and all reports that I get from the experts. This will help you should you at some point in the future decide to rezone the property yourself, or should you elect to sell to someone who is interested in commercial development.

Newton: What happens to the $25,000 if you do get the rezoning?

You: Well, then I will be in a position to close and the $25,000 deposit is credited against the purchase price.

Newton: Let me think about it. The gravity of your offer requires some thought.

Newton does think about it, and in future conversations the two of you reach an understanding that is embodied in a typical Option Agreement, the key terms of which are:

1. Price: $3 million (well more than the property is worth for residential purposes).
2. Option Payment: $25,000 (note that this is less than 1 percent of the sales price).
3. Time to close: one year. Optionee (the Purchaser; the landowner is the Optionor) can close earlier, with 30 days prior written notice if he chooses (perhaps you get the rezoning in four months, no appeal is filed, and you want to close sooner than one year).
4. The Optionee forfeits the $25,000 Option Payment if Optionee does not close.
5. If the Optionee does close, the $25,000 Option Payment is credited against the purchase price.

Options

6. If the Optionee does not close, Optionee delivers to the Seller (Optionor) copies of all studies done by the Optionee's experts.
7. The Optionor agrees to cooperate in all respects with the Optionee's efforts to rezone, including attendance at public hearings.

What have you accomplished? Well, you've tied up what is potentially a $3 million property for up to one year, and for a relatively small amount of money for a deal of this magnitude ($25,000). You know that you have a tough row to hoe ahead of you as you attempt to get the property rezoned, but if you're successful, you have a great piece of property that is particularly valuable to you, given that Mr. Retailer is in your pocket. True, if you're not successful with the rezone you lose about $100,000—$25,000 of Option money and the cost of your lawyers and experts—but you have assessed the risk-reward scenario and have concluded that is a risk worth taking.

Have we achieved the stated goal in this book: ADDING VALUE, in this case to the process of acquiring real estate? I would answer "yes" and here is why:

1. We've put ourselves in a position to do a very lucrative deal. We know there is risk, but we can quantify it (the amount of the Option Payment and costs associated with the Due Diligence and rezoning of the property).
2. We can use the period that we have the property tied up (the Option term) to do our homework on the costs of building Mr. Retailer a store, exploring financing options, and other relevant matters. Presumably we have a pretty good feel for these numbers before we enter the Option Agreement, but we can use the Option Term to really refine things. Remember, we are *not* obligated to buy (even if we get the rezoning). If we conclude that the cost of Mr. Retailer's store makes the deal unfeasible, even if we get the zoning, then we can drop the deal and we lose only our Option Payment and some expenses.
3. It is possible that we're underpaying for the property. Option Agreements usually come into play when development is involved. Often the Seller has no interest in taking on the development and therefore does not really have a good idea as to the value of his land—if rezoned and developed. All Mr. Newton knows is that we paid more than he could get from a residential developer. What he does not know is how valuable his land is for a retail development.

So we have added value to the process of buying this land with the use of an Option Agreement. We tied up a piece of land that can make us a lot of money. We are at risk for the Option Payment but we have a huge upside. We may have underpaid for the land.

Are there other ways to accomplish the same things, with even less risk to the Purchaser? Yes, there are. In the next chapter we'll go into Real Estate Contracts that include zoning contingencies, and you'll see that a clever real estate player can sometimes create a virtual Option for himself without even risking any Option money. But for now let's go back to our conversation with Mr. Newton to illustrate what I consider to be a critical component of success as a real estate entrepreneur, to wit: the way you communicate with the other party to a potential transaction.

Always Selling

It is my view that businesspeople must always be aware of the words they're using when speaking to someone with whom they hope to do a deal. In the case above, the real estate player must choose carefully the words he uses with the potential seller, Mr. Newton. In short, the real estate player must keep in mind that he is *always selling*, and therefore must constantly be thinking about the way he's coming across.

Let's analyze how you handled the conversation with Mr. Newton and why you selected the words you used. In order to facilitate our review, I've highlighted certain words you used that, in my view, were very well chosen.

1. Early on you wanted to establish for Mr. Newton the benefits of doing a deal with you . . . so in your second sentence you referred to the fact that the conversation could mean "a lot more money" to him.
2. You also wanted to sell Mr. Newton on the fact that the rezoning would not be easy, a lot of costs would be associated with it, and therefore you were assuming a lot of risk in just taking this idea forward. Note the several times you referenced "risk" and needing to "get lucky." You also indicated that lots of time and effort would be required for the rezone and that it would require someone "strong enough to take on the fight" who was "young and energetic."
3. Finally, you wanted to persuade Mr. Newton that the type of deal you were proposing is standard fare for the sale of property like his. Note your respectful use of the words "as you know," not only showing him the deference a younger person should show to an elder, but also suggesting that like any intelligent person, he knows that Options are common and often used ("developers usually get") when a landowner sells to a developer.

Later in the book I will address the art of persuasion (selling someone on something); but for now, as you read hypothetical conversations in subsequent chapters, always consider the words that are being used and whether the speaker is trying to subliminally affect the other party's decision.

Before we leave the topic of Options, let me tell you about a real-life deal that returned $2.5 million on an investment of $100,000 in about 18 months' time. But for my knowledge of Option Agreements, I might never have made that deal.

Options

In the early 1990s Wal-Mart enlisted the help of my partner and me to help them find sites to build stores in New York and Connecticut. Wal-Mart did not work exclusively with us, and if someone else brought them a deal, they listened. But what they did do, in return for our committing to work hard to find them good sites, was educate us about the kind of sites they wanted and the general location where they wanted to be. With that information and a good understanding of Option Agreements, my partner and I felt we had something of real value.

One day we come across an interesting piece of land, 90 acres just off the Interstate, in Albany, New York. It was surprising to us that this land had not been developed, and based upon our understanding of Wal-Mart's site criteria, we know that it will be of interest to them.

We go to the City Assessor's Office and learn that the land is owned by a wealthy farmer who had no interest in developing it. We also learn that in order to get it approved for retail, we'll need several zoning and other regulatory approvals (e.g., wetlands, traffic, drainage, sewer). We know you can never be sure about getting those approvals, since zoning and other boards are very sensitive to neighbors' issues, and a development on 90 acres could potentially upset a lot of neighbors.

We negotiate an Option Agreement with the landowner that gives us two years to close at a price of $7 million. We put down $100,000, which is nonrefundable; in other words, we lose this money if we do not close. Our timing was good because the landowner had recently been contemplating what to do with the land but had no interest in developing it himself, primarily because he didn't want to risk getting into a dispute with his neighbors (he lived nearby). So he gave us an Option on his land.

Now we're off and running (as fast as we could) because we only had two years to get all of the approvals we needed. We hired a good local attorney (critical when dealing with zoning and other regulatory issues) and, as if we had the approvals in hand, began talking to prospective tenants.

Needless to say, our first stop was Wal-Mart. They were not upset that we took this opportunity for ourselves. They are not in the real estate business and did not care who owned the land; so long as they got the deal they wanted, they were okay with our being the developer. They committed to taking two 100,000 square foot stores—one a Wal-Mart and one a Sam's Club. Needless to say, having these deals in hand made our discussions with other "big box" prospective tenants that much easier.

In the ensuing six months, we signed up letters of intent with two other large retailers, one a supermarket and the other a home improvement company. We now had 400,000 square feet spoken for of the 650,000-square-foot total we could develop.

Fortunately, our zoning and regulatory applications were also going well. A "power center" this huge represented a lot of jobs, and that out-weighed concerns of traffic and other municipal issues. As it appeared that we were going to get the approvals we needed, we had to start thinking about our next step, since a deal of this size was beyond our capability. Not only did we need to close on the land for $7 million, but we also had to look at developing 650,000 square feet of retail space—at a cost of another $40 million or so.

Without the capability to do this project ourselves, my partner and I felt that we had taken this deal as far as we could with our own money. We approached a major developer, and with tenant interest of 400,000 square feet (all good credits) and the necessary approvals in the offing, the developer paid us back all our expenses and gave us a profit of $2.5 million—not bad for 18 months of hustling.

The point is to show you what a powerful tool Option Agreements can be. Had we not been able to tie the land up with only $100,000 and not had two years to try to get all the necessary approvals and to confirm tenant interest, we would never have pulled this deal off. That's why you need to be comfortable with and knowledgeable about Options.

Conclusion

Top real estate entrepreneurs make clever use of Option Agreements. They understand that there is great value to having control over another person's real estate. They understand that while they have control pursuant to an Option Agreement, they can attempt to add value with a minimum of risk to themselves.

If they're successful, great . . . they exercise their option to buy and take advantage of the value they have added. If they're unsuccessful, well, they lose some money, but not nearly as much as they would have had they purchased first and then attempted to add value.

Good real estate entrepreneurs evaluate risk and reward. Option Agreements are a perfect forum for this exercise. How much are you willing to risk in order to attempt to add value to a particular piece of real estate? The answer is what you will pay for an Option Agreement tying up another person's property.

Okay, so on to another way to tie up property and attempt to add value: the Real Estate Contract with a contingency.

5

Contracts with Contingencies

The good real estate player must understand the concept of contingencies. This is a little confusing, so let's go slowly.

Mortgage Contingencies

A contingency is an event that must happen before the obligation of a party to a Contract matures. Usually the obligation is that of the Purchaser. The mortgage contingency is the most common example. As we have seen the typical mortgage contingency reads:

> The Purchaser's obligation hereunder is conditioned upon [contingent] its ability to obtain a mortgage of $X with Y terms. If the Purchaser does not obtain this mortgage, then its herein obligation to purchase expires and so long as the Purchaser gives the Seller written notice not later than ____ that it did not obtain the referenced mortgage, then the Seller shall immediately return to the Purchaser its down payment and the rights and obligations of the parties to each other shall thereafter cease and terminate.

As you can see, the Purchaser's obligation to purchase does not mature unless he obtains a mortgage commitment for the agreed-upon loan. If the Purchaser does not get the referenced mortgage, then Purchaser does not have to buy if he does not want to. But—and this is an important point—the Purchaser can always waive his right to terminate the Contract. Note that if the Purchaser does not give the Seller written notice that he did not get the mortgage in question, then the deal goes forward. In other words, only the Purchaser can avail himself of the use of the mortgage contingency. It does nothing for the Seller.

Now, if you were the Seller in a Contract with the indicated mortgage contingency, how might you want to change the language? Wouldn't you want the Purchaser under some type of affirmative obligation relative to his obtaining a mortgage? Would not you want Purchaser at least obligated to use, say, "best efforts" to obtain the mortgage in question? If I were the Seller in the above example, I would want to add to the mortgage contingency clause this sentence:

> Purchaser agrees to make immediate application for the referenced mortgage, to prosecute same with diligence, and to do all things in its power and use its best efforts to obtain the mortgage in question.

This language puts pressure on the Purchaser. He cannot just diddle along, halfheartedly attempting to get a mortgage, and then at some point decide that if he does not want your property, he can just opt out of the deal because he did not get a mortgage commitment. As a Seller, I do not want anyone having unfettered control over my property.

Similarly, if you were the Seller in the above example, would you not want to have some say over the amount of $X and the terms of Y? Let's say you're selling a small office building for $1 million and the Purchaser suggests that the mortgage contingency clause stipulate that the Purchaser has to be able to attain a mortgage of $900,000 amortized over not less than 35 years and at an interest rate of not more than 7 percent. In other words, Purchaser wants a clause that provides that if it does not get a mortgage commitment for $900,000 at the referenced terms or better, it can pull out of the deal.

Well, again, I do not want a Purchaser having control over my property with no corresponding obligation. So I call a few banker friends of mine to find out whether it's likely that any Purchaser would get a loan for $900,000 with a 35-year amortization and a 7 percent interest rate. I'm told that the $900,000 is more than most banks will give, and although the 7 percent is reasonable, no banks in the area are "going out" (amortizing the loan) 35 years. Had I not done that research I might not have realized that by agreeing to the amount and terms suggested by the Purchaser, I was putting myself in a bad position. The Purchaser, knowing in advance that he could not get the loan in question, would have a free Option over my property. If he wanted to go forward, Purchaser would waive the contingency and buy, and if he didn't want to, he would invoke the contingency, have no obligation to buy, and get his entire down payment returned. Purchaser would have control of my property for some period of time while deciding what to do, and if he did not want to buy, Purchaser would just invoke the unrealistic mortgage contingency clause to walk from the deal.

Think back to the last chapter. What the Purchaser really has with a poorly drafted (by the Seller) contingency clause is an Option Agreement but with no Option Payment. The Purchaser has some amount of time to consider buying or not, but unlike a true Option—where he would lose his Option Payment if he did not buy—with an unrealistic contingency clause Purchaser can decide to walk *and* get back 100 percent of his deposit.

As I said above, the mortgage contingency is usually not a concept that advanced real estate players can use to their advantage. That is because Sellers of higher priced properties do not generally like the idea of going to Contract with a Purchaser who needs a mortgage contingency. The assumption in the higher reaches of the real estate world is that if you can buy a property for, let's say, $5 million or more, you do not need to condition your obligation on your ability to obtain a mortgage, that is, you should know that you can obtain a mortgage or you shouldn't be buying properties with sales prices in the millions.

Zoning Contingencies

On the other hand, zoning contingencies can be very helpful to the large and clever real estate entrepreneur. To understand how, let's revisit our negotiation with Isaac Newton in the previous chapter on Options.

Let's go back to our first call to Mr. Newton. As you will recall, you have a friend, Mr. Retailer, who is willing to build a 40,000-square-foot store on land owned by Mr. Newton, if you can get Newton's property rezoned. You want to tie up Mr. Newton's land while you take the property through the rezoning process but you prefer not to put down any Option money (the $25,000 Option Payment in our example).

So here's how you might approach the conversation with Mr. Newton:

YOU: Hi. My name is Joe Entrepreneur and I believe you own the five acres on the corner of Main and Broad Streets. I would be interested in purchasing that piece if you would consider selling it.

NEWTON: Well, I have thought about that in the past.

Confessions of a Real Estate Entrepreneur

YOU: Yes, it's a nice piece of property, and I may have a user for it if it can be rezoned. And, as you know, this land is worth much more if commercially zoned.

NEWTON: Yes, I know that.

YOU: Well, I'm young and strong and willing to take on the fight of trying to get the land rezoned, and I'd be willing to enter a Contract with you to show you my good faith so long as, of course, the Contract has a standard zoning contingency in it.

NEWTON: What price are you willing to pay?

YOU: Well, I haven't completed all of my homework, but my preliminary analysis indicates that I could pay up to $3 million if I get the land rezoned. And, as I know you are aware, that's much more than a residential developer could pay.

NEWTON: When would you close?

YOU: I would be willing to close within 30 days of getting the zoning approval and after the expiration of the appeal period . . . just in case someone files an appeal.

NEWTON: How long do you think all of that would take?

YOU: Well, as I'm sure you know, rezoning can take a while. But best case, I hope we'd be able to close in nine months, but I can't be sure.

NEWTON: What kind of down payment are you willing to make?

YOU: I want to show you that I am serious, and I would put down $300,000.

NEWTON: Let me think it over.

Newton thinks it over, and eventually you and he agree on a Contract with the following zoning contingency in it:

> Purchaser's obligation hereunder is conditioned upon its ability to get the land rezoned from Residential II-A to Commercial B zone. Purchaser agrees to make immediate application for said rezoning and Seller agrees to sign whatever documents Purchaser needs in order to submit said application to the Town Zoning Board. Seller agrees to appear at any public hearing, as requested by Purchaser, in support of said application. Purchaser agrees to close not later than 30 days after a favorable decision by the Zoning Commission is published and any appeal period has expired with no appeal being filed. In the event that the Purchaser is not successful in obtaining the referenced rezoning, and gives notice to Seller to that effect by _____, then the Purchaser may terminate the herein Contract,

and the Seller shall immediately return to the Purchaser the Down Payment herewith and the rights and obligations of the parties to each other shall thereafter cease and terminate.

Does this look like a fair agreement from Newton's point of view? Well, let's analyze what you've accomplished and contrast it with an Option Agreement.

1. You've tied up the property without any time limit at all. Other than the fact that you agree to make immediate application for the rezone, there is no outside date by which you must either fish or cut bait. Suppose, for example, that your first application for rezone is denied but you want to go back in and try again. There's nothing in the zoning contingency language that would prevent that. The only outside limit on this clause is either (a) getting the successful rezone, and the appeal period expiring with no appeals, or (b) you giving notice that you do not want to continue with the transaction. Needless to say, a Seller would be well advised to tighten this paragraph by (a) putting an outside time limit on it and/or (b) stipulating that the Purchaser only has one crack at a rezone and that if he is denied or an appeal is filed, he must either terminate the deal by giving written notice or waive the contingency (dropping his right to pull out) and close.

2. You've tied up the property with no money at risk. In our example, you agreed to a deposit equal to 10 percent of the sales price. That $300,000 is really irrelevant and is much different from an Option Payment. Note that the Option Payment (the $25,000 in Chapter 4) goes to the Seller NO MATTER WHAT. Either the Optionee (Purchaser) does not close and forfeits this money, or does close and this money goes to the Seller as a credit against the sales price. *But* in the Contract with a contingency, the deposit money is never at risk. If the Purchaser does not get the sought-after rezone, and decides not to pursue the purchase, then the deposit money is returned in full to the Purchaser. If the Purchaser gets the rezone, then he closes and the $300,000 is credited against the sales price. So using the Contract with a zoning contingency is a big plus for the Purchaser.

Why will a Seller agree to a zoning contingency instead of an Option Agreement or at least require the forfeiture of some amount of the Deposit on Contract? Well, here again, not all people in the real estate transaction world have the same level of sophistication. I've seen many situations when a real estate entrepreneur can persuade a Seller to enter a Contract with a zoning contingency that provides for a return of the entire deposit if the desired zoning is not obtained. My hope is that by the end of this book you will be a competent real estate player, able to think creatively and use all the tools we discuss to craft such a Contract favorable to you. Perhaps the party on the other side of your table is not as knowledgeable as you are, which you will find is true in some cases. On the other hand, you'll also be dealing with people who are very sharp and experienced, and your knowledge will be necessary to make sure they do not take advantage of you.

For the moment just take it at face value that there will be times when the opposing party will not see the important differences between the Option approach to purchase and the Contract/contingency approach. Those are the situations when your knowledge of the strategies we're reviewing will be particularly helpful.

Other Contingencies

There are many types of contingencies you might use to create a favorable Contract for yourself. Consider the following two situations:

Suppose you're trying to create an assemblage of two parcels into one larger land area on which you could develop an office building. You go to the owner of Parcel #1 and agree to pay him "more than it is worth" (of course when part of a new assemblage, it will be worth even more) if he will enter a Contract with you that includes a contingency as to your ability to tie up Parcel #2. The contingency might look like this:

> Purchaser's obligation to purchase the Property is contingent upon its ability to get Parcel #2 under Contract.

Again, the theme is the same: Your obligation to buy Parcel #1 is dependent upon your ability to acquire Parcel #2. You have some time to try that, and if you're unsuccessful, you give the Seller of Parcel #1 notice that you're invoking the contingency and terminating, and you get your money back.

A second example might be an effort to buy a property with known environmental issues. This property may be worth a lot of money to you if you can get the environmental problems solved for under $100,000. But until you tie up the property and meet with the State and/or Federal authorities, you don't know if that is possible. And further testing may be required. Since this is such a valuable property (if you can accomplish the required cleanup at a reasonable cost), you would even risk some Option money, but here, as in our other examples, you'd be better off if you could convince a Seller to give you a Contract with a contingency that says something like:

> Purchaser's obligation hereunder is dependent upon its confirmation that the required clean-up can be accomplished for under $100,000.

The point is, there are many ways to use the contingency approach. Your goal is to try to tie up a property while you ascertain whether you can do what you need in order to add the value you seek to attain. And what you're trying to do in negotiating the contingency clause is to give yourself as much control as possible over the contingency event, thereby giving you lots of control over the deal with nothing at risk.

For example, in the effort to create an assemblage above, your obligation to buy Parcel #1 is dependent upon your ability to buy Parcel #2. But the contingency language does not stipulate at what price. That is not good for you since there is a price for everything. The owner of Parcel #2 may say to you, "Sure, I'll sell to you . . . for $100 million." The owner of Parcel #1 then says, "Hey, you cannot invoke the contingency clause, because you are *able* to buy Parcel #2 . . . you just do not want to pay the Seller's price."

What you want instead is a phrase in the contingency clause that says:

Purchaser's obligation to purchase Parcel #1 is contingent upon its ability to buy Parcel #2 at a price *not in excess* of $X.

Now you have a lot of control. If you can buy Parcel #2 for $X or less, you do so and then close on Parcel #1 and have your valuable assemblage. But if you cannot buy Parcel #2 for $X or less, then you pass on the deal, invoke your contingency clause, and get your deposit back. Your use of Contracts with contingencies to tip the balance of a deal in your favor is only limited by your creativity and ability to persuade a Seller as to the fairness of your proposition.

Overview

My premise throughout this book is that you need to know as much about the real estate business as you can in order to be a successful real estate entrepreneur. You need to be conversant and comfortable with all the techniques and strategies for tying up a property with the least cash at risk. You need to know how to answer every one of a Seller's objections and concerns. You need to know how to persuade a potential Seller to see things your way. Not every strategy will work with every Seller or every situation: you need to be able to think creatively and shift from one strategy to another when one is not working and another may. My point: learn everything you can about what works in the real estate world, and be prepared to pull from your quiver that arrow most likely to land you in the bull's-eye.

Conclusion

We saw in Chapter 4 the value of tying up another person's real estate with an Option Agreement. Contracts with well-crafted contingency clauses can be more powerful than Option Agreements because if the contingency does not occur, then the Purchaser has no obligation to buy and therefore gets back all of his or her deposit. One might argue that Contracts with contingencies are a risk-free form of Option Agreement. In both cases, however, the goal is the same; to find a way to tie up another person's piece of real estate, and then, "on his nickel," to try to create or add value. If it works, great, you're off and running. If not, you may lose some money (if you had to rely on an Option Agreement), but your exact loss is defined in advance, and that is a great advantage to someone in a risk-reward assessment business like real estate entrepreneuring.

Okay, now let's jump to development and see how many extremely wealthy real estate players ADD VALUE.

6

Development

Some of the wealthiest people in America are real estate developers. These are people who take on the risk of finding and buying a piece of land and then building multimillion-dollar shopping centers or office buildings or industrial parks—with the thought that when they're finished, they will be able to lease or sell (for a profit, of course) what they have created. Talk about risk! And the reward is commensurate.

There are many ways to create value when engaged in the development process. As an example, let's start with your effort to purchase land to build a 40,000-square-foot store for your retailer friend, Mr. Retailer.

As you'll recall, Mr. Retailer wants to open a 40,000 sf store in your community. He wants a 20-year Lease and will pay a rent of $20/sf triple net (as you will recall from Chapter 3, this means that in addition to the rent he has agreed to pay for all operating expenses of the property, including real estate taxes).

As we said before, leasing is done on a per square foot basis ($X/sf). When determining the annual rent that a tenant will pay, you multiply the square footage of the area being leased (in our example, 40,000 sf) times the dollars per square foot that the tenant is willing to pay (in our case

$20/sf). So Mr. Retailer is willing to pay $800,000 per year in rent (40,000 × $20/sf), plus operating expenses and real estate taxes. The owner of this property will therefore be receiving a *net operating income* of $800,000 per year.

Okay, back to the deal at hand. We know that if we can acquire the land Mr. Retailer likes and build him the store that fits his specifications, he will pay $800,000 in net annual rent. That sounds good. Now let's make sure the numbers work.

In our example the cost of the land is $3 million. Assuming we're successful in getting it rezoned and in getting what is usually called "site plan approval"—the zoning commission's consent to a specific use of the parcel, that is, building a 40,000 sf retail store with certain areas for parking and loading—we estimate that the costs of development are as follows:

Hard Costs of construction	
(building the store: $100/sf × 40,000)	$4,000,000
Site Work	400,000
Soft Costs (legal, permits, architects, etc.)	250,000
Interest (on borrowed money during construction)	200,000
Miscellaneous/Contingency	250,000
Subtotal	$5,100,000
Land	3,000,000
TOTAL PROJECT COST	$8,100,000

One way to analyze this deal is to look at the cash on cash return (i.e., no debt). In other words, if we just go to our checkbook and write a check for $8.1 million, what kind of return are we earning? Well, since Mr. Retailer will be paying $800,000 per year in rent, we're earning about 10 percent per year on our investment. Not bad, but let's see if we can improve on this return by putting some debt against the property.

Financing

There is not a successful real estate player in America who does not have a good understanding of how to use debt (leverage) to his advantage. If you want to be a successful real estate entrepreneur, you too need to have a good understanding of the financing options for the properties you buy or develop. So let's take a short side trip and discuss financing.

Few people will want to spend $8 million of their own money (assuming they have it) to buy the land and build the store. Most likely there will be an acquisition loan (when the land is purchased) and a construction loan (to build the building). Once the project is finished and the tenant is in possession of the building, the developer will generally pay off these loans by refinancing and putting permanent (long-term) debt on the property.

Loan-to-Value Ratios

Fortunately, Mr. Retailer is a good credit risk and there are many lenders who will give us 70 to 75 percent of the appraised value of the property once the building is completed and the retailer is in possession and paying rent. For the moment let's assume that the appraised value of the completed project is the cost of our project ($8.1 million). This means we can get a loan of $5,670,000 to $6,075,000. Let's say we select a loan of $6 million, a 74 percent loan-to-value ratio.

Recourse versus Nonrecourse

Will this loan be recourse or nonrecourse? Well, with a good credit tenant, this loan is most likely nonrecourse. (During the construction phase, however, there's always some type of personal risk to the developer, i.e., the nonrecourse aspect of the loan does not kick in until the building is finished and the tenant is in possession.)

The lender's point of view is that our loan is safe because we have a strong credit agreeing to lease the property (for 20 years). Therefore, a lender does not also need the individual who owns the property (or, more likely, owning the entity that owns the property) putting his personal assets at risk. Of course, that doesn't mean that the lender would not always prefer to have the developer's personal assets at risk on the loan (recourse or guaranteed). Over time, however, lenders have gotten comfortable with making loans for this type of property on a nonrecourse basis, and so any lender who asks for recourse will not be competitive.

Interest Rates

Okay, so what kind of interest rate can we get? Usually, for commercial loans, a lender will offer you a fixed rate for 5 or 10 years based on some spread (often called a margin) over an index. A commonly used index is the 10-year rate on U.S. Treasuries.

Let's say you want a 10-year fixed rate. Prospective lenders will look to the interest rate on a 10-year Treasury bill and they may say to you: "That rate is presently 4.25 percent and we propose a margin of 145 basis points over the 4.25 percent, or a fixed rate of 5.70 percent. We'll give you a 20-year loan, with interest changing in year 11 to 145 basis points over the then 10-year Treasury rate and remaining at that rate for the remainder of the term."

You can negotiate, of course. Basically the discussion will be about the margin. The margin (in our example 145 basis points) is how the lender makes its money— the lender's cost of funds may be ±4.25 percent, and by lending to you at 5.70, it earns a spread equal to the margin. The smaller the margin, the lower the rate, so you should speak with several lenders to get a sense of what kinds of margins they may be offering.

One other point about margins: In our example we've asked for a loan of $6 million, which is a 74 percent loan-to-value ratio. But if you elected to take less than 75 percent, say $5.5 million, lowering the loan-to-value ratio from 74 to 68 percent, you'd have a good argument for a lower margin since the risk to the lender goes down as the amount you borrow decreases. Why? Well, in case all goes wrong, the lender will have to resell the property, and the less the debt, the better. If the building fetches only $5.7 million after repossession and resale (remember, in our scenario, all has gone wrong, which means there's some organic problem with the property, e.g., maybe retail does not work at this location), then the lender who loaned $6 million loses money, while the lender who loaned $5.5 million is okay.

Another way you may be able to negotiate a lower margin is to agree to increase the pace at which you amortize your loan. In our example, with a margin of 145 basis points, I'm assuming a 25-year amortization. But if you're comfortable with a faster 15-year amortization (with larger principal payments, the lender's risk is lowered), you can argue for a lower margin, and lenders are generally responsive to this position.

Back to the lender's loan proposal: What happens to the interest rate after 10 years? There are a variety of ways lenders approach this issue, and one method is to reset the rate in year 11, again at 145 basis points over the *then* Treasury rate and to fix the rate for another 10 years. The point to keep in mind is that the interest rate will no longer be fixed in year 11 of your loan, and you need to pay attention to the mechanism that the lender will use at that time to establish a new rate. Obviously, the mechanism must be fair so that, should you still have this loan, you are not overwhelmed with a very high interest rate in year 11.

Amortization

What will be the rate of amortization—the amount of debt reduction the lender will want you to pay every year? As you know, lenders want to get their money back and they do not want to wait until you sell the property. So they establish an amortization (repayment) schedule, and there are many different types of such schedules.

In our example we're assuming a schedule that amortizes the loan over 25 years with 300 (12 × 25) fixed monthly payments, meaning that at the end of 25 years, the loan balance with the last payment will be zero. This type of loan is sometimes called "self-amortizing" because it pays itself off. There are tons of different types of amortization; the point is to understand the requirements on how your loan balance is to be repaid.

Development

When real estate entrepreneurs look at interest rates and amortization, they sometimes use the term "constant of the loan." This is the total of annual interest payments and amortization as a percentage of the loan amount. So, for example, if you borrow $1 million and your first year annual interest and principal payments are $85,000, then your constant is 8.5 percent. Figuring out your constant can be helpful in comparing one loan against another. If a lender wants a very quick amortization (say 10 years), your constant will be very high (perhaps resulting in a low or negative cash flow) and that loan may not be attractive *even if* its interest rate is lower than another proposed loan.

Back to our deal: Assuming a loan of $6 million at an interest rate of 5.70 percent and a self-amortizing schedule over 25 years, it's easy to calculate the annual payments on this loan, and calculators will do the math for you in seconds. The monthly payment in the initial 10-year period is $37,565.31, or a debt service of $450,783 per year. (Note that in year 11, assuming the interest rate changes, the lender will reset the amortization schedule/monthly payment in order to pay off the balance of the loan in 15 years.)

Prepayment Penalties

As a borrower, be aware of prepayment penalties, which are probably in your loan documents. A prepayment penalty is assessed when you pay off your loan sooner than the lender wants you to. Why would the lender care? Well, your loan is an asset for the lender, who wants its money at work. In addition, the lender has costs in making a loan. It does not want to spend this money and energy and then have you repay the loan shortly thereafter. What's more, a lender will sometimes borrow money to make you a loan. In our example, where the lender is offering you a 5.70 percent rate for 10 years, it may have borrowed $6 million for 10 years with restrictions on its prepaying its loan. This is sometimes called "matching funds." Since it cannot repay its loan (without penalty) before the end of the 10-year term, it puts restrictions on you doing the same.

What do prepayment penalties look like? There are different types, but the following would be a common prepayment penalty for a 10-year fixed-rate loan:

In the event that the Borrower repays the loan within the first 10 years thereof, it will pay to the Lender, in addition to the principal balance due, the following prepayment premium [they never call it a penalty]:

Years 1 to 5 of the loan:	5 percent of the loan balance
Year 6 of the loan:	4 percent of the loan balance
Year 7 of the loan:	3 percent of the loan balance
Year 8 of the loan:	2 percent of the loan balance
Years 9 and 10 of the loan:	1 percent of the loan balance

Confessions of a Real Estate Entrepreneur

Now that we've gone into the financing elements, let's return to analyzing our deal.

> Assuming we can obtain a $6 million nonrecourse loan at 5.7 percent interest and a 25-year amortization, we should reexamine the return on our investment. Now, our equity in the deal is not $8.1 million, but $2.1 million. What is the return on our equity?
>
> Our net operating income is $800,000. Our debt service is $450,000. Our cash flow is therefore $350,000. So our annual return on equity is $350,000/$2,100,000, or 16.7 percent. Not bad. And, in reality, the return on our equity is even higher because included in our debt service is some amount of principal reduction, and this money should not be deducted from cash flow to determine return on equity since it is lowering our loan balance.
>
> Accordingly, we might analyze our annual return on equity as follows: Interest of 5.7 percent on a $6 million loan is $342,000 (the $108,000 difference between $450,000 and $342,000 is principal). So I suggest that true annual return on equity is:
>
> Cash flow of $458,000 ($800,000 − $342,000)/$2,100,000
> = 21.8 percent

Not bad. But we can do even better, as you will see shortly.

Capitalization Rates

Remember I said at the beginning of this chapter that lenders will advance up to 75 percent of the appraised value of the property? Up until now I just assumed that the appraised value and the cost of the property were the same. But that is not necessarily true. Suppose that the appraised value of our property was $10 million. How could it get that high?

Well, let me give you one way an appraiser would value the property. Many appraisers will look at the net operating income of the property ($800,000) and divide it by something called a **cap rate**.

What is a cap rate? Used all the time in the real estate world, it is short for **capitalization rate**, and it means the rate that a purchaser would be willing to receive as a return on its cash to own a particular property. Cap rates go up and down as the economy strengthens or weakens, as interest rates go up and down, and as the investor community perceives the safety (or not) of a specific piece of property. Different types of properties generally fetch different cap rates.

Development

For instance, a trophy office building in a superb location and with an excellent tenant mix is going to be valued with a comparatively low cap rate—perhaps a 7 cap rate. That means in order to value this property, the net operating income it produces is divided by 0.07. In other words, an investor will be willing to receive a 7 percent return on its money (assuming an all-cash purchase) to own this property. So, let's say that this particular building has a net operating income of $1 million. An investor, willing to accept a 7 percent return on its money, will pay $14,285,000 for this building. In other words, the investor will accept a 7 percent return on its capital in buying this particular property. Since the net income generated is $1 million, the investor is receiving a 7 percent return on its investment of $14,285,000. Another way of saying the same thing is that the investor bought this property with a 7 percent cap rate.

Let's compare a less attractive property: an industrial building in a declining area of the city that also has a $1 million net operating income. This building is dated and is leased to a single tenant with okay but not great credit. An investor looking at the property will want a higher return on his investment because he believes there is considerable risk. If the tenant defaults or leaves the building, for example, it will not be easy to re-lease and once again achieve a $1 million net operating income. And so the investor community will want a much higher return on this property and will require a cap rate of, say, 13 percent.

Accordingly, the price that the investor community will pay for this property is $7,692,000 ($1,000,000/0.13), obviously significantly less than what the investor community will pay for the trophy office building, even though both properties have exactly the same net operating income. The difference is essentially the investment community's assessment of the predictability and reliability of the $1 million net income generated from the two different buildings over a long period of time (and with something factored in for the building's future value). With the office building, the investment community is confident that the $1 million (or more) will be there year after year. With the industrial building, the investment community is not so sure, and therefore wants a higher going-in return.

Okay, now back to our example.

As indicated, we have $800,000 of net operating income and a completed cost of the project of $8.1 million. We want to get as much financing as possible, so we go to an appraiser (a reputable appraiser, one with whom the lender community will be comfortable) and we ask him how he might value our property. He will usually reply that there are two or three standard methods: net income analysis, cost basis, sales comps. The net income analysis is what we are discussing—a cap rate type analysis. Cost basis is not often used—basically, this is the methodology of valuing a building as a function of its replacement cost. Sales comparables—tying the value of one property to similar properties that have been recently sold—is only as good as the number of true comparables. And so appraisers often rely heavily on the income analysis.

Knowing that, we begin a discussion with the appraiser. We ask him what kind of cap rate he might use for a property like our retail development, with a good credit tenant. He indicates that his range would be 7.5 to 8.5 percent if the credit of the tenant is truly high quality.

We now go to the lender community. Although generally the lender is required to hire the appraiser, and the borrower can only make recommendations as to which one, often, if the appraiser is credible and has a good reputation, the lender will go along with the appraiser the borrower prefers. We select a lender who is willing to extend us a loan on a 75 percent loan-to-value basis, and we ask the lender to hire the appraiser we spoke with, and the lender does so.

The appraiser visits our property, reviews the Tenant's credit, and decides that the correct cap rate is 8.25 percent. So he divides our net operating income of $800,000 by 0.0825 and gets a market value for our property of $9,700,000—not bad, since the property only cost us $8,100,000. In theory, at least, we have already added $1,600,000 to the value of this property.

The lender reviews the appraisal and gets comfortable with it. The lender indicates that it is willing to extend a loan of $7,275,000 ($9,700,000 × 0.75). Now let's look at our return on investment.

The loan proposal for a $7,275,000 loan has an interest rate of 5.85 percent (slightly higher than the rate proposed for a $6 million loan; even though the loan-to-value ratio is the same, lenders feel more comfortable with less debt than more). The monthly payments for this loan, with a 25-year amortization, are $46,208, and the annual payment is $554,497. Now we have cash flow equal to $245,503 ($800,000 − $554,497). But we only have equity (cash in the deal) of $825,000 ($8,100,000 − $7,275,000). So our annual return on equity is a whopping 30 percent ($245,503/$825,000). Now, take a moment to do the math if we delete the principal reduction (amortization) portion of our debt service:

Interest on $7,275,000 = $425,600 ($7,275,000 × 0.0585)
Cash Flow = $374,400 ($800,000 − $425,600)
Return on equity = $374,400/$825,000 = 45.3 percent

So, the actual return on equity in this deal is 45 percent per year. Not bad, and a good way to get rich!

Rental Increases

But I have even more good news. As with most long-term leases, there are periodic increases in the rental due to the Landlord. Before signing the lease with Mr. Retailer we suggest that he will achieve higher sales every year as his business gets established and his following grows. We suggest that he pay us an annual increase on his rent of 2.5 percent per year. He won't agree. However, he does agree that the rent may be increased by that amount every other year. We agree.

So the rental he will pay us over the first 10 years of the lease is as follows:

Years 1 and 2:	$800,000
Years 3 and 4:	$820,000
Years 5 and 6:	$840,500
Years 7 and 8:	$861,512
Years 9 and 10:	$883,050

Now remember that our loan has a 10-year fixed rate (5.85 percent), so our interest costs do not increase during this period. *But* as our rental income increases, our cash flow increases, and so does our annual return on equity:

Years 1 and 2:	45.3 percent
Years 3 and 4:	47.8 percent
Years 5 and 6:	50.3 percent
Years 7 and 8:	52.8 percent
Years 9 and 10:	55.4 percent

I think you must be getting the picture. The potential rewards to a capable real estate developer can be huge.

Conclusion

Lots of people in the United States have gotten very wealthy by understanding and executing a plan of real estate development. The key, of course, is to find a good piece of land and to understand what can be developed and at what cost. The developer must also have a good feel for the rental market. What will the completed building rent for?

In our example above, we knew exactly what the retailer would pay, since he was "in our pocket" when we purchased the land. But that's not always the case. Although a good developer will have a sense of what he can rent his completed building for, markets go up and down, and often there is risk involved in erecting a speculative (without a lot of preleasing) building. Often a developer even has to guess two or three years in advance of completion what rents and demand will be. That is all part of the risk-reward equation. And if a developer gets it right, he will be rewarded very, very handsomely.

Here's some good news: you do not need to undertake new construction in order to receive the type of returns we discussed in this chapter. In the next few chapters we review deals with huge returns but with somewhat less risk than new construction: these are tales involving the revitalization of existing structures.

7

Revitalizing Existing Properties

$\mathbf{D}$evelopment does not always mean new construction. In fact, in my area of the country, the Northeast, there is a tremendous amount of a different type of development: the revitalization of existing properties. What I'm talking about is the paradigm added value play: finding a property that is not selling or renting for what it might or should be, and doing those things to it that boost its value.

The most obvious case of this is finding a property that is, let's say, physically challenged. Perhaps it needs a lot of renovation. Sometimes the problem is just cosmetics and the work needed is pure aesthetics; one piece of good news for you: most purchasers and tenants can't envision what a property might look like with just some cosmetic upgrades. This is an opportunity because if you can see what a run-down or unattractive property might look like and know what it would cost to get it to that point, you have a talent that will be very valuable in added-value plays.

Physically Challenged Real Estate

One of the most famous real estate books ever written is William Nickerson's *How I Made One Million Dollars in My Spare Time*. Like many real estate entrepreneurs, I read this book when I ventured into the real estate game. The premise of the book is simple: take a two- or three-family house with units that are renting for, say, $1,000 a month, clean up the units, repaint the house, increase the rent. One of Nickerson's points was that residential tenants want an attractive place to rent and yet many owners do not do the things they should to make their property as attractive as possible. What's more, often the things the property needs are not that expensive (e.g., painting, upgraded appliances, new kitchen cabinets).

Nickerson's point was that you can ADD VALUE to real estate without spending a lot of money by purchasing properties that are cosmetically challenged, redressing and rerenting them, and then perhaps reselling at much higher numbers. And if you do it right, the cost of the cosmetic improvements is generally insignificant compared to the increase in value that results from the enhanced desirability of the apartments.

Nickerson's general premise is followed by multimillionaire real estate developers who purchase and rehab office buildings, strip shopping centers, and apartment buildings.

Here's an example of a deal I was involved with that illustrates the point:

An office building was for sale in the town in which I lived. It was well located but never seemed to rent well. There was always a FOR RENT sign in front, and the tenants were paying comparatively low rents—about $15/sf **gross plus utilities**. As you'll recall, a gross rent means that the Landlord is paying all of the building expenses (in contrast to a net rent, where the tenant pays, in addition to the base rent, all operating expenses and taxes). Operating expenses and taxes can vary in different areas of the country, of course, but in my community they were about $5 per square foot at the time. So the net rental the owner of this building was achieving was only about $10/sf. The building was 7,000 sf, which means the net operating income was $70,000 per year. As I mentioned, the building was in a good area of town, and the economy at the time was stable, and this building was being marketed at a 10 percent cap rate, or $700,000. My partner and I bought it for $650,000 . . . no great deal on the face of it.

But fortunately for me, I had read Nickerson's book about residential properties, and, like many other real estate players around the country, I figured that Nickerson's points could be applied to commercial property as well. So before committing to purchase, I sat in front of the building and asked myself why this building always had a lot of vacancies and never achieved the level of rent that it might. Well, this is not brain surgery by any stretch, and after about 15 minutes it was clear to me that although

Revitalizing Existing Properties

the building potentially had great charm (many years before, prior to being renovated for office usage, it had been a large, beautiful residence), the current owner was doing nothing to display the building in its best light.

The building sat behind a strip shopping center, the largest tenant of which was a restaurant such that everyone entering the office building would pass the rear of the restaurant and see and smell the garbage generated by this popular establishment. In addition, the building entrance was immediately behind the middle of the strip center and overlooked its rooftop air-conditioning and heating units—noisy and unattractive, to say the least. What's more, the front door of the building was a cheap, battered wood thing that may have been there for 50 years. Ditto the windows. And the building had not been painted for quite some time—peeling was everywhere. You get the idea.

Before buying, I had done some rough numbers as to what it would cost to renovate the property. I concluded that with expenditures of less than $100,000, I could change its image. And so, after closing, I hired a contractor and here's what we did:

- Planted the tallest hemlocks we could find along the front property border (behind the strip shopping center)—and voilà, the strip center was no longer visible, and the noise and smell from the restaurant were diminished as well.
- Replaced the front door and created an attractive portico outside and foyer inside so the immediate entrance into the building was greatly enhanced. (Remember the saying, "You only get one chance to make a first impression," and now the look and feel of the entryway into the building were greatly improved.)
- Replaced the old windows with new windows that were in keeping with the style of the property.
- Installed new trim around the windows and roofline.
- Gave the building a new paint job.

Total cost: $75,000.

Then we took down the old FOR RENT sign and put up a new (attractive) one. Soon we started getting calls and lookers. Our asking rent? Twenty-two dollars per square foot gross plus utilities.

In one year we filled the vacant space in the building with tenants paying the higher rent, and by the end of year two we had replaced (or raised the rents of) the existing tenants so that our entire rent roll was now $22/sf gross plus utilities. Since the operating expenses of the property were still $5/sf, the net rent from the property two years after I purchased it was $119,000 ($17/sf × 7,000 sf). And with a much better look and feel to the building, the investor community now saw this property in a different light, such that the cap rate we could use to value the property for sale or finance was now 9.5 percent.

Therefore, given the new net operating income and the new cap rate the market used, the new market value was $1,250,000! Net ADDED VALUE: $525,000 ($1,250,000 − $650,000 − $75,000). Not bad for two years.

By the way, just for fun, you might calculate the return on equity. The building was purchased with $150,000 of equity and $75,000 for renovation. So total equity invested was $225,000. In two years, putting aside cash flow, the building had increased in value $525,000, or $262,500 per year. Therefore, the return on equity in the two years of our ownership was more than 100 percent per year. I hope that some of you are saying, "Wow, what a great deal." Yes it was, but believe me, there are players in the real estate game doing deals like this all the time (and much larger deals). No matter the size of the deal, the concept is the same:

Find a property that is not renting for what it should be and so long as the cost of changing its image (in order to improve its value) makes sense in light of the projected new value of the property, buy it.

Other Types of Hair

Many real estate players will use an expression about a challenging deal, "The property has hair on it." That generally means that the deal is ugly (think hairy gorilla) for some reason. It might be because the building is physically challenged, or it might be something else: a construction issue, a title problem, an environmental concern, a tenant revolt . . . anything that depresses the price of the property.

These are the kinds of deals that my partners and I love. As entrepreneurs, we operate under the presumption that there is enormous money to be made finding deals with hair on them, especially if the property is in the hands of an "institutional" (nonentrepreneurial) owner. Institutional investors often own a large number of properties, many of which are located far from their corporate headquarters. Often, they do not have the time or the manpower to deal with problems that can arise with a property and so they may neglect to do the things a local entrepreneur would do. At times this can cause an artificial depression in the value of the property. I say "artificial" because the problems that are depressing the value may not be fundamental or organic to the deal. A change of ownership, with a new, entrepreneurial approach to the problems, can mean huge added value in a very short period of time.

Here's an example:

Revitalizing Existing Properties

My partners and I located a 50,000 sf office building owned by a local developer who had gotten into trouble building too many new (speculative) buildings. He was cash tight and was not doing what he needed to do to attract and retain tenants in his building. As a result, there was a lot of vacancy in the building, and the developer was behind on his mortgage payments, and his lender started a foreclosure action.

In addition, it was commonly known that there had been an oil spill on an abutting property and that his property had been affected. Finally, there was some indication of physical problems with the property: the three-level parking garage was showing signs of concrete and rebar deterioration.

The institutional lender who had started the foreclosure was staring into the face of a crummy rent roll, a potential construction issue, and an ongoing State investigation into an environmental condition on the property. That is "hair"! Just the kind of property an institution located a thousand miles away did not want to deal with.

I was aware of the foreclosure and contacted the attorney for the institutional lender. I asked him if the lender might want to sell the loan to my group. Note that the lender could not sell me the property; it did not own it. All it owned was the Promissory Note and Mortgage on the property. That is all it had to sell.

The loan balance on the Note was about $5 million. But with all the problems this property had, it might have been worth only half that. And the lender knew it. What's more, the lender had litigation to deal with since the property owner was contesting the foreclosure. Two million dollars later, my group owned the lender's Promissory Note and Mortgage Deed.

Now, here's a critical point: This property was 10 miles from where my partners and I lived. We knew all the players in the market and the individual who owned the property. We sat down with him. We treated him with respect, since we could relate to the difficulties he was experiencing (in contrast to the corporate vice president of the lender, located a thousand miles away, who did not know the property owner from Adam . . . all he knew was that the guy was causing him a problem). We had a couple of meetings and worked out a stipulated foreclosure, that is, the owner stopped contesting the foreclosure, and as a result the change in title procedure (the foreclosure action) whisked through court. In 30 days we owned the property. And again, being local, we were able to immediately get contractors and consultants to the site—meeting with them at 5 a.m., if they wanted—to get an assessment of the construction and environmental issues. Little by little we got our hands around the potential problems (the lender's VP had not even begun to evaluate the problems), and bit by bit chipped away at them, finding solutions in each case. Then, being local (are you getting the point?), we started a new leasing program and began renting vacant spaces.

Our total expenditure to resolve the foreclosure, construction, and environmental issues was $500,000. So we were in the deal for $2.5 million. A year later the property was worth $7 million.

Now, I didn't tell you this story to pound on my and my partners' chests. That is not the intention of this book. I told you this story to illustrate the following points:

1. Constantly be on the prowl for undervalued property—have your eyes and ears open at all times.
2. Deals with hair on them are especially intriguing.
3. Use what you have that the owner (or lender) may not have: entrepreneurial energy, local market knowledge, creativity, and the focused intensity that comes with spending your own money (contrast the institutional owner or lender). Often you can solve problems without spending huge dollars; in many situations it is just a matter of rolling up your sleeves and getting a little dirty—something that a corporate executive a thousand miles away is generally reluctant to do.
4. The results of your hard work can be a lot of ADDED VALUE.

Buying a "hairy" deal is a form of real estate development. You may not be building from the ground up, but you are undertaking construction, marketing, environmental, and legal issues all the same. Your skill at managing and overcoming these issues is what will make the deal successful or not. As you can see, deals with "hair" on them, and other artificially depressed properties, can be potentially as lucrative for the real estate entrepreneur as new construction.

Besides the upside potential of development deals, there's another reason these deals present a real opportunity to you: MOST PEOPLE ARE AFRAID OF THEM. There are tons of people buying and selling real estate, but only a small percentage of them are willing to take on the risks and complexities of a development deal, be it new construction or the purchase of a "hairy" property. So by educating yourself on the opportunities these kinds of deals present, you put yourself in a position that many real estate investors are neither interested in nor capable of handling. This gives you a kind of "niche" to take advantage of.

One last point: Developers take RISK. Much more risk than the investor who buys a well-leased building and sits with it. This latter type of investor generally knows a property's downside and is comfortable with the more limited upside that comes with a safer deal. This is the type of investor who will buy one of your developments when you're done with it and have made a large profit for yourself.

On the other hand, this more conservative investor can sleep at night. Developers don't always get much sleep, since the level of their risk is high. Think about it: Given that I had to move quickly on tying up the 50,000 sf office building in the example above, I could not do all the due diligence I would have liked relative to the "hair" on the building. I had an idea of what was involved, but I did not have all the facts. Fortunately, the potential problems were solved for $500,000, but what if the solutions turned out to be four times that amount? What if the State DEP decided to shut down the property for some time due to the oil spill next door? What if the leasing program for the property was so delayed by the rebuilding of the parking garage or cleanup of the environmental problems that it took us years to get the vacant space rented? Or worse, what if we lost tenants during the work and ended up with an empty building?

Any or all of those scenarios could have played out and my partners and I could have lost a lot of money. That is what risk is about, and this deal illustrates the risk-reward equation quite well. Needless to say, the more you do these types of deals, the better you get at it. In the deal described above, we were savvy to the types of issues we were facing when we laid out $2 million to buy the building. We had dealt with these problems on other properties and we had some sense of what things cost. Over time you too will develop a sense of what costs what and will be able to move quickly when you need to.

So, if you're prepared to get into the development arena, be prepared for risk. It is part of this game. Your willingness to live with it (and perhaps contend with sleep deprivation) is what will separate you from the pack and position you for the huge rewards that can come from a successful development deal.

Conclusion

Locating and acquisition of an existing property that is artificially depressed in value is a form of development. Although the real estate entrepreneur does not construct this property from the ground up, he takes steps to blow life into it, to address whatever problems are depressing the value. Sometimes construction is involved, sometimes legal issues, sometimes marketing. In all cases, you exercise entrepreneurial skills to overcome the problems. And if you do things well, your reward can be huge . . . greatly out of proportion to the amount of time or capital you invest, or even the risk that you take on.

Now we're going to look at another type of development deal: so dramatically changing the look and feel and use of a property as to convince the investment community that the old property is gone and something "new" stands in its stead.

8

A Complete Makeover

$\mathbf{A}$nother type of development deal is what I call the Complete (or Extreme) Makeover. This may or may not be a property with hair on it. The Complete Makeover deal is the purchasing of a property that is perceived one way by the investment community and then, through some combination of renovation, marketing, and repositioning, completely changing this perception.

Self-Storage Facilities

A great example of how fortunes were made by remaking real estate is the evolution of the self-storage facility. About 50 years ago some enterprising real estate player got the idea of buying a big, old industrial building and renting it out in sections to people who needed storage. Let's assume that he bought a 75,000-square-foot building and determined that he could rent it out in storage rooms measuring 8-by-10 (80 square feet). He did not know what to charge for the rooms so he arbitrarily chose a rent of $120 per month. He advertised his storage rooms in the local newspapers, and before he knew it, people were showing up and renting the rooms. Soon he increased his rentals to $150 per month, and people were still showing up. At some rental amount, he found that people would leave personal possessions in their attic, basement, or garage instead of renting from him, and that's when he stopped raising prices.

Let's look at some numbers:

Let's assume that the real estate entrepreneur was able to rent storage rooms for $150 per month, that his 75,000 sf building could be divided up into 500 storage rooms of 80 sf each (40,000 sf), and that the balance of his building was needed for shipping and packing areas, corridors, and administrative offices. Finally, let's assume that on average he could achieve an 80 percent occupancy, that is, 400 rooms rented over the course of the year.

So his annual revenue looked like this: $400 \times \$150/\text{mo} \times 12 = \$720,000$.

Now, since our real estate entrepreneur was one of the first to create a self-storage facility, the building he purchased was priced as an empty industrial building (which it was, of course), let's say at $20/sf, or $1.5 million.

Within a year our real estate friend was making this kind of money:

Annual room revenue		$720,000
Ancillary income (boxes, insurance)		25,000
Total		$745,000
Annual Expenses:		
Personnel	$120,000	
Real estate taxes	25,000	
Utilities	35,000	
Insurance	10,000	
Advertising	10,000	
Maintenance	15,000	
Total	$215,000	$215,000
Net Operating Income		$530,000

Assume that our real estate player spent $10/sf on the building to create the 500 storage rooms and the administrative and loading areas . . . about $750,000. Therefore his total investment was $2,250,000 ($1,500,000 for the building and the $750,000 for construction).

Assume that he bought this property with a 70 percent loan and that the lender also financed 70 percent of the improvements to the building (the storage rooms). Therefore the loan amount is $1,575,000 ($2,250,000 × 0.7), and let's assume that his constant on the loan (percentage of the loan that represents interest and amortization) was 8 percent. Therefore, his debt service is about $126,000/year.

A Complete Makeover

So his Cash Flow is about $400,000/year ($530,000 − $126,000).
Since his equity in the deal is $675,000 ($2,250,000 − $1,575,000),
his return on equity is a spectacular 60 percent per year:

$400,000/$675,000 = 60 percent . . . NOT BAD!

What's more, with time he may improve his occupancy rates, and any incremental revenue falls right to the bottom line. And unlike office buildings or shopping centers, where landlords and tenants usually sign long-term leases, locking the landlord into fixed rents over an extended period, the self-storage operator is free to raise room rents every six months or so if and when the market warrants it. Finally, using a cap rate of 10 percent, this self-storage facility is theoretically worth $5.3 million to an investor; in other words, our real estate entrepreneur added value of $3 million!

Are these numbers crazy? No, these are realistic numbers for the business opportunity that existed for perhaps a decade or two in the United States. But over time this opportunity diminished. Why? Two reasons:

1. Eventually the country got saturated with self-storage facilities. There was only so much demand for self-storage in a given geographic area. So although the first ones in an area did well, there was a limit on how many facilities could service a particular region.

2. Sellers wised up. People who owned empty buildings and who would have historically sold them at some cap rate on projected warehouse or factory rental income saw what was happening to their friends' empty buildings: entrepreneurs were turning them into self-storage facilities and making a ton of money. Sellers decided that their pricing model was therefore wrong. They figured that a well-located empty building should now be priced as a potential self-storage facility—a much greater value than what a traditional cap rate analysis would yield on an empty warehouse or factory. As a result, the opportunity for entrepreneurs to make huge profits on these types of deals decreased.

This phenomenon makes an important point about real estate entrepreneuring. One of the ways entrepreneurs have made millions of dollars in real estate is by buying a property based on one pricing model and then selling it based on another pricing model. Self-storage entrepreneurs were buying buildings that were priced on potential net income from a large factory or single-tenant warehouse user (e.g., the 75,000 sf building in our example above was priced at $20/sf because that was the right number given rents being paid by these types of users). They were then completely changing the rules of the game: converting the building to a self-storage facility and then operating them or selling them at numbers that had no connection to the basis upon which they were purchased.

But this opportunity can only last as long as Sellers of empty buildings remain uninformed as to the potential conversion possibilities. We will see more of this phenomenon below.

The self-storage story reveals something else about entrepreneuring. As you might expect, there were only so many empty buildings that entrepreneurs could buy. And if there was still demand in an area for storage units, these entrepreneurs were going to figure out a way to service the demand (and make money doing it). So they started to build self-storage facilities, the original, newly constructed facilities looking like rows of garage units. These did well, but then some entrepreneur decided that people wanted a nicer facility to store their important personal items. So some entrepreneurs began building self-storage facilities that resembled attractive office buildings, with beautiful lobbies and clean restrooms. Wow, the business had come a long way. But that is what happens. Someone somewhere is always thinking up a better (and more profitable?) way to do deals. That someone could be you.

For the moment, let's focus on the principle I want to make in this chapter: the Complete Makeover. Here's the point illustrated by the self-storage story: **if you can purchase property that is priced on one model and effect a dramatic change in the use and perception of the property, you may make a lot of money.** Because, as in our example, once your Complete Makeover is completed, the investment community no longer sees it as a large industrial building. Instead, where that building once stood there's now a profitable self-storage facility that bears no economic resemblance to its prior usage.

Factory Outlet Centers

I was an early player in a different type of makeover opportunity. Unfortunately, although I did one very successful deal, I did not recognize what a huge opportunity I was staring at. Just by way of reminder, the deal that I am about to describe is not meant to show how smart I was. I have made a lot of stupid deals, and I'll get to those later in the book. In some respects, with little money to lose (at the beginning of my career), I was able to take risks that others might not. And I got very lucky. But at least I was in the game swinging.

A number of years ago in Norwalk, Connecticut, a city near where I lived, there was a large factory building (165,000 sf) for sale in a good location (right off Interstate 95). It was occupied by a retail tenant, a deep discount type operation called The Factory Store, which sold low-end merchandise. This company had a lease on the building, with about five years to go on the lease.

A Complete Makeover

All the "smart" money had passed on this property, since the seller was asking an "outrageous" price of $1.5 million based on the rent that The Factory Store was paying. My partner and I had total liquid assets of $25,000 and maybe a collective net worth of $200,000. We had done a couple of small office building deals and we decided that we were ready for bigger things.

So we put in an offer to the Seller:

Price: $1.6 million

Terms: 60-day Option Agreement with a Deposit of $25,000

Financing: Seller to take back a first mortgage of $1.1 million, interest only, for five years

Why did we offer more than the asking price? Because we knew we could never get traditional financing, and so we thought that maybe the Seller would finance the building if we sweetened the offer (we knew he had no mortgage on the property). He took our offer. **Step #1.**

We used all of our cash ($25,000) to put down on the Option Agreement. We realized that this money was at risk and that if we could not close within 60 days, we would lose that money. Nothing like entrepreneurial optimism! Now what?

We thought about trying to raise $500,000 from investors, since this was the amount we needed to close (actually $475,000, because our Option payment would be applied to the sales price upon closing). But early in our careers, and with no track record or experience, we did not think others would be interested in investing with us.

We bounced around other ideas and began to panic, since we had no idea where we could find that kind of money. So, as a diversion, I went to see the owner of the company that operated The Factory Store (the tenant in the building), a man whom I had never met (he has since become a friend).

Here's how the conversation went:

ME: Hi, my name is Jim Randel and I want to introduce myself, as I will be buying the building in Norwalk, Connecticut, that your company leases.

HIM: Oh, that's nice . . . glad to meet you.

ME: Are there any problems with the building that I should know about?

HIM: No, not really.

ME: Oh, that's good . . . Do you and the owner of the property get along?

HIM: Yes.

Confessions of a Real Estate Entrepreneur

ME (just fishing): Are you going to want to renew when your lease expires?

HIM: No . . . we're not happy in that location.

ME (a teeny, tiny little bell starting to ring in my head): You're not . . . oh . . . you do intend to honor your lease, however?

HIM: Yes, of course, but I might be interested in leaving the building early if you would like me out.

ME (the sound of the bell getting louder): Oh, well, I don't know about that . . . maybe, maybe we could work out some kind of termination agreement with you, but we went to contract on this building knowing you would be there. So we would need some kind of substantial payment for that.

HIM: We might be receptive to that.

ME: (Bell in my head really clanging now.)

And from there he and I reached an agreement: that upon our closing the purchase of the building, we would terminate his lease. What did we get in return? He paid us a $200,000 termination fee and gave us a $300,000 loan, to be secured with a second mortgage on the property. **Step #2!**

Oh boy, now we might be getting somewhere. We knew that if we could figure out how to get the deal closed, we could go to the owner of The Factory Store and get $500,000 from him for terminating his lease. Somehow we had to figure out how to get a $500,000 loan for a day. We needed to find a banker who liked entrepreneurs, and since we didn't know any bankers, we started calling banks out of the yellow pages. After several less-than-promising calls, we reached a young lender (one of my best friends today) who was bored when my call came in and so, just for sport, decided to speak with me:

ME: Hi, my name is Jim Randel, and I am a young real estate investor and I need someone to consider a kind of crazy request.

HIM: All right, I have nothing to do right now . . . what's up?

ME: Well, I'm under Contract to buy a building for $1.6 million. The Seller is willing to take back a first mortgage for $1.1 million. I need $500,000 to close, which I do not have. But the tenant in this building is willing to pay me $500,000 to terminate its lease, actually pay me a $200,000 termination fee, and loan me $300,000 as a second mortgage behind the Seller's first. So, if you'd loan me $500,000 for a day, I could buy the building then terminate the lease, get $500,000 from the tenant and immediately repay your loan.

A Complete Makeover

HIM: You're right . . . that is a crazy request.

ME: There must be some way to get it done.

HIM: Would the retailer put the $500,000 in escrow before closing so that immediately after you get the Deed from the Seller you go into the escrow agent's office, display the Deed, sign the Termination Agreement, receive $200,000, execute the Note and Second Mortgage Deed, and get the $300,000?

ME: I'll ask.

And that's exactly what happened. The owner of The Factory Store agreed to put the $500,000 in escrow so that once we displayed a Deed to the escrow agent (confirming our ownership of the property) and signed the Termination Agreement and Loan Documents, the Escrow Agent would release the $500,000 to us. With that agreement in place, the lender agreed to loan us $500,000 for one day, the understanding being that within that day we had to buy the building, terminate the lease (and get the $500,000 from the tenant), and then repay the loan.

Here's what happened:

1. Lender cuts a check for $500,000 to my partner and me. He gives it to his attorney who gets in the car with us and drives with us to the closing. He does not even let us touch the check.

2. We drive to the Seller's attorney's office. We give the Seller the $500,000 (actually $475,000), the balance being for closing costs (legal and bank fees). We sign the $1.1 million Promissory Note and First Mortgage Deed to the Seller. He gives us the Deed to the property. We now own it.

3. We drive to the Escrow Agent's office. We display the Deed showing that we are now the owners. We sign the Termination Agreement and the Promissory Note/Second Mortgage Deed to the tenant. The tenant is now released from his remaining lease obligations and has a $300,000 second mortgage on the property. The Escrow Agent hands us two checks, totaling $500,000 and payable to us. The lender's attorney takes the checks out of our hands and has us endorse them to the bank. Our two-hour loan is now repaid and we own the property. **Step #3.**

Oh wow . . . are we excited. We now own a 165,000 sf building in Norwalk, Connecticut. But our elation is short-lived.

The next day we go to the building and walk through it. We panic again. With nothing in the building, it looked frighteningly humongous (four acres under a roof). Nothing there but us and the pigeons. Now what were we going to do? We have mortgage payments due on our first and second mortgage in 30 days and real estate taxes due in a couple of months. We of course have the building insured and we owe an insurance premium. And we have very little cash left to our names.

So again we start thinking out loud. "How about an indoor baseball field? A giant flea market? The largest restaurant in the world?" While we're panicking, I get a phone call from a real estate broker in Boston.

BROKER: I heard that you just bought the old Factory Store building off Exit 16, I-95.

ME: Yes, that's true.

HIM: Well, I represent a manufacturer of men's clothing that wants to open a factory outlet store in that area. Are you interested in leasing to them?

ME (never having been to a factory outlet store): How much space do they need?

HIM: About 5,000 square feet.

ME (trying to think on my feet): Do factory outlets stores like to be located near each other?

HIM: Sure, you should drive around Maine where a bunch of them are located. Or go to Utica, New York, and see what one developer did, locating a number of factory outlets under one roof in an old building like yours.

ME: I'll get back to you.

So my partner and I hop on a plane to Utica, New York, and we visit an old factory building that looks something like ours, and there are about 20 factory outlet stores in it. And lots of people shopping. Our panic turns to excitement. We can do this . . . the owner had taken a building just like ours and divided it into individual retail spaces separated only with Sheetrock and chicken wire. So we hurry back to Norwalk, Connecticut, and I call the broker from Boston.

Me: We're interested in leasing to your men's wear manufacturer. By the way, do you know other factory outlet stores that might be interested in coming into our building?

HIM: Yes I do.

And so we were off and running; converting an old factory into something completely new: a factory outlet shopping center. And, of course, with any project like this, luck is a factor (which should be pretty obvious by this point in the story). At that time, manufacturers who had for years opened outlet stores in out-of-the-way locations (like Utica, New York) so as not to offend their retailer (department store) accounts, were getting more aggressive. Since the department stores

A Complete Makeover

were hard to deal with (they controlled distribution), manufacturers decided that they needed to have their own distribution channels (i.e., their own stores).

Norwalk is in the middle of Fairfield County, Connecticut, which is a high-income metropolitan area. At the time there were several department stores within a 20-mile radius of our building, and five years earlier (manufacturers were not as yet totally fed up with department stores) I don't think we would have been able to pull off a factory outlet shopping center in Norwalk. But our timing was good (like we intended it that way!) and we began to market our property to manufacturers around the country.

Within a year we were fully leased: 165,000 sf of retail area leased at an average of $10/sf (triple net). Now, you do not have to think too hard to realize that our purchase of the factory building was turning out quite well. We purchased the property for $1.6 million (about $10/sf). And we spent maybe another $200,000 on Sheetrock, chicken wire, and brokerage fees. So our total investment in the property at this time was $11/sf. Now, one year after purchase, we were leasing the property for a net rental of $10/sf. In other words, our net operating income in year two was about $1.6 million, the price we had paid for the property!

Five years later we sold this property for $10.6 million.

I tell the details of this deal for a couple of reasons:

1. To illustrate how profitable it can be if you buy a building that is priced as one type of property, in our case an old factory (leased to a low-end retailer), and then sell it as an entirely different type of property: a shopping center! Without a lot of physical modification to the building, we accomplished this makeover primarily with a new positioning and marketing of the building.

2. Luck is a factor in any success story. Without a whole lot of luck flowing our way, we would never have pulled this deal off: luck in finding a seller who would take back the first mortgage of $1.1 million, in buying a building whose existing tenant gave/loaned us the money to purchase, in finding a banker willing to listen to our crazy request and figure out a way to get the loan done. And luck in finding a use for this huge, outdated property. *But,* and here's one of the most important factors in entrepreneurism: *If you're not out there swinging, you will never hit a home run.* Yes, luck is important, but it won't help you if you're not in the game trying your best. The point is that you have to play to win . . . do your best every day. Get up off the ground when you get knocked down (as you most certainly will). Never quit. And someday, hopefully, a lucky break will come your way, and whoosh . . . you're off to the races.

3. I was not as smart as I should have been.

At the time we developed this property, the factory outlet boom was just beginning. Having developed a highly successful center in Norwalk, I knew all the manufacturers who were interested in opening stores around the country. I had relationships with the decision makers, who were willing to tell me where they wanted to locate. But I was spoiled and shortsighted. I had just purchased a building for $10/sf and leased it out for $10/sf. I wanted to do more of those types of deals, and I was too dense to see that in order to expand the business I would eventually have to build new facilities for the outlet stores. Maybe it would cost me (at the time) $100 per square foot to purchase land and construct a new building for these outlet centers.

With financing, I would have been earning a very nice return on my investment, and with time (as happened) rents would increase and I would be earning a really excellent return on my investment. But I was only thinking about more home runs. I wanted to find factory buildings in other towns where I could duplicate my Norwalk experience. But finding this type of factory building in all the areas that the outlets now wanted to be (e.g., Orlando, Florida) was not realistic, and so while I sat on my hands, other developers tied up pieces of land around the country and started building outlet centers. Duh . . . In a way, I was a victim of my own success. Having made an incredible score on one deal spoiled me. I wanted more incredible scores and was missing the forest for the trees. In the ensuing 10 years, while I did only one more deal (buying another factory building in Hartford, Connecticut) others stepped into the vacuum and started building new centers around the country. Had I done the same, taking advantage of the lead I had established, I would be a very wealthy man right now.

Lesson? Don't be greedy. I could have made good deals building outlet centers, but I wanted each deal to be a grand slam home run. I got greedy and lost out on an enormous opportunity.

One more reason I told the story of this deal:

4. I want you to know another one of my huge screwups: One of our first tenants in the Norwalk Factory Outlet Center was a small bed and bath type store called Bed, Bath & Beyond. This may have been their first store. The owners, Len Feinstein and Warren Eisenberg, were wonderful guys and we all got along very well. One day we had lunch and they asked me to become the exclusive real estate guy for their young company: finding and building them locations around the country. I passed and completely missed one of the most exciting growth opportunities a person can have in his lifetime. Shame on me.

Why tell the stories of my mistakes (two huge ones)? Because any entrepreneur who claims to always hit the ball out of the park is lying to you. It is the nature of entrepreneurism that some deals will work and others will not. YOU WILL MAKE MISTAKES. The key is not to let these mistakes—be they financial or emotional (I was devastated as Bed, Bath & Beyond continued to grow and grow and grow)—beat you. Get out of bed and continue the fight. What counts most? Perseverance and heart. Those are, in my view, the most important characteristics of a great entrepreneur. Yes, you will screw up at times, losing money and missing opportunities. But every successful person has done the same. Just stay with it.

We will speak more to entrepreneurism in later chapters.

Conclusion

Another development opportunity is to dramatically make over a property in order to change its perception (and value) in the real estate world. Self-storage facilities and factory outlet centers are no longer a big opportunity. But I'm sure there are other new exciting opportunities waiting for some creative entrepreneur (you?) to take advantage of. Remember that beauty is in the eye of the beholder. So, think outside the box: Can you so change the look, image, feel, and positioning of a property as to change how others (tenants and buyers) see it? If so, maybe you have a makeover opportunity right in front of you.

You know, telling you about my humongous mistakes has been a bit of a catharsis. Why don't we take a little side trip and laugh (cry?) at some of the other dumb mistakes I've made.

9

Other Mistakes
I've Made

$\mathbf{P}$erhaps this is an appropriate time to talk about other mistakes I have made in the real estate game. I hope that you will learn from my errors.

Another Big Factory Building

There was a time when I thought I could not make a mistake. I had recently sold the Norwalk Factory Outlet Center for $10.6 million. I was thinking, "Wow am I smart! I bet that everything I touch will turn to gold." WRONG. Anyway, with my big head blocking my judgment, I got caught in a deal that in hindsight made no sense.

A good real estate broker brought me a deal in Shelton, Connecticut, a factory building in a very good location. The property was zoned for industrial but was directly across the street from a successful shopping center and right in the heart of what would be the future growth of retail in Shelton; so, I assumed that obtaining a rezone of the parcel to retail was not going to be a problem. The broker who brought me the deal had done his homework and knew exactly what to say when we met to discuss it.

HIM: Wow, that was some deal you did in Norwalk. What a score!

ME: Thank you. Thank you.

HIM: You certainly have a knack for adding value, particularly converting industrial buildings into retail uses. And that's why I've brought you this deal. It's a 110,000-square-foot industrial building on 10 acres and in the direct line of retail growth going on in the city. The seller knows that the buyer of this property will have to be someone like you who is really good at adding value to these factory type properties. (Boy, was this guy playing me or what?)

ME: Thank you. Thank you.

Anyway, you get the picture, and you will not be surprised to hear that I did put a group together to buy this property. All of us agreed with the general premise that the property was right in the middle of the retail growth in Shelton. And we figured that if we could buy it at a price commensurate with its industrial usage, we would make a nice profit once we converted it to some type of retail usage.

Now I do not want to suggest that we did not do some homework. We were impressed with ourselves but not stupid. The building was leased to an industrial user for six months beyond the closing date. We reviewed the lease and the creditworthiness of the tenant. We did an engineering study of the building. And environmental. And we got a survey confirming that the property was a usable, rectangular 10 acres. What we did not do, however, was consider the politics of rezoning the property from industrial to retail. We did know that the city of Shelton was in favor of more retail, but we didn't do as much homework as we should have relative to the rezoning of the property. We should have dug deeper and asked the following questions:

How long would it take us to get the retail zoning?

Was getting the rezoning a guarantee?

Who might object and fight us?

Was the building rentable to industrial users in the interim and at rents that made sense in terms of the price we were paying?

Soon after we closed, we applied to the city to rezone the property from an industrial usage to a retail usage. We argued in the public hearing that the highest and best use of this property was clearly retail. We argued that the citizens of Shelton were in need of additional retail options (the shopping center across the street being the only real choice). The zoners agreed. We got the approval.

Unfortunately, a few days later we also got our comeuppance when we learned that the owner of the shopping center across the street had started an action in court to contest the rezoning. He claimed that we obtained our approvals wrongfully and asked the court system to overturn them. We hadn't planned on that! Maybe had we not been so taken with our "talents" and "golden touch" we might have considered this possibility. **Mistake #1.** Once we thought about it, it was fairly easy to see that the shopping center across the street from us was so successful, in part, because it had a monopoly on retail in the area. The owner of the center, and its major tenants, were not happy about seeing competitive retail uses open across the street. And so the battle was on.

Here's a suggestion you should take seriously: If you're going to buy a property that you need to rezone, do not underestimate the difficulties in doing so. First of all, the zoners may not see things the way you do. Second, interested neighbors can take an appeal and hold you up in court. I knew this intuitively. I just got caught up in my own silliness, thinking I had some kind of real estate magic touch. And now you know why I spent so much time in earlier chapters explaining how to use Option Agreements and Contracts with Contingencies. These devices are not only opportunities to tie up a property and add value by getting a rezone. They are also techniques for protecting your backside; that is, protecting you from buying a property BEFORE you know what you can do with it. If you meet resistance to the zoning or rezoning approval that you're seeking, while you have the property tied up with an Option Agreement or Contract, meaning BEFORE you have closed, you can still walk away from the deal.

Mistake #2: We did not do our homework on the industrial market in this city. Since we hadn't considered the prospect that the zoning approval would be denied, or appealed, we didn't bother to research in depth the prospects of re-renting the building once the existing tenant's lease expired (six months after closing). Had we done so, we would have thought harder about buying this building. This city, like many others in lower Connecticut, was experiencing an exodus of industrial users to areas with cheaper land and labor. The fact was that the industrial tenant market in Shelton was very thin, and the prospective tenants for a building like ours were few and far between.

While we were fighting the appeal of our zoning approval, the lease of the tenant in our building expired and the tenant left. We now had an *empty* 110,000 sf building, costing us about $50,000 per month in debt service, taxes, and insurance. Our grand plan for a conversion to retail was tied up in litigation and we could not find any tenant interest for even half our building, let alone the entire 110,000 square feet. What's more, most tenants of this magnitude wanted a five-year lease, and often a five-year option term as well, and if we did find a tenant, we'd be in a position where we had to put our retail conversion program on hold for five or more years . . . In short, we were in a really, really bad position.

How did we survive? Well, now (at last) some good news:

We found a good lawyer and researched the zoning appeal. Appeals to a zoning approval are very dangerous to a developer because they can tie up a property for years and stop a development from proceeding. And in many cases (such as ours) the motivation of the appellant (the party instituting the appeal) is such that there is no discussion or compromise. In our view, the owner of the shopping center across the street from us was appealing just to keep more retail out of the area. There was no talking with him. He did not want us to exist. Even if he could only hold us up for a couple of years, he was happy because it was two or three more years that his tenants had a monopoly in the market, and those few years represented a lot of money to them.

Thank goodness we found a twist in Connecticut law distinguishing appellants to zoning approvals based upon how close their property is to the property that was rezoned. In Connecticut, property owners within 100 feet of a property being rezoned have an inviolate right to maintain an appeal; the logic being that these people are the most affected by a rezoning. To be distinguished were property owners not within 100 feet of the property: although they have a right to appeal as well, they must prove to the court that they will be significantly impacted by the rezone.

Although an eyeball assessment of the distance from our property to the shopping center across the street told us it was within 100 feet, *just to be sure* we had a surveyor make a measurement. As it turned out, the shortest distance between our property line and that of the shopping center was 110 feet, and that 10 feet may have kept us out of real trouble. Because the shopping center owner did not have an absolute right to take an appeal, we got before a judge fairly quickly and took the position that the appeal should not be allowed.

Although you might think that the shopping center had a good argument that it would be significantly impacted by additional retail across the street, the law is not about anticompetitive behavior. By "impact," the law is concerned that the area does have, for example, adequate traffic flow such that more retail would not cause a traffic nightmare for adjoining properties. But that was not the case in our situation. The only "impact" to the shopping center across the street was the additional competition. Fortunately for us, although the shopping center owner cited traffic and made all the other usual arguments, the judge could see what their appeal was about and he dismissed it summarily. *Thank goodness!* Note that had the shopping center been within 100 feet of our property, he could not have done that and would have had to schedule a hearing on the merits of the rezone, which could have delayed matters for at least another year. Again, a story of luck but not all luck: FOR THE MOMENT, THINK SCRAPPY.

A divine force intervened. Shortly after the appeal against our rezone was filed, there was a fire in Shelton. An industrial building about three miles from ours was burning. I was in the city that day and could hear the fire engines. That evening I checked the news and heard that a 100,000 sf building near ours had been badly damaged. At 6 a.m. the next morning I was at the burned building thinking, just maybe, the occupant would need temporary space. I got lucky. The president of the company that occupied the building was there. I introduced myself.

ME: Hi, I'm Jim Randel. I'm really sorry about the fire.

HIM: Thanks.

ME: How are you going to keep your operation running?

HIM: Well, it's a little early to make any decisions . . . Right now we're trying to assess the damage to our equipment and inventory.

ME: Can I take your card and call you in a few days? I own a 110,000-square-foot building down the street . . . it happens to be empty.

And two weeks later his company was renting our building on a one-year lease. The rent he paid us, about $600,000 for the year, met our carrying costs and saved us money while we fought off the appeal to our zoning approval and moved our retail plans forward.

But even with the good fortune of the early dismissal of the zoning appeal and finding a tenant after the fire, we lost a lot of money. By the time we were able to get the zoning approval final and obtain site plan approval, we'd lost a lot of time and momentum. We eventually got the approvals we needed and sold the property, but even so, we lost about $1 million on this deal. And it could have been a lot worse.

What Did I Learn from This Experience?

Well, first and foremost I learned never to believe your own press clippings. Yes, I'd had several very successful deals up to that point, and good for me. But that did not, by any stretch, mean that I was some kind of real estate genius. I'd created some good deals and executed on them, and fortunately, things worked out. But each deal is different, and as such has the potential for huge reward or huge loss. Had I approached the deal in Shelton the way I did the successful deals, doing a ton of due diligence and questioning all my assumptions, I might never have bought the building and/or incurred the loss I did.

Second, I learned that a real estate entrepreneur can never take anything for granted. Even though it was clear that the people in Shelton wanted more retail, as did the zoning officials, I should not have taken for granted that the zoning approval would whisk through. Any good businessperson needs to consider not only the good stuff that can occur, but the "what ifs," that is, the bad stuff that can happen. Had I done that, I would have thought about a possible appeal to the zoning approval and realized that the shopping center owner across the street had all the reason in the world to slow down a retail development that would compete with his property. Dumb . . . dumb . . . dumb!

Third, I learned to never, never, never stop hustling. Above, I mentioned being scrappy. Some of the best real estate entrepreneurs I know are also the

> I was talking with a broker friend of mine the other day about one of the young brokers in his office who had enjoyed great success very early in his career. My friend described the young broker this way:
>
> "You know, Jim, he's just one of those people . . . He'll ask someone for something and they'll tell him NO 10 times in a row, and you know what he *hears*? 'How about coming to my house for dinner next week?' That's why he's done so well so fast."

scrappiest people I have ever met. They fight and fight and fight . . . and then fight some more. They never take no for an answer.

Scrappiness is critical to the real estate entrepreneur. One reason I got into trouble with this deal was that I forgot about being scrappy while doing my due diligence. Fortunately, when I realized I was in serious trouble, my instincts came out: I found the right zoning lawyer. I suggested we check the 100-foot zoning requirement for appeals of approvals. I went to the burning building at 6 a.m. and found the president of the company that had been displaced by the fire. Finally, my scrappiness saved me. But I was way too late in finding myself. The point is that if you want to succeed in the real estate game, especially in the arena of bigger and more complicated deals, you have to get up each day with the same attitude: "I'm in a race for my life. I've got to run as hard and as long as I can. I do not believe my own BS. I only believe in hard work and hustle." Then you'll do fine.

Residential Land Development

Here's another mistake I made. The story is fairly short . . . but not sweet. This deal also occurred during the time when our group was making a lot of money and we thought we were really, really smart.

One day one of us came across a *Wall Street Journal* article advertising a 70-acre piece of land for sale in Newtown, Connecticut. The property was a magnificent horse farm, with beautiful stables and an indoor/outdoor riding area. The location was great. We decided that since we were so good at buying, renting, and/or selling office, distribution, and industrial buildings, we would be good at residential subdivision and housing development as well.

So we bought the land for what we told ourselves was a bargain price of $2.5 million. We had done our homework and concluded that we could subdivide this property into 20 large parcels. Each homeowner would have a great piece of land, with access to the stables and riding areas. We concluded that we could sell each lot for about $500,000; we did the math and congratulated ourselves on our great purchase:

Other Mistakes I've Made

$500,000 \times 20$	$10,000,000
Land cost	$2,500,000
Estimated roads/Infrastructure	$2,000,000
Taxes, insurance, interest (during development)	<u>$500,000</u>
Estimated profit	$5,000,000

Wow, how easy was this! Unfortunately, we missed a few things:

1. Getting all the subdivision approvals took about a year longer than expected.
2. We had greatly overestimated how quickly we would sell the lots. Our expected sell-out of 18 months turned into four years. Hence, our carrying costs (while we owned the land) were much higher than we'd estimated.
3. Since residential land development was not our thing, we hadn't done a competent job of determining the cost of installing roads throughout the 70-acre parcel. Not that we had done *no* homework. We talked to road builders and learned that the cost of roadway was $X per linear foot. In assessing the project, we had laid out on the survey where we thought the roads would go, measured the linear feet, and came up with a projected estimate of $2 million for needed roadways and related infrastructure. Unfortunately, we goofed in laying out the roads. In order to get an accurate estimate of the location and length of the roads we would need, we should have worked at the site, hiring land planners or road builders to stake the lots and then determine how the roads would weave through the 70 acres. Had we done that we would have learned that the roads we laid out on paper were not practical given the contours and topography of the site. When we learned where the roads would actually have to go, given the peculiarities of the land, our estimate for roads and infrastructure was much lower than it should have been.
4. Residential land development is a scary proposition for the real estate player. Unlike a commercial property where you presumably have rents coming (i.e., cash flow), residential land development is all or nothing. You have nothing coming in (and a lot going out) until you start selling lots. None of us had the patience or stomach for this kind of business with sporadic and unpredictable revenue. When we saw that the lots were not selling as quickly as we hoped, we dropped the price just to get some money coming in the door.

Result: a $1.5 million loss.

Lessons from This Deal

1. You're not as smart as you think you are. Do your homework, and then when you think you've done enough, do some more. Speak with people who have done the type of deal you're considering. Had we just done that, some

experienced land developer would have told us that the only way to accurately measure road cost is to walk the property with a road builder.

2. Be cautious about venturing into unfamiliar areas of real estate development. To the extent that you can, stick with your expertise, or at least with deals where there is a natural connection or progression from what you've been doing. For example, if you have been buying and leasing office buildings and a strip center is brought to your attention and the numbers seem to work, well, I don't have a huge problem with your buying the strip center. The general concepts of office building purchase and leasing are similar to those for retail purchase and leasing. But when you stray, as we did, into residential land development, you are venturing into unfamiliar water and you may be swimming with the sharks. My suggestion: if you're going to take on a project out of your comfort zone, partner with an experienced developer. Stay with what you know and/or only stray when the segue from one type of deal to another makes sense.

3. I personally learned another huge lesson in this residential land deal. In prior transactions with my partner, I'd taken the lead and he was a bit more passive. He had found this deal and wanted me to come into it, and though I didn't know much about the deal, I felt that since he and I were partners in previous deals, I should follow his lead into the residential land deal. Now, don't get me wrong. My partner is a very smart guy and has made a lot of money in the real estate game since the time of that residential deal. But I was way too passive! Although I would most likely have made the same mistakes in the due diligence had I been doing it, I somehow would have felt better if the screwups were all mine. What I rue most was my decision to follow someone else's lead. As an entrepreneur, you must have great confidence in your own talents. Entrusting yourself completely to someone else's deal is, in my judgment, a mistake.

What I Learned about Myself

I never again want to be a passive investor in someone else's deal because there is no upside for me. If the deal is a bad one, I lose money and kick myself for playing a passive role. If the deal is a good one, I make money but do not get the same enjoyment from the process (that I would if I were leading the deal) since I had no part in the success. That is critical to me (and perhaps to many entrepreneurs). It's like I got lucky in the stock market by throwing a dart at a board and coming up with the right stock. What fun is that? In short, as an entrepreneur, do *not* live by the bromide: "Lead, follow, or get out of the way."

Here's what the Entrepreneur's Rule should be: "Lead or get out of the deal."

It cost me $750,000 to learn that lesson. You have just learned it for the egregiously inexpensive price of this book.

Another Mistake I've Made Several Times

One thing that I see a lot of entrepreneurs do wrong, and I did several times earlier in my career, is trying to stretch a single into a double and getting thrown out at second base. One of the hardest things to learn as an entrepreneur is where to position yourself in a negotiation. Whether you're a seller, buyer, landlord, or tenant, one of the things you must learn to do is to decide, BEFORE negotiating with the opposite party, EXACTLY what you will or won't do, and how to communicate that to the other party. Here's an example:

> Several years ago I owned an office building with a 5,000 sf vacancy. A broker brought me a potential tenant and I made the judgment that this prospect was very interested in my building. My asking rent was $25/sf gross plus utilities, and the prospective tenant offered $20/sf. Now, even though I knew that $20/sf worked for me, I decided to counter, and I told the prospective tenant's broker that I would accept $23/sf for the first year with $1/sf per year increases thereafter, "but not a penny less." In other words, I thought I had a very interested prospect and so I played the negotiating game.
>
> A few days went by and I didn't hear from the prospective tenant's broker. A little surprised, I called him:
>
> ME: Hey, Bill, I'm surprised that I haven't heard back from you. I could tell that your customer was very interested in my building and I thought we had the makings of a deal.
>
> BROKER: Well, Jim, to tell you the truth, they did really like your building but you were a couple dollars per square foot higher than they wanted to pay and so they asked me to show them a few other buildings and they found one they liked.
>
> ME (sickening feeling creeping in): Have they made an offer on another building?
>
> BROKER: Yes, in fact the offer has been accepted and Lease Agreements are being drafted.
>
> ME: Well heck, Bill, I don't want to lose this deal. Suppose I go down to their offer of $20/sf? Can we get this deal done?
>
> BROKER: No, Jim, I don't think so. These people are very honorable and they've signed a Letter of Intent. I'm afraid it's too late.
>
> ME (to myself): Dumb! Dumb! Dumb!

Now, it's pretty obvious what I did wrong: (1) I misjudged the tenant's level of interest, and (2) I set my "not a penny less" price higher than I would, in fact, have happily accepted. Misjudging the prospect's interest was not why I was angry at myself, however. Misjudging people is something we all do in all areas of life. The reason I was upset with myself was that I did such a poor job of negotiation and communication.

As mentioned, I would have been fine with a rent of $20/sf. I tried, however, to stretch a solid single into a crowd-pleasing double. And I got tagged out at second. Shame on me! This is a mistake that I see entrepreneurs make ALL THE TIME. A guy is selling a building. He's asking $500,000 and he gets an offer of $450,000. He counters at $475,000 even though he would be happy at $450,000. He loses the deal. A woman is making an offer to buy a building. The asking price is $2 million. She offers $1.7 million even though her analysis indicates that she can make this deal work very well at $1.9 million. She loses out to another buyer. And so on.

Maybe you're thinking that I'm speaking against typical, everyday negotiation. One party asks X. The other party offers 75 percent X. There is a counter at 90 percent X and the parties agree. And, of course, that does happen every single day. *But* what also happens is that people get too cute. They try to get that last dollar and lose out on an opportunity where they could have made hundreds of thousands or millions of dollars. That, to me, is a bad risk-reward analysis. DON'T RISK THOUSANDS IN ORDER TO SAVE HUNDREDS.

My rule now is that I decide exactly what I can accept or pay before opening my mouth. I do not, of course, always offer the asking price or accept the first offer I receive. But neither do I try to grossly undercut an asking price or push an offer that is close to what I can live with. If the ask or offer is close to my number, I'm going to make the deal somehow, some way.

In the example above (where I had space for lease at $25/sf), I could have done a much better job of negotiation and communication. (Can you see areas for improvement?):

1. I could have accepted the $20/sf offer right away. Once I got the number that worked for me, I could have said to myself: "I'm where I need to be, take the deal."
2. I should never have used the expression "not a penny less." That communicates to the other party that I am rigid at $23/sf. Even if I want to try a counteroffer, I should phrase it to the other party with some "wiggle room":

   ME: Look, Bill, I really was hoping for $23/sf. Do you think you can get that? Please give it a try and then get back to me.

   This leaves the door ajar for further discussion.
3. I should NEVER have waited a few days for the prospective tenant's response. Those couple of days of silence was a bad sign that I did not pick up on. Once I had an offer that could work for me, time was the enemy. In contrast, today,

Other Mistakes I've Made

whenever I decide to push a little bit by stating a number that is less than I will pay, or more than I will accept, I NEVER let much time go by with the other party. Time is an invitation for them to reconsider and/or go look for other deals. In the example above, what I should have done is called the prospect's broker back soon after making my counter:

ME: Bill, it's been a couple of hours and I wonder if you've had a chance to speak with your client.

Based on what he tells me (and in this case, presumably, that he was asked to show the prospect other buildings), I can immediately regroup and drop my price to $20/sf and make the deal. Never assume in these situations that "no news is good news."

As a principal, a broker, and a lawyer, I see people making this mistake over and over and over: trying to be too clever in a negotiation. Just this month I was representing a tenant (as the broker) who was interested in leasing an established developer's vacant building. My client was willing to pay $28/sf in the first year of a 10-year lease with reasonable increases thereafter. The developer and I had a conversation and he was adamant:

HIM: Jim, I have a lot of interest in this building. Please tell your client in the nicest way possible that I will not go below $30/sf in the first year.

ME: Joe, I think you're making a mistake . . . in fact a very common mistake that way too many real estate entrepreneurs make. (No, I did not really add that last part.)

HIM: Jim, I have to draw a line in the sand, and that is mine.

ME: Okay.

Fast forward two weeks: My client decided not to lease the building and to keep looking. When they considered the developer's rent of $30/sf, they took a second look at the traffic patterns and demographics of the location and determined that even their offer of $28/sf was too high. So we're still looking. As you might have guessed, I eventually got a call from the developer:

HIM: Jim, what's the scoop? My broker tells me that your client has passed on the deal.

ME: Yes, Joe, they did not want to pay $30/sf.

HIM: Yes, I gathered that. So I am now willing to accept $28/sf.

ME: Too late, Joe. They've concluded that your location is not right for them.

HIM: What about $26/sf?

ME: Sorry, Joe.

This is a scenario I see over and over. I think of it like clearing the dinner table. I know that I can reasonably carry four glasses from the table. But on occasion I decide to push it and try for six. Sometimes I make it. Sometimes I drop (and break) several of the glasses. I should have limited myself to four glasses. Think about that the next time you're negotiating.

Conclusion

As a real estate entrepreneur, you're going to make mistakes. Anyone swinging for the fences is going to strike out. But you cannot fear striking out or you'll never get into the batter's box. What you can do is maximize your potential for success and minimize your potential for failure if you:

1. Never take anything for granted.
2. Hustle, hustle, hustle . . . and then hustle some more.
3. Stick with what you know, or if you're going into an area or type of deal that is totally unfamiliar, partner up with someone who has knowledge and experience in that area or kind of deal.
4. Don't be a passive investor. Either take the lead or get out of the deal.
5. When you get a deal that works for you, don't try pushing a single into a double. A hit is a hit.

Wow, I'm glad that I got this chapter out of my system. On reflection, I hate talking about what a jerk I've been. Let's get back to some more cool deals I've done.

10

Buying Wholesale, Selling Retail

For years now real estate players have made a ton of money buying properties wholesale and selling them retail. The best example of this is the purchase of an apartment building that is then "condominiumized" and sold off as individual condominiums. What happens is that a real estate player buys the units at a wholesale price (in bulk) and then sells them off at retail prices (individually). Enormous money has been made doing this!

Dividing One Building into Two

Before we discuss condo converting, I thought I would tell you a story of how I learned this most simple lesson: buy wholesale, sell retail. The story of this deal is also discussed later in the book in another context, but here I want you to focus on the fundamental reason we were able to turn a nice profit: buying wholesale and selling retail.

Years ago some brokers brought me a building for sale in Milford, Connecticut. It was a 200,000-square-foot distribution center with a single tenant whose lease was about to expire. The asking price was $7 million, which was a fair price given that the tenant in the building had made it clear that it would not be staying once its lease was over. There was not much demand in the Milford market from 200,000 sf users, and so re-leasing the building was going to be problematic. Fortunately for us, the seller of the property was "institutional" (read "nonentrepreneurial") and was not looking to add value. The seller just wanted to sell.

Here is an easy rule to remember: **Whenever you come across a seller who is not entrepreneurial, there may be an opportunity for you.**

Hammering at the fact that there were so few 200,000 sf tenants in the market, my partners and I were able to convince the seller to sell us this building for $6.6 million. But we had done our homework. Though finding a 200,000 sf tenant would be problematic at best, if we could divide the building into two 100,000 sf spaces, we'd have a much better chance to lease it. Simple, you laugh . . . and you are absolutely right. But the seller could have done this research too. He just did not have the entrepreneurial energy to take on the creation of a 200-foot-long, 35-foot-tall, fire-rated demising wall in order to create two 100,000 sf spaces out of one 200,000 sf space. But to us this was all part of being entrepreneurs, and we got it done in two months at a cost of about $250,000. Shortly thereafter we had the building leased to two 100,000 sf tenants, and about a year later we sold the property for $10.2 million. The secret: we bought wholesale (200,000 sf) and sold retail (100,000 sf).

Condo Conversions

The economics of condominium conversion are pretty simple. Let's look at an example of a deal that I was involved with at the beginning of my career:

I put together a group to buy a 40-unit apartment building. The net operating income of the building was about $100,000 and we bought the property for $1,250,000, about an 8 percent cap rate. We operated the building for a couple of years, built the net operating income up to $130,000, and then sold, again at about an 8 percent cap rate, for $1.6 million. So we made a nice $350,000 profit.

But the individual who bought the building from us was a lot smarter than we were. He had done a better job of paying attention to what was going on in the Connecticut residential market, and he realized that our building was a good candidate for a condo conversion.

Here is how he analyzed our property:

Buying Wholesale, Selling Retail

- Our building contained 30 one-bedroom units and 10 two-bedroom units. Our prospective buyer estimated that after turning our apartment building into a condominium—so that each of the units could be purchased separately (as a condominium unit)—and upon renovation, he could sell the units as follows:

  One-bedrooms $100,000
  Two-bedrooms $135,000

- He did an engineering study and concluded that the building was in good shape and that all he would need to do to put the units in marketable condition was repaint, recarpet, and install new kitchen appliances and bathroom fixtures. He budgeted $20,000 per unit for this work. In addition, he had a general line item for the common areas in the building: repaint, refloor, cosmetic upgrades (trim, etc.). This line item was $100,000. He felt that he could sell units to one-third of the existing residential tenants, and therefore he needed to budget for carrying the building with some number of units empty (tenants who left because the building was "going condo"), for brokerage expenses in finding and selling to new buyers, and for marketing. The line item for this last category was $100,000.

- Finally, there's the cost of converting the building to a condominium. An apartment building cannot be sold in pieces. Each unit needs to become a separate piece of real estate, what is commonly known as a "condominium unit." Every State has certain requirements for converting an apartment building into individual condominium units. Generally, a **Declaration of Condominium** needs to be filed with the Secretary of State's office and in the Town/City land records. This document defines the condominium units, identifies the common areas, and calls for the formation of a condominium association, usually a corporate entity that owns the common areas (and which is itself owned by the condo unit owners). The expenses of converting a building to condominium ownership are not usually that high. This line item was $25,000.

So here is what the prospective buyer's pro forma looked like:

SALES:

30 one-bedroom units at $100,000	$3,000,000
10 two-bedroom units at $135,000	1,350,000
Total	$4,350,000

Confessions of a Real Estate Entrepreneur

EXPENSES:

Acquisition	$1,600,000	
Unit renovations (at $20,000/unit)	800,000	
Common area upgrades	100,000	
Down time, brokerage	100,000	
Legal/Declaration of Condominium	25,000	
Contingency/Miscellaneous	200,000	
Total	$2,825,000	2,825,000
Projected Profit		$1,525,000

And his numbers turned out to be accurate. About 18 months after purchasing the property from us for $1.6 million, he was able to sell out the 40 condominium units at the projected prices and make himself $1.5 million. This is an example of profiting by buying wholesale and selling retail.

Why did I not do the "condominiumizing"? Well, at the time I was not familiar enough with the mechanics and opportunities of doing so, and frankly, I just missed the boat. Since then, of course, I have educated myself, and have recently put together three deals to purchase apartment buildings that we will eventually "condominiumize."

Is the residential condo conversion play over? I certainly do not think so. Buildings all across the United States are being condo converted as you read this page. What is happening, however, is that the profits one can make from condo-converting an apartment building are decreasing. Why? Because most owners/sellers of apartment buildings are now aware of the potential value of their properties on a condo-conversion basis. Whereas our group in the above example was not on top of what was going on in Connecticut at the time, sellers today are for the most part very savvy to the condo-conversion phenomenon and they price their properties accordingly. This decreases the potential profit to the condo-converter, although in my view there is still plenty of money to be made.

Remember when we discussed self-storage facilities and the money one could make by buying an industrial building that was being sold at a price based on its rental value as an industrial building, then turning it into a self-storage facility? Well, that is the same story here. Creative entrepreneurs are always thinking about new ways to use real estate or ADD VALUE. It is of course a common theme in this book: turning an industrial building into a self-storage facility, turning a factory into a factory outlet shopping center, turning an apartment building into condominiums. In each case the theme of the opportunity is the same: *buy on one pricing model and sell on another.* It's a great way to get rich.

Buying Wholesale, Selling Retail

What happens eventually, of course, is that sellers wise up. We saw that in the story of self-storage facilities. And it happened in the pricing of buildings that could be converted to outlet malls. And it's the same in buying apartment buildings for condo conversion. Today, finding a seller of an apartment building who has not analyzed his property as a potential condominium conversion is rare. That means the size of the opportunity has diminished because now sellers are selling *potential condo conversions,* whereas years ago they were still selling *apartment buildings.* What's the lesson? Watch for new opportunities and be creative. And when you see something that makes sense, move quickly and aggressively. Don't let the sellers catch up.

The good news is that there is always opportunity in the real estate game. The concepts stay the same; the application just changes. For example, there is a push in some areas of the country now for the condo conversion of office buildings. As of this writing, the demand is not nearly as clear as it is for residential condo units. But based on the deals being done in some areas, it does appear that there is a demand for office condominiums. And so my company has begun its research of that phenomenon in the areas in which we invest. If we can find an office building at some fair cap rate that has potential for conversion to office condos, we would be very happy to purchase the building and pursue its "condominiumization."

Do office condominiums make sense? Yes, for the same reason that residential condominiums make sense: people prefer to pay off a mortgage than to pay rent. A tenant has nothing to show for years of paying rent, but a condominium unit owner will presumably have paid down a mortgage and/or (hopefully) experienced price appreciation and increased equity. This is a compelling argument for ownership over rental. People are comfortable with the condominium concept. Real estate ownership is one of the embedded principles of our economic thinking, and people expect to make money from the ownership of real estate. I presume that most business owners own their own home (house or condo) and so understand the benefits that can come from real estate ownership. Office condo ownership is just like owning your own home . . . only in this case the property owned is the business's home.

What are the issues with office condominium ownership? Well, in my view, one issue is that business life is perhaps not as static as family life. A business can grow or contract quickly based on a lot of factors. Although families also expand and contract, the increase or decrease is usually predictable and happens slowly. So when one purchases a residential condominium unit, he generally has a pretty good idea as to how many bedrooms and bathrooms and square feet he will need for the foreseeable future. It is therefore unlikely that the residential condominium owner will need to sell because a year after buying he has too much or too little space.

Businesses, on the other hand, do expand and contract quickly . . . and at times due to unexpected circumstances. A business owner may be reluctant to purchase an office condominium that turns out to be too large or too small shortly after purchase. And he may not want to be stuck with having to sell should a need for more or less space arise quickly (condominiums are very hard to expand or contract unless one can buy out or sell to an adjoining owner).

Now, one could argue that this rigidity is the case whether a businessperson buys or rents. A business owner who signs a long-term lease is making a commitment to a particular amount of real estate, and if the business needs to grow or shrink, he still has a commitment to the square footage leased. But expansion or contraction in a rented building can be handled because when one person owns the entire building, he can more easily expand or reduce leased spaces. This flexibility in a rental versus a condominium may be a factor in the growth (or not) of the popularity of office condominiums.

My opinion: I believe that more business owners will eventually get comfortable with the idea of owning their own space. And that means that more real estate players will be looking to buy office buildings or flex buildings or industrial buildings that can be converted into and sold off as individual condominium units. But of course only time will tell. As a friend of mine says: "Whereas everything is clear in the rearview mirror, the game is to anticipate what is coming at you around the corner."

Conclusion

Real estate entrepreneurs who got into the residential condo conversion game EARLY made tons of money. They bought properties wholesale and sold them retail. They purchased apartment buildings at some multiple of net operating income and then sold them on an entirely different basis. Sooner or later the seller community caught up, and now apartment buildings that have conversion potential are priced accordingly—the huge markups are no longer easy to find. But perhaps office condo conversions are the next wave. Or maybe strip shopping centers where the owner converts each store into an individual condo and sells it to a user. I'm not sure what will be the next opportunity to buy wholesale and sell retail. I JUST WANT TO BE THERE FIRST.

The condominium conversion phenomenon taught us that getting to the party early was a good thing. Buying at one pricing model and selling at another (higher) pricing model is what a real estate entrepreneur strives for. How to get in the game early? Well, watch for new ideas, and if they appear to have "legs," capitalize on them quickly. That's what the next chapter is about.

11

The Next New Great Idea

$\mathbf{A}$s we have discussed, 30 or so years ago converting apartment buildings to individual condominiums was the new, cool idea. And real estate entrepreneurs who were early to the condo-conversion game made tons of money buying property based on the numbers of one business model and then selling based on numbers of an entirely different business model.

Today, converting apartment buildings to condominiums is no longer a new idea and sellers have caught up with the pricing model. One of your goals as a real estate player is to keep up with and perhaps create new ideas. Here is one that seems popular right now.

Condo Hotels

I own property in Miami Beach, Florida, where we are beginning to see a new phenomenon: condo hotels, sometimes called "condotels." Here is the proposition: you buy a condominium unit, just like you would in any condominium development, but instead of living in a building run by a condo association, you live in a building that is run as a hotel. And if you elect to put your unit in the "hotel pool," it can be rented out on a daily basis just like any other hotel room. Theoretically, there are several advantages to the owner of a condo-hotel unit:

1. *Increased services.* Since you're living in a hotel, you have access to house-keeping, to room service, to security, and to all the amenities a hotel generally offers the public (e.g., spas and restaurants). These services are not generally available to you if you live in a typical condominium building.
2. *Daily rental.* The big marketing pitch of the condo-hotel developers is that as the owner of a condominium in their hotel, your unit can be rented whenever you do not wish to stay there. This, they claim, will cover some or all of the cost of ownership of your condo unit.

Here is a typical sales pitch, from a five-star condo hotel being developed in Miami:

Hotel-condominium units are for sale at a price of $1,000 per square foot. A typical one-bedroom unit is about 650 square feet, so the selling price is $650,000.

Your common area maintenance charge (similar to that of any other condominium property) is $700/month and your projected real estate taxes are about $1,000/month.

Assuming that you obtain a 75 percent loan-to-value mortgage ($487,500), the debt service on your mortgage (assuming a 6 percent interest rate and 30-year amortization) is $2,922/month. Therefore, the total carrying costs of your hotel-condo unit are about $4,600/month (not calculating anything for a return on your equity of $162,500), or $55,000/year.

The developer suggests that you will probably use the condo 30 percent of the year, or about 100 days, and rent it out the other 265 days. The developer points out that the room rent for your condo will be $500/night, and since the hotel is projected to achieve 70 percent occupancy over the course of the year, the hotel operator should be able to rent out your room 70 percent of the 265 days that you are not using it, or about 185 days. So if the hotel rents out your room 185 nights, your condo will earn $92,500/year (185 × $500).

The developer informs you that the hotel operator does earn a share of your room's revenue, in this case (1) 10 percent off the top for credit card charges and reservation services, and then he (2) splits the balance of the room revenue with you on a 50-50 basis. In our example, your revenue share is $41,625 ($92,500 × 0.9 × 0.5). And, as the developer of the condo hotel will quickly point out, this $41,625 covers most of your annual carrying costs of $55,000/year *and* you get to use your unit 100 days per year almost "for free."

The Next New Great Idea

Now all that may sound pretty good, and it does seem to be working, since people are buying condo-hotel units all around the United States. But before purchasing from the developer in our example, you might want to do some homework. For example, the first two questions I would ask are (1) whether $500/night on average is realistic and (2) whether the hotel operator will in fact achieve a 70 percent occupancy with your unit *(at the times you do not want to use it)*. The $500/night may be realistic in season, but perhaps not when you put your unit in the "hotel pool" for rental (off season?). Similarly, over the course of the year, the hotel operator may achieve a 70 percent occupancy, but if you analyzed just the off-season months (when you are not interested in using it), the occupancy rate may be much lower.

After you do your homework, you may conclude that the condo-hotel investment is a great one. It does make fundamental sense when one considers the typical use of a vacation home. Most people probably do not use their vacation home more than, say, one-third of the year, so if an owner is able to create economic value out of the two-thirds of the year when he or she is not there, that is a good thing.

If the condo-hotel phenomenon catches on, then as we've seen with other examples (such as buying an apartment building and selling it off as individual condominium units), there will be an increasing number of real estate entrepreneurs purchasing hotel properties based on the numbers derived from one business model (operating a hotel), and then selling off the hotel rooms at numbers that are tied to an entirely different business model. The same theme we have been seeing time and again.

What's Next?

What will be the next wave in real estate? Where are the opportunities? Unfortunately, I do not know for sure, although I do believe there will always be opportunities. Our job, being the good real estate entrepreneurs that we are, is to find the opportunities and make a lot of money before others rush into the vacuum.

Here's one project I'm working on that may get your creative juices flowing. I've been buying property in an area where parking is at an enormous premium. There is just not enough of it. There are parking garages, of course, but these are often full, so people cannot rely on getting a space when they need one. My idea is to build a parking garage and then SELL the spaces: "parkominiums," to coin a word. Our budgeted cost to create a parking space is about $10,000 plus the cost of the land. So if I can find land with a cost per space of, say, $10,000 and then build the garage, I'm in for $20,000 per space. My guess is that I can sell these spaces for about $50,000. Not a bad business model if I can pull it off!! Check back with me this time next year.

Conclusion

Our company is always watching for new ideas, looking for new ways to use real estate. For creative ways to buy real estate based on one business model and then to sell it based on another (more profitable) model. For strategies for buying property at wholesale and then selling it at retail. For a better technique for doing something that has been done one way for years and years.

The great thing about being an entrepreneur is that there is no one right path. Any way that drops money to the bottom line is, in my view, a "right way." So don't be stuck in thinking that you need to do something as others are doing it or in the way it has always been done. In fact, it seems to me that those who are thinking against the grain—"Forget how it's always been done, I want to do it in a new and different way"—are sometimes the most successful entrepreneurs. Here's hoping you come across an idea that is new and exciting. By the way, just in case you want to share it with me, my e-mail is jrandel@randrealestate.com. Thanks!

Similar to finding the next new great idea is discovering the next new hot area of the country. Twenty years ago, if I had recommended that you buy in the meat-packing district of Manhattan or the South Beach area of Miami Beach (or many other areas that experienced an upward spike) and you had done so, you would be thanking me right now. Well, the next chapter is to get you thinking about where the next new hot area may be so that hopefully you will be writing me thank you notes years from now.

12

Buying Ahead
of the Crowd

As you know, fortunes are made in business when one can anticipate the direction of growth and demand. Any stock picker who can accurately predict investor demand will be rich very quickly. In some ways the same applies to real estate.

Many real estate entrepreneurs have made a lot of money buying properties in front of the crowd. There are examples throughout the country where once blighted areas formerly of no interest to homeowners or investors are now popular with both. And those who bought even five years ahead of the crowd made a lot of money.

Wherever you live, there must be areas near you that have potential which is yet to be realized. Where is the direction of growth in your area? Where is there potential for rehabilitation and gentrification in areas that today are blighted, seedy, or unsafe? How do you know which areas will experience rehabilitation? Well, of course, you cannot be sure. As mentioned in the introduction, everything is risk-reward. You do your homework and then you place a bet.

I have watched areas around the country evolve from not-so-desirable to highly desirable. I went to college and law school at Columbia University, which is located on the Upper West Side of Manhattan. Thirty years ago the area was a bit squishy (some sections being unsafe at night). Co-ops and condos could be purchased for a song in many buildings. Today the value of these properties has increased 10 to 20 times or more.

Confessions of a Real Estate Entrepreneur

Had I paid attention, I would have seen signs that good things would eventually happen to this area. The university was buying up property and renovating. Run-down buildings were being razed. Newer and better stores and restaurants were opening. Crime areas were being better policed, and young adults with families were starting to move in. What's more, I knew intuitively that New York City would always be an international and financial center and that there would be a constant demand for housing in Manhattan. When I was at Columbia, the East Side was much more popular than the West Side, but had I been paying attention, I would have concluded that sooner or later rising prices on the East Side would drive people to the West Side. It did not matter that I missed the signs, since I didn't have any money anyway. But it still bothers me that I was so blind to what was going on.

Of course, there are many other areas of the country that are today like the Upper West Side of Manhattan was 30 years ago. For the last five years I have been investing in Miami Beach, specifically South Beach, the five-square-mile area at the southernmost tip of Miami Beach.

What do I like about South Beach? Well, first let me say that I am by no stretch the first person in this market. There have already been two or three waves of price run-ups; I just wish that I had been investing sooner. What I like about South Beach is that I see many of the signs I saw years ago on the Upper West Side of Manhattan. Everywhere I look there are signs of renovation and rehabbing. Formerly vacant and boarded-up properties are being totally rebuilt. It seems there are new stores and restaurants opening every six months. Some of these stores are national chains that will only open in high-income areas. Crime areas have been addressed. New five-star hotel chains have opened recently (Ritz-Carlton, W Hotels, The Setai, and The Regent). There is money flowing into the area from all directions. While there is no Columbia University to serve as the foundation of stability, the magnificence of the beach and ocean draws lots of people to southern Florida.

Also, the press loves South Beach . . . as do celebrities. Every week or so, there is some newspaper or periodical writing about some celebrity or rich person moving into Miami Beach. This brings more celebrities, more rich people, and crowds of normal people who just like to be near the rich and famous. The city of Miami has greatly improved its reputation, and there are currently thousands of new condominiums either in development or on the drawing boards for downtown Miami. People with a lot more money than I have are placing big bets on the city. And as the reputation of the city of Miami improves as an international community, Miami Beach attracts more capital from all over the world.

Are there still problem areas? Yes. There are still parts of South Beach that need to be upgraded. But all around these areas there are signs of improvements. In my opinion, sooner or later these areas will be squeezed out of existence. I also believe, of course, that the movement of retiring baby boomers from the North and Midwest into south Florida will help. All of these factors tell me that Miami Beach is a good investment. (By the way, since I started buying there in 2001, oceanfront properties have appreciated from values of about $500/sf to $1,000/sf or more . . . in other words, one would have doubled his money by doing nothing except buying.)

As I began to invest in Miami Beach, I also did my homework into demographic trends such as population movements, household incomes, rental rates per square foot (as against other metropolitan areas), and so on. I tried to quantify on paper what my eyes were telling me, and nothing I learned changed my viewpoint. And so I am buying. Ten years from now we can look back and see whether I was right or not. In addition, I'm trying to find the next South Beach. I have now started to research what is commonly known as "North Beach." This area, stretching from about 71st Street to 85th Street in Miami Beach, has similarities to what South Beach looked like10 years ago, and the real estate there is much cheaper. So I've begun to make offers. Again, only time will tell if I am right.

Most assuredly there are areas near you that have the potential to be the next Upper West Side of Manhattan. Today you may need to take a leap of faith to start buying in these areas. Looking forward is hard to do. It's a bit of science, a bit of art, and a bit of guesswork. But if you're right, you may find your investment increasing in multiples that will dwarf a similar investment in an already safe and established area. Here we go again: risk-reward.

A Big Error Some People (Including Me) Have Made

Making money by purchasing ahead of the crowd is just another way of guessing which way the wind is blowing. Whether you're investing in a mature real estate market (e.g., where I live in Fairfield County, Connecticut) or one in transition (like South Beach), what you're really trying to do is anticipate price increases (or not).

In that regard, I have found that I (and others), who have been in a discrete real estate market for a long time, often fall prey to something I'll call the "I remember when" syndrome. Here's how this malady works, as illustrated by another pretty good-sized error I recently made:

> About two years ago there was a portfolio of seven office buildings on the market in Fairfield County. The asking price for this portfolio was about $38 million, and all the "smart" investors in the County looked hard at buying it. But most of us, including yours truly, could not get to a price over $35 million. In fact, here was a frequent refrain in our conversations with one another: "Who in the heck is going to pay $38 million for those properties? My gosh, I can remember when you could have bought all

of those buildings for a total of $15 million." And we walked away from the deal, shaking our heads and laughing.

And so along comes an investor from outside the area. He pays the $38 million and does all the right things to the property. Two years later (after having spent about $5 million), he sells the portfolio for about $55 million, laughing all the way to the bank.

Now what does this illustrate? I think it highlights something very, very important for entrepreneurs who have been buying in one area over an extended period of time. BE CAREFUL NOT TO GET SO CLOSE TO THE TREES THAT YOU MISS THE FOREST!

I think it's human nature to at times miss what's happening in your own backyard. I'll presume that prices have risen in your backyard over the last five or ten years. You've seen prices rise and rise and yet somehow you just cannot believe that they will continue to rise. So you get conservative. You find yourself talking yourself out of deals because you think that prices have got to stop somewhere. And you may be right. But the way to make that determination is not to think to yourself: "Wow, these prices have gone up so much over the last five years, how much higher can they go?" Rather, you must do an analysis based on supply and demand, the direction of interest rates and the economy in general, the fundamentals of the property under consideration, and so on. Do not do what I (and many others in Fairfield County) did: miss the forest for the trees (and blow a great opportunity) because we could "remember when."

Frankly, that is exactly what I think is happening in South Beach right now and why I like investing there. There have already been two waves of price increases in South Beach. The early players (the real risk takers) made a fortune when the next wave of buyers came in, buying at prices that the early players thought were ridiculous. Now a third wave is buying, and I am in it. I look at prices in South Beach, and compared to other well-located metropolitan areas, they look inexpensive to me. But to the early investors and even to the next wave, the prices I'm paying look dumb, dumb, dumb. Well, you know what, that's okay with me because I believe that there are about two or three waves yet to buy in Miami Beach, and I plan on selling to them. And the earliest buyers and even the next wave, who would never pay the "ridiculous" prices I am paying, may just discover that they missed an even bigger run-up than what they experienced. In short, they may be victims of the "I remember when" syndrome.

Conclusion

Anyone who can anticipate the direction of demand will make a lot of money. In the world of the real estate entrepreneur, the game is to be five or more years ahead of the demand. Then buy all you can and wait. If you're right, sooner or later the magnetism of the area in which you purchased will draw more and more people, capital, and energy. And you will be the beneficiary of having outwitted the herd.

Okay, now let's switch gears a little bit. Maybe you already sense that I am fascinated by superb salespeople. People who know exactly how to push your buttons, such that you end up doing just what they want you to do. Well, that's my lead-in to brokerage . . . where some of the smartest, most entrepreneurial people I have ever met are brokering their way to millions of dollars a year.

13

Brokerage

I'm going to take a break from talking about deals and instead discuss the people behind many of the deals: real estate and mortgage brokers. I started my career as a real estate attorney, and certainly having that perspective helped me a lot. Shortly after beginning my own legal practice, I got my real estate brokerage license, and I'm very glad I did. What's more, in hindsight, I believe there is perhaps no better point of entry into the real estate game than real estate brokerage.

Real Estate Brokerage

The job of the real estate broker is to connect people to each other. Whether it is a seller looking for a buyer, a buyer looking for a property, a landlord looking for a tenant, a tenant looking for space to lease, a developer looking for opportunities, or an investor looking for investments, the job of the real estate broker is to match people with their needs.

What is great about brokering is that no capital is required. Just people skills, salesmanship, and an understanding of the real estate business. And let's be honest with each other. The real estate business is not brain surgery. The concepts are basic, the math is simple, and the business is far from high tech. In my view anyone with about six months of real estate education can jump in and be successful.

Confessions of a Real Estate Entrepreneur

As you will see in this and later chapters, I am a great believer that success is a function of hard work, perseverance, and integrity. And real estate brokerage is the perfect forum for someone with these skills to succeed. You do not have to have capital. Or connections. Or an Ivy League education. What you need is a fire in the belly and a desire to hustle. What could be better than that?

Before we get into how real estate brokers make money, let me address the terminology of the business. Generally when one enters the real estate brokerage business, he or she has to sit for a certain number of classroom hours and then an examination. Upon passing the exam, this individual earns what is called a **salesperson's** license. After some period (it varies from state to state) acting as a salesperson, the individual may then take a test to be licensed as a **broker.** Some people do it, some don't. The distinction of being a broker is that he or she can operate a real estate office or company under his or her name, while the salesperson has to be aligned with a broker in order to function. For purposes of this book, however, I am calling everyone a real estate broker, since that is the common term used in the industry even when an individual is only licensed as a salesperson.

Let me give some examples of how real estate brokers work and how they earn money. Most top real estate brokers specialize in either leasing or sales. A leasing broker will, as it sounds, work on lease deals: representing either a landlord wanting to lease his building or a tenant looking to find space to occupy. A sales broker will represent buyers and sellers of investment properties. And then there is the residential brokerage business, about which many books have been written.

Leasing Brokers

Representing the Owner of a Building.   Property owners hire real estate brokers to lease vacant space in their buildings. The property owner signs a Commission Agreement engaging the broker to lease his building. The main points of the Commission Agreement will be:

- Owner hires Broker to find tenants for his building.
- The duration of the Agreement is usually six months to one year.
- If during the term of the Agreement the Owner signs a Lease with a tenant, the Owner will pay the Broker a commission. (Most Commission Agreements also have a "tail," a provision that says if a Lease is signed after the Commission Agreement expires but with a tenant who saw the building during the term of the Commission Agreement, then the Broker still earns a commission.)
- How the commission is to be calculated. As we will learn, commissions are tied to the total rent the tenant will pay. (I love this part—it means there is almost no limit on the size of a commission.)

Brokerage

Here's an example of how a leasing broker makes money:

Our real estate broker friend, Bill, has been hired to help a property owner ("Owner") lease vacant space in Owner's office building. There is 10,000 sf vacant in this building, and Owner wants to ask $20/sf gross plus utilities for the space. Generally, before Bill even takes the assignment, he will have a discussion with Owner to determine what Owner wants to ask for the space. If Owner is not realistic, there's no point to Bill taking on the assignment. For example, if the true rental value of the space in Owner's building is, say, $15/sf, then Bill may be wasting his time working on this assignment.

Sometimes owners need to be educated about the market. A broker can do that by showing an owner comparable office buildings for lease so that the owner can form his own judgment as to an appropriate asking price.

Usually an owner will ask the broker for assistance in setting the asking price and/or the "concession package." "Concessions" mean incentives used to induce a tenant to lease; for example, periods of no (or low) rent and/or money to assist the tenant with relocation and/or the building out of its new space. The goal of the leasing broker is to help the owner position the space to lease as quickly and as well as possible.

Now, back to our example:

Anyway, let's assume that Bill is comfortable with Owner's asking price of $20/sf. Now Bill has to find tenants. He's done some homework (e.g., checked with an architect) and determined that Owner's 10,000 sf vacancy can be divided into two spaces of 5,000 sf each, so Bill is looking for two tenants of 5,000 sf or one tenant needing 10,000 sf.

Bill puts a sign up in front of the building. He puts an ad in the local newspaper. He purchases a mailing list of companies in the area with 20 or more employees (presuming they require at least 5,000 sf of office space) and sends out a flyer to these companies. He puts information on the computerized "listing service" used by other leasing brokers in his area. Bill even hosts an open house at the building, hoping to attract to this event leasing brokers who represent tenants that might be interested in the building. Bill knows that part of the success with representing a building is not only attracting prospective tenants directly, but also getting assistance from other leasing brokers working in the market (since they are in touch with individuals and companies that may want to lease Owner's space).

Confessions of a Real Estate Entrepreneur

Let's say Bill gets lucky and gets a call off his newspaper ad. It's the CFO of a company in need of 10,000 square feet.

CFO: I saw your ad in the paper and I'm wondering if you can give me information about the office space for lease.

BILL: Yes, I'm happy to. It is located at 123 Main Street, which, as you probably know, is within walking distance of lots of restaurants, banks, and stores. The building was recently renovated with all new heating and air-conditioning. The Owner is prepared to make deals ... he's less interested in the last dollar of rent and more interested in finding good quality tenants.

CFO: What is the asking rent?

BILL: Twenty dollars per square foot plus utilities. Just so you know, we did a market survey of all comparable buildings before setting the asking rent and we've targeted an ask that is 10 percent below comparable properties.

CFO: That sounds interesting. Can I get some period of time between taking occupancy and having to pay rent? We have some unique needs and I presume we'll have to remodel the space for our particular usage.

BILL: Yes, we're offering four months of free rent but if you want to pay a little more in terms of rent, I can get you even more time. [As we discussed in Chapter 3, sometimes landlords will trade "free rent" for higher face rent.]

CFO: Okay, well perhaps I should make an appointment to come see the space.

And so Bill meets the CFO at the building, points out all the benefits of the space, structures a deal that works for both Owner and the CFO, and a 10-year Lease Agreement is signed. (Wow, this is an easy business, wouldn't you say?)

Let's say that the Lease Agreement calls for a starting rent of $20/sf, increasing by $1/sf per year for every year of the Lease Term. Remember, the tenant also gets four months of free (no) rent. Now, how does Bill get paid?

As indicated, commissions are calculated off the total rent paid by the tenant to an owner. In Bill's area of the country brokers get paid 5 percent of the gross rental *to be paid* by the tenant for the first five years of the Lease Agreement and 2.5 percent of the gross rental *to be paid* by the tenant for the second five years. Note that I italicized "to be paid." That is a great part of the leasing brokerage business: the broker usually gets paid once the Lease Agreement is signed, receiving a per-

Brokerage

centage of the rents the tenant WILL (if all goes well) pay to the owner over the ensuing 10 years; that is, once the Lease Agreement is signed, the broker has earned the commission and is paid in advance for rent to be received over time by the owner. Here's what the Commission Invoice from Bill to the Owner will look like:

COMMISSION INVOICE

Rent in year 1: 10,000 sf × $20/sf [$200,000 − $66,666 (four months free rent)]	$ 133,334
Rent in year 2: 10,000 sf × $21/sf	210,000
Rent in year 3: 10,000 sf × $22/sf	220,000
Rent in year 4: 10,000 sf × $23/sf	230,000
Rent in year 5: 10,000 sf × $24/sf	240,000
Total rent years 1 through 5	$1,033,334
Commission rate (5 percent)	× 0.05
Commission due	$ 51,666
Rent in year 6: 10,000 sf × $25/sf	$ 250,000
Rent in year 7: 10,000 sf × $26/sf	260,000
Rent in year 8: 10,000 sf × $27/sf	270,000
Rent in year 9: 10,000 sf × $28/sf	280,000
Rent in year 10: 10,000 sf × $29/sf	290,000
Total rent years 6 through 10	$1,350,000
Commission rate (2.5 percent)	× 0.025
Commission due	$ 33,750
Total Commission Due	**$85,416**

Not bad for one deal.

How much of this commission does Bill take home? Well, if he's a licensed broker who owns his own company, he takes home all $85,416. But most real estate brokers work for a real estate company, that means they have to share their commissions with the company. The split varies depending on the length of time a broker has been with a company, his success over the years, and his performance in a given year. Splits vary at the low end from 50-50 up to 80-20 (80 percent to the broker). In our example, Bill's split is 60-40, so on this deal he earns $51,249 ($85,416 × 60 percent).

Overrides. Now let's consider a scenario where the CFO of the company in our example came to Bill through another real estate broker. Let's assume the CFO has hired a leasing broker to help him search for space, and that broker, Charlie, is the one who called Bill. How did Charlie learn about the space? Maybe the ad. Maybe the computerized "listing" service. Maybe from an e-mail or flyer Bill sent to all brokerage companies in his market. Whatever. Remember that part of Bill's job is to get the word out, not just directly to prospective tenants, but also to all leasing brokers in the market who may be representing prospective tenants. In any event, Charlie calls Bill and here is how their conversation might go:

> CHARLIE: Hey, Bill, how you been? [Most leasing brokers in a given market know each other.]
>
> BILL: Fine, how about you?
>
> CHARLIE: Fine . . . I'm curious about the 10,000 sf space you're advertising.
>
> BILL: [Same sales pitch as above.]
>
> CHARLIE: That sounds pretty good . . . What commission are you offering outside brokers?
>
> BILL: Full commission to you, Charlie. I will get an override.

And that's what Charlie wanted to hear: that he would get a full commission (no split of a commission with Bill). So, in our deal Charlie will receive $85,416. And Bill will get what is called an **override**, usually a half commission . . . in our example, $42,708.

What is the logic of this arrangement? Well, owners have learned that in order to lease their buildings they need the assistance of all the leasing brokers in their market. And in order to ensure this cooperation, owners know they need to provide a healthy incentive to any broker representing a tenant. In most office markets this incentive is a full commission to the broker representing a tenant. (For some reason, the override concept is not widely accepted in the retail world; usually a 5 percent commission is split 50-50 between the broker representing the property owner and the broker representing the tenant.)

Now, if an owner pays the broker representing the tenant a full commission, his broker will still need to be paid, and hence the evolution of overrides (half commissions) to the owner's broker when another broker is representing the tenant. (Customs vary in different areas when the owner's agent and leasing agent are associated with the same company.)

Representing Tenants. Some brokers ("tenant brokers") concentrate on representing individuals or companies that need to lease space. They assist a prospective tenant with the location, analysis, and negotiation of Lease

Brokerage

Agreements. Sometimes a tenant's broker will negotiate an extension with an existing landlord, that is, the tenant does not even move, it just hires a broker to handle its negotiations.

In our example above Charlie was hired to work for the CFO in assisting him with finding 10,000 square feet of office space. Charlie was happy with this assignment because he was pretty sure he would make a commission (remember that brokers are in an "all or nothing" business—they only want to spend their time and energy where it's likely they will earn a commission). Most tenant brokers will expect that their client will work only with them, and they often ask for an exclusive "search assignment" agreement.

Sometimes a tenant's broker will work for a company that already has good space but wants to test the market to see if it can get a better deal elsewhere. So the company hires a broker to show it other spaces and get proposals from other landlords. But what if the company, after considering all its options, decides to stay put? How does the broker earn any money? Well, he may be paid by the company's existing landlord on an extension of the company's lease. Alternatively, some tenant brokers ask for "no go" fees in their search assignment agreement, a clause which says that if the company elects not to move (and if the company stays put, the broker does not earn a commission from the company's existing landlord), then the company will pay the broker a fee for his time.

Leasing brokerage can be very lucrative, and top leasing brokers make a lot of money. In larger cities, where the potential leases can be for significant amounts of space, top leasing brokers make several million dollars a year. There are even brokers who have years in which they make $10 million or more.

In addition to the large incomes a successful leasing agent can earn, there is another benefit to a career in real estate brokerage: it is a logical point of entry into the real estate ownership and development worlds. As a leasing broker, you will have access to incredible market information about companies that need real estate. And there may be times when you can turn this information to your advantage.

Insinuating Yourself into a Deal. A very successful broker friend of mine talks about the art of insinuating himself into a deal. He takes a small piece of information or a passing connection with someone and turns it into an opportunity to do a deal.

Here's an example:

Charlie, our tenant broker, is looking for new clients. He learns through a golfing buddy that a friend of a friend is in charge of Human Resources at the ABC Insurance Company and that ABC might be looking for new office space. So Charlie calls the HR executive (Bob Jones) at ABC and here's how the conversation goes:

Confessions of a Real Estate Entrepreneur

CHARLIE: Hi, Mr. Jones, my name is Charlie Brown and we have a mutual friend in Linus Smith. Linus plays golf with Clark Kent, who I guess you know. I don't really know Clark but I hear he's a good golfer, and I'm planning to have Linus set up an outing with Clark in the not too distant future.

JONES: Yes, Clark is a friend of mine and a very good golfer. Don't let him tell you that he's a seven handicap.

CHARLIE: Thanks for the tip. Anyway, I'll only take one minute of your time. Linus is under the impression that ABC may be considering relocating. I'm a real estate broker with a specialty in representing companies considering relocations. My job is to know about every office building in the market, what it rents for, who the good landlords are, what kinds of concessions one can extract from them, and so on. In short, my job is to help you consider your options and, should you decide to move, to get you the best deal possible.

JONES: Yes, that sounds like what we need, but the truth is, we were thinking that perhaps it's time to build our own building. We don't really have the expertise for this and would like to find someone who can help us.

CHARLIE: Well, if you have the time, I can explain to you in detail how I can also help you in that regard.

JONES: Sounds good.

Okay, Charlie struck gold, and of course most initial calls do not go nearly this well . . . but hey, I make the examples and I didn't want to take you through the tedium of all the unproductive calls a broker needs to make. The point is what Charlie learned from the call: that ABC Insurance may want to find a piece of land and construct its own building. This is a natural segue for Charlie to take his first step as a developer.

Charlie knows that ABC Insurance currently occupies about 10,000 square feet of space. He meets with the zoning office in his town and learns that in order to construct a building of 10,000 sf or more, ABC will require a piece of land of at least one-half acre. He does his homework on available parcels of a half acre or more within a 10-mile vicinity of ABC's present location and goes back to meet with Mr. Jones, armed and ready for business.

There are many different directions in which the next conversation with Jones can go. Charlie can act solely as a broker and attempt to broker the sale of a parcel of land to ABC. Or he can attempt to work his way into a development role. He does know that ABC is considering

132

constructing its own building, so he is morally obligated to present to them any opportunities to purchase land that he knows about (with him earning a commission, of course). But he may discover in conversations with the CFO that ABC does not relish the development role (tying up the land, taking it through zoning, meeting with architects, overseeing contractors, etc.) and that they would be willing to give him a piece of the deal if he undertook these jobs. In other words, Charlie may find himself in a position to trade his services for a piece of ownership of ABC's new building, an opportunity he creates for himself by leveraging his expertise as a real estate broker.

By the way, Charlie may not know a lot about development, such as zoning, construction, etc. Still, like most good real estate brokers, he is an extremely confident individual who will figure that he can learn as he goes. And for the opportunistic real estate broker looking to get into development, the chance of acquiring equity in a decent-sized office building (leased to a good credit tenant) will be a welcome challenge.

Okay, let's assume that ABC does not want to take on the development chores itself and is open to Charlie playing some type of role. Let's review how the conversation with Charlie and Bob Jones might play out:

CHARLIE: Bob, I do appreciate the opportunity to participate in ABC's purchase of land and construction of a new building. Here are my thoughts as to how we might do it. Since you have concluded that the ideal size for ABC is 15,000 square feet, I think the best land for us [look how quickly he has started using the word "us"] is the Frances Street piece, which is one acre. My estimate is that the total cost of land and construction for a 15,000-square-foot building at that location will be about $2.5 million. If ABC is willing to put up that money, I will take on the developer's role.

JONES: Will you earn a commission on the sale of the land to us?

CHARLIE: Yes, I'm entitled to a $50,000 commission, but I don't think there's anything unfair about me receiving that. If you do not buy the land, I have other interested clients, and I can sell it to one of them.

JONES: Oh, okay.

CHARLIE: I've checked around, and a standard developer's fee for a project of this size is $100,000, 4 percent of the total cost of the project. I will waive that fee for a piece of the deal. If ABC's equity in the deal—the money above its mortgage—is say $400,000, then including my $100,000, total equity is $500,000 and I would like to own 20 percent of the completed property.

JONES: Well, on first blush that sounds fair, but let me think about it. However, we will need some kind of buyout clause in case we want to acquire your ownership.

CHARLIE: That's okay. If you want to buy me out, we can get the property valued and you can buy me out for 20 percent of its value over the mortgage.

JONES: Well, that seems reasonable, but who will do the valuation?

CHARLIE: Any of the top real estate brokers in the area will be able to give us a valuation very quickly.

JONES: Well, since you're probably buddies with all the real estate brokers in the area [Bob is no dummy], why don't we use an appraiser?

CHARLIE: Okay, sure . . . no problem. I would just like one more point: that I can extricate myself from the deal at any time with, say, six months prior notice. In other words, I can ask you to buy my share of the equity at whatever the then market value of the property may be.

JONES: Done.

And so ABC and Charlie write up their agreement.

What has Charlie accomplished? Well, he turned a hoped-for leasing assignment into a commission on the sale of land and equity in a good real estate property. He did this by selling himself as a developer. That may have been a little questionable (given that he had no experience in this regard), but as a smart, hardworking guy, Charlie will most likely do a good job for ABC. What's more, he's created a situation where he can liquefy his investment at any time with six months' notice. Perhaps he waits a couple of years for the office market to appreciate and then he exercises his "put" to ABC and receives a nice check for his 20 percent interest.

Yes, Charlie had to hustle to create this deal for himself. And, of course, he will have to work hard to get the land approved for the 15,000 sf office building and to get the building designed and built. But if you're not into hustle and hard work, you're wasting your time reading this book, because that's what real estate entrepreneuring is all about! The goal of the real estate entrepreneur is to bootstrap his or her way into good deals, bigger deals, more lucrative deals. And hard work and hustle are the steps on the ladder.

By the way, Charlie enjoyed his role as a real estate developer, and he learned a lot . . . all on ABC's nickel. In fact, he is now so confident of his new abilities that he's thinking about taking an option on a piece of land near ABC's new headquarters. He will need to get it rezoned, and see if he can find a company willing to occupy it (he will most likely not build "on spec," i.e., without a tenant already in hand). Charlie realizes that he will have to risk some option money (about $25,000) and some legal and architectural fees (about $25,000). But, if he does get the project built and leased, he believes he will be able to sell it for a significant profit.

Here's the point to take away from this example: Information in the real estate business is very valuable. Charlie learned from a friend of a friend that ABC might be moving. That in itself was worth something because even if ABC had not hired him and given him a piece of the deal to develop its building, he still might have made a brokerage commission on the sale of land to ABC. From his initial meeting with Bob Jones, Charlie was able to parlay his general knowledge of the real estate market (although he puffed up his development skills a bit) into a piece of the action.

Charlie is a fictional character, *but* many, many real live real estate brokers have converted their knowledge about and contacts in a specific real estate market into highly lucrative careers as real estate developers. Information and contacts are two great doorways to get you into this very profitable area of the real estate game.

Selling Brokers (Often Called Investment Brokers)

As I indicated above, commercial real estate brokers tend to become either leasing brokers (representing owners and tenants) or selling brokers (representing sellers and buyers). Yes, of course, there is crossover in many communities, but in the larger cities, where the bigger dollars are at stake, there tends to be specialization. So let's look at what a selling broker does and how he makes money.

A broker who concentrates on the sale and purchase of real estate can work for the seller or for the buyer. Similar to the situation with leasing brokers, the broker who works for a seller will want a commission agreement spelling out how the broker gets paid for a sale. And the broker who works with a buyer may want an exclusive representation agreement committing the buyer to work with only that broker for a specific period of time.

Selling brokers can make a lot of money, since they earn commissions based on the sales price of the properties being sold. The commission rates can range from 6 percent of the sales price for properties of say ±$1 million down to 1 to 2 percent of the sales price for properties of $10 million or more. Customs vary from state to state, but most of the time the sales commission is split 50-50 between the broker representing the seller and the broker representing the buyer.

Since a selling broker needs to have a good understanding as to the valuation of commercial real estate, this is an appropriate time to discuss a common analysis used to evaluate commercial properties: the **discounted cash flow analysis.** Pay attention, since this is very important stuff for both the real estate broker and the real estate principal (sellers and buyers).

Discounted Cash Flow Valuation. Most buyers of investment-grade properties will evaluate a property with what is commonly known as a discounted cash flow analysis. In its simplest form, this is a present valuation of the income stream that the new owner of the property can expect in the five to ten years after his purchase. Let me take you through the important steps a buyer will make in performing this analysis:

Let's assume that our buyer is considering the purchase of a 5,000-square-foot office building with five tenants. The potential buyer will initially decide how long he intends to own the property. For simplicity's sake, let's assume that our potential buyer intends to hold the property for five years and then sell. Now he will create a **spreadsheet** (also called a **Pro Forma**) that projects his income stream from this deal over that five-year period.

Analyzing the Lease Agreements, he can determine what rents the tenants will be paying over the ensuing five years. When a tenant's lease does not run five years into the future, the buyer will need to make judgments as to where rents will be in the future. And looking at past operating expense figures, he can make some estimates about future costs. In our example, the potential buyer uses 2005 expenses (obtained from the seller) and increases these by 3 percent per year beginning with 2006. The same with real estate taxes. Finally, our buyer is using a December 2005 closing date, so his first month of ownership will be January 2006.

Our buyer's first stab at a five-year Pro Forma will look like this:

	2006	2007	2008	2009	2010
Gross rents	$100,000	$105,000	$110,000	$115,000	$120,000
Operating expenses	$ 28,000	$ 28,840	$ 29,705	$ 30,596	$ 31,514
Real estate taxes	$ 12,000	$ 12,360	$ 12,730	$ 13,112	$ 13,506
Net operating income	$ 60,000	$ 63,800	$ 67,565	$ 71,292	$ 74,980

Our buyer knows that a prudent purchaser should assume a certain amount of vacancy and deduct some amount from projected gross rents to account for those times when the building will not be 100 percent leased. Sometimes vacancy is the result of a tenant who gets into financial trouble and leaves the building (without meeting its rent obligation). Sometimes the reason for vacancy is that a tenant's lease expires and the tenant does not renew, thereby creating a gap between when the expired tenant's rent stops and rent comes in from a replacement tenant. In any event, the standard that buyers assume for vacancy is in the range of 3 to 5 percent of gross rents. Our buyer decides to use 4 percent. So our buyer plugs in a vacancy factor and his Pro Forma now looks like this:

	2006	2007	2008	2009	2010
Gross rents	$100,000	$105,000	$110,000	$115,000	$120,000
Vacancy (4 percent)	$ 4,000	$ 4,200	$ 4,400	$ 4,600	$ 4,800
Operating expenses	$ 28,000	$ 28,840	$ 29,705	$ 30,596	$ 31,514
Real estate taxes	$ 12,000	$ 12,360	$ 12,730	$ 13,112	$ 13,506
Net operating income	$ 56,000	$ 59,600	$ 63,165	$ 66,692	$ 70,180

Our buyer still has more work to do, however. In analyzing the Lease Agreements provided by the seller (always part of the usual due diligence package presented by a seller), the prospective buyer learns that the leases of three of the tenants in the building will expire within the indicated five-year period. In his initial stab at a Pro Forma (above), he assumed that all three would renew their Lease Agreements. But he knows that is not realistic, and now it's time to refine his Pro Forma.

Let's assume that three leases expire during the five-year Pro Forma period (just for simplicity I've made all expiration dates December 31) as follows:

The lease of a 1,000 sf tenant expires 12/31/07

The lease of a 2,000 sf tenant expires 12/31/08

The lease of a 750 sf tenant expires 12/31/08

Our buyer needs to make a judgment as to which of those tenants will renew and which will not. In his opinion, the tenant whose lease expires 12/31/07 is not doing too well. He has visited this tenant's space several times and there are only two people working there. The phone is never ringing and the buyer has not seen any visitors come to the space. He believes that this tenant will leave the building when the Lease expires. Therefore, he knows that he will probably have down time (vacancy) as well as expenses to re-lease the space: brokerage commissions and costs to retrofit this space for a new tenant (repaint, recarpet, etc.).

Therefore our buyer has to make assumptions about what he will pay in 2008 by way of brokerage commissions and retrofit expenses. He believes that those expenses will be $5/sf and $10/sf respectively—both incurred in the year of the re-leasing. Since these are not traditional operating expenses, they are often "below the line" of Net Operating Income (NOI), and when deducted from the NOI, you have the "Adjusted Operating Income." As indicated, the space in question is 1,000 square feet and the prospective buyer's Pro Forma would now look like this:

	2006	2007	2008	2009	2010
Gross rents	$100,000	$105,000	$110,000	$115,000	$120,000
Vacancy (4 percent)	$ 4,000	$ 4,200	$ 4,400	$ 4,600	$ 4,800
Operating expenses	$ 28,000	$ 28,840	$ 29,705	$ 30,596	$ 31,514
Real estate taxes	$ 12,000	$ 12,360	$ 12,730	$ 13,112	$ 13,506
Net operating income	$ 56,000	$ 59,600	$ 63,165	$ 66,692	$ 70,180
Brokerage	$ 0	$ 0	$ 5,000	$ 0	0
Retrofit	$ 0	$ 0	$ 10,000	$ 0	$0
Adj. operating income	$ 56,000	$ 59,600	$ 48,165	$ 66,692	$ 70,180

Notice that our buyer has not increased his vacancy in 2008. He could have. If he believed that it would take six months, for example, to re-lease the vacated space, he might have changed the 2008 gross rental figure, reducing it by the six months when no rent will be coming in from the empty 1,000 sf space. Just to keep things simple, I'm assuming that our buyer believes he can re-lease the space immediately, so there is no gap between the time the existing tenant stops paying rent and the new tenant starts paying rent.

Now our buyer has to make some judgments about the other two tenants whose Leases expire 12/31/08. He visits both spaces. He talks to the seller about these tenants and he gets the seller's permission to speak with the tenants themselves. After meeting with them, he concludes that the 2,000 sf tenant will most likely renew but the 750 sf tenant will not. Once again, therefore, he must add brokerage and retrofit expenses to the Pro Forma, which now looks like this:

	2006	2007	2008	2009	2010
Gross rents	$100,000	$105,000	$110,000	$115,000	$120,000
Vacancy (4 percent)	$ 4,000	$ 4,200	$ 4,400	$ 4,600	$ 4,800

Brokerage

Operating expenses	$ 28,000	$ 28,840	$ 29,705	$ 30,596	$ 31,514
Real estate taxes	$ 12,000	$ 12,360	$ 12,730	$ 13,112	$ 13,506
Net operating income	$ 56,000	$ 59,600	$ 63,165	$ 66,692	$ 70,180
Brokerage	$ 0	$ 0	$ 5,000	$ 3,750	$ 0
Retrofit	$ 0	$ 0	$ 10,000	$ 7,500	$ 0
Adj. operating income	$ 56,000	$ 59,600	$ 48,165	$ 55,442	$ 70,180

Our buyer is almost finished. He knows that over the first five years of his ownership he will probably have to make some major repairs and/or capital expenditures (new equipment). He estimates that the total cost of these repairs/expenditures will be about $15,000 or $3/sf. He does not know exactly when these will need to be made so he spreads this $15,000 evenly over his five-year Pro Forma. Therefore, we have another line item to add:

	2006	2007	2008	2009	2010
Gross rents	$100,000	$105,000	$110,000	$115,000	$120,000
Vacancy (4 percent)	$ 4,000	$ 4,200	$ 4,400	$ 4,600	$ 4,800
Operating expenses	$ 28,000	$ 28,840	$ 29,705	$ 30,596	$ 31,514
Real estate taxes	$ 12,000	$ 12,360	$ 12,730	$ 13,112	$ 13,506
Net operating income	$ 56,000	$ 59,600	$ 63,165	$ 66,692	$ 70,180
Brokerage	$ 0	$ 0	$ 5,000	$ 3,750	$ 0
Retrofit	$ 0	$ 0	$ 10,000	$ 7,500	$ 0
Repairs/Cap X	$ 3,000	$ 3,000	$ 3,000	$ 3,000	$ 3,000
Adj. operating income	$ 53,000	$ 56,600	$ 45,165	$ 52,442	$ 67,180

Finally, our buyer needs to make an assumption about the sale of this property. He assumes he will sell the property in January 2011 for a price equal to his 2010 Net Operating Income ($70,180) divided by a cap rate of 9 percent. He also assumes selling expenses of 4 percent (brokerage, legal, conveyance costs).

So our final Pro Forma looks like this:

	2006	2007	2008	2009	2010	2011
Gross rents	$100,000	$105,000	$110,000	$115,000	$120,000	
Vacancy (4 percent)	$ 4,000	$ 4,200	$ 4,400	$ 4,600	$ 4,800	
Operating expenses	$ 28,000	$ 28,840	$ 29,705	$ 30,596	$ 31,514	
Real estate taxes	$ 12,000	$ 12,360	$ 12,730	$ 13,112	$ 13,506	
Net operating income	$ 56,000	$ 59,600	$ 63,165	$ 66,692	$ 70,180	
Brokerage	$ 0	$ 0	$ 5,000	$ 3,750	$ 0	
Retrofit	$ 0	$ 0	$ 10,000	$ 7,500	$ 0	
Repairs/ Cap X	$ 3,000	$ 3,000	$ 3,000	$ 3,000	$ 3,000	
Adj. operating income	$ 53,000	$ 56,600	$ 45,165	$ 52,442	$ 67,180	
Sale in year six						$779,777
Selling expenses (4 percent)						$ 31,191
Net proceeds						$748,586
Income stream	$ 53,000	$ 56,600	$ 45,165	$ 52,442	$ 67,180	$748,586

Though this Pro Forma is by no means an exact picture of what will happen over the first five years of our buyer's ownership, it does represent the buyer's best guess based on the information he knows today. Now, he asks himself this

Brokerage

question: "Given that I expect a revenue stream generated by my operation and then resale of this building of $53,000, $56,600, $45,165, $52,442, $67,180, and $748,586, and given that money today is more valuable than money in the future (assumes inflation), how do I value this income stream?"

Well, first he needs to decide on a **discount rate**, which will be his assessment of what kind of return he desires to achieve on his investment. This rate takes into account his confidence in actually receiving the projected revenue income stream, current interest and inflation rates, and his view of the overall economy in general. The lower the discount rate (i.e., the lower the return that a buyer will be comfortable with), the higher the price he will pay. Our buyer decides that he wants to do this deal, but only if he can earn an annual return of between 10 and 14 percent on his capital (we are assuming an all-cash purchase). So he uses his HP calculator (or his Excel software, etc.) to determine the net present value of the projected revenue stream assuming discount rates of 10, 12, and 14 percent.

Here is what he will learn:

Discount Rate	Present Value of Revenue Stream
10 percent	$628,981
12 percent	$575,294
14 percent	$527,514

The above dollar amounts tell him the *present value* of the projected revenue stream for the indicated discount rate.

If the buyer is optimistic about his prospects with this property and the economy in general, and will accept a 10 percent annual return on his investment, he will pay about $630,000 for the property. As you can see, the higher the return the buyer desires, the lower the price that he'll pay. Which makes sense.

Now it's one thing for the buyer to do a Pro Forma and determine that he will only pay $X. The seller may have his own ideas of the value of a property and may be just as facile with Pro Formas as the buyer is. The seller may believe that the building is worth $700,000, notwithstanding the buyer's discounted cash flow analysis. This discussion between the buyer and seller (or their respective brokers) is all part of the jockeying that occurs prior to an agreement being reached.

As you might expect, there are software packages that make this kind of analysis quite easy to do. Many people in the industry use a software called ARGUS which allows a prospective buyer to make all sorts of assumptions about the property

Confessions of a Real Estate Entrepreneur

being considered; plug these in and the ARGUS software does the rest. For example, in a building with many tenants, ARGUS will ask the potential buyer to make a general assumption about tenant renewals, brokerage expenses, retrofit costs (for an existing tenant who stays) and new fit-up costs (for a new tenant). Once those assumptions are plugged in, ARGUS spits out the expected revenue stream.

I recommend, however, that a beginning real estate entrepreneur learn how to do the discounted analysis himself using Excel software, for example. And if considering a multi-tenant building, I would recommend that the analysis proceed tenant by tenant (most ARGUS analyses I've seen make a general assumption about ALL tenant spaces in regard to such items as probability of renewal, cost to retrofit, etc., but these general assumptions may not be accurate as to specific tenant spaces) and, as to each rented (or vacant) space, ask these questions:

- Will this tenant renew?
- If so, what kind of rent and concessions package will I need to give? Will I have a brokerage expense in renewing the lease, and if so, how much?
- If not, how much down time will there be before a new tenant is in place and paying rent? What costs will I incur in re-leasing this space in terms of fit-up money and brokerage fees?

This more specific analysis will be very helpful to you, forcing you to think through each tenanted (or vacant) space and the costs of re-leasing should you lose tenants.

As you start performing these analyses, you may also hear the term **Internal Rate of Return,** or **IRR.** This concept is similar to the discount rate. It basically analyzes the capital you invest at the beginning of an investment, how and when you receive income and principal back on this investment, and tells you what your rate of return will be over the course of the investment. Suppose instead of net present valuing the revenue stream as we did in our example above, you work backwards from the projected revenue stream, already knowing what you will have to pay for the building. The IRR tells you your return on investment over five years given the indicated revenues. To me it is very similar to the discount rate (although I have seen people use it differently in that they gradually reduce the investment amount as revenue comes in, causing a recalculation of the return on a declining investment amount). In my view, if you know how to do a discounted present value calculation, you will be fine.

Wow, have we learned a lot! Having made it this far, you're well on your way to success. Discounted cash flow analysis is about as complicated as it gets in the world of real estate entrepreneuring so if you're still with me, HURRAH . . . I like you . . . you have perseverance.

Back to Brokerage

The reason I included the discussion on net present valuation (NPV) in this chapter is because any broker who is involved in investment sales must be conversant with this analysis. Whether representing a seller or a buyer, the broker must be able to help his clients prepare, review, or revise an NPV spreadsheet.

Okay, back to the above example. Our buyer has reviewed the Pro Forma he prepared and concluded that he will pay $650,000 for the 5,000 sf office building (although the 10 percent discount rate indicated a price of $628,981, the buyer was forced to stretch to get this deal since the seller was not willing to go below $650,000). The seller agrees and we have a deal. The seller had previously given you, the broker, a Commission Agreement to sell his building, and let's assume that the buyer does not have a broker and is representing himself (generally this means you are entitled to the entire sales commission). Note that at times there may also be what is called a "dual agency," where one broker represents both sides of the transaction. This situation can be a little scary since you never want one of the parties coming back and saying that you did not adequately represent his interest, and when you're on both sides of the transaction, that can become an issue. The key is to obtain the consent of both parties with full disclosure as to how you're going to handle your dual agency.

Since this is a relatively small deal, you were able to negotiate a commission equal to 5 percent of the sales price, and so you earn $32,500 on sale, payable at closing. And good for you, you are now developing a track record and a reputation for successful sales. What's more, since you're familiar with discounted cash flow analyses, you're starting to make bigger deals. Although the commission rates generally drop for larger deals, the sales prices are higher, so the commissions can be very lucrative. Last month, for example, I put together two friends of mine, one interested in selling his building and the other interested in buying. I helped put together a Pro Forma for both parties and discussed with each the different assumptions I was making. Eventually they both got comfortable with my analysis and the deal closed at $4 million. My time invested was about 25 hours. My take: a $160,000 commission.

Needless to say, the brokers in large metropolitan markets who specialize in selling buildings for $20 million, $50 million, and $100 million-plus are making huge sums of money. Yes, it takes time (and maybe luck) to get into the league of these brokers . . . but someone is going to make this money, why not you?

Why I'm a Brokerage Fan

There are many reasons that I'm a big fan of the commercial real estate brokerage business:

- It does not require any capital. All that is at risk is your time. It does not require a college or business school education. Success is a function of one's work ethic, hustle, street smarts, and skills at networking and deal making.
- It is a great way to acquire information and contacts that can then be parlayed into real estate ownership positions. We spoke about the leasing broker who parlayed information about a particular company's need for space into an equity position in a deal. That happens with selling brokers too. I know of situations where a selling broker will be asked to find an individual or company a building to buy. He does so and then asks the potential buyer whether he can "throw his commission" into the deal. In other words, the selling broker is converting his commission into equity. Needless to say, the broker only does that when he really likes the deal and thinks that the eventual value of his equity position will far outstrip his commission.
- I believe that having a good sense of real estate brokerage will make you a better real estate entrepreneur. For example, my company owns a Class C office building that has constant tenant turnover. We knew that would be the situation when we purchased the building, and frankly not all real estate owners could be successful with this property. In our case (we have an in-house brokerage capability), although we need to constantly find tenants to replace those who leave, we've been very successful with this property. Our ability to handle a building that requires active leasing and re-leasing gives us a leg up on our competitors. When this building was being marketed for sale, other investors looked at this property and shied away from it. As we were not afraid of the leasing challenge, we stepped up and bought it, and given our knowledge of the brokerage business and leasing market, we've worked it into a real financial success.
- The number one reason that I love the real estate brokerage business is that there is no connection between the amount of time one invests in a matter and the potential reward. As a real estate attorney, I have been trained to "sell my time." I'm always cognizant of the fact that my income is limited by the number of hours in the day that I have to sell. This limiting business model is obviously not unique to attorneys and applies to anyone who sells his time (e.g., doctors and consultants).

Selling Time

A friend of mine says that business is "about selling the minutes of your life." By that he means that one factor to success in business is valuing every minute of your time during the workday, making sure you get the most you can out of each minute. If you actually sell your minutes (like an attorney), there is a cap on your income because there are only so many minutes in the day. In my view, a better model is the real estate brokerage business, where one can earn a commission that has

Brokerage

absolutely no relation to the time one invests. See my example above, where I spent about 25 hours putting my two friends together on a $4 million deal, and earned a commission of $160,000 (if I were selling my time, that comes to $6,400/hour). But that is not my best story. Here's one where I earned $375,000 per hour:

About five years ago a friend of mine asked for a recommendation of a good commercial real estate broker in New York City. My friend ran a company that leased space in New York City and his lease was expiring. He was considering moving his company's headquarters and he wanted to see his options. So I gave him the name of another buddy, a guy running a real estate brokerage company in the City and a very well-respected leasing broker (no matter what the opportunity, I would not recommend someone unless I felt he or she would do an excellent job). So that the two of them could get to know each other, I set up a breakfast in the City and the three of us had a nice two-hour breakfast meeting. After the breakfast, Friend #1 hired Friend #2 to help him analyze the prospect of relocating his company.

Friend #2 (the leasing broker) told me I was entitled to a referral fee for bringing him this matter. He sent me a letter acknowledging that he would pay me a 15 percent referral fee on whatever his company would earn. Fifteen percent didn't sound like a huge amount to me, but I didn't push. I said, "Okay."

After the breakfast meeting I lost touch with the matter. I knew that Friend #1's company was a big user of space, but I didn't consider what that meant in terms of dollars and cents if a deal was made to move his company into new space. Then one day a year later I get a phone call from Friend #2, and here's how the conversation went:

FRIEND #2: Hey, Randel, how you doing?

ME: Fine, how about you?

FRIEND #2: Oh, very well . . . Hey, we recently signed a Lease Agreement for new space for your friend's company. It turned out to be one of the larger deals done in the City this year.

ME: Oh, that's great. Is my buddy happy?

FRIEND #2: Oh yes, he loves the new space and he's very appreciative of the work we did for him.

ME: Great . . .

FRIEND #2: And by the way, I'm about to send you a check for your share of the leasing commission.

ME: Oh, that's nice [at this point I was still thinking, 15 percent . . . not that much].

FRIEND #2: Do you want me to tell you how much your check is?

ME: Yes, sure.

FRIEND #2: How does $750,000 sound?

I fell off my chair.

As it happened, Friend #1's company signed a long-term lease for about 400,000 square feet of space. The total commission on the deal was $5 million. My 15 percent did not seem so small anymore.

What did I learn from this experience?

1. Sometimes you get lucky, but as with all my stories, you have to be in the game to get lucky—you have to be constantly working to make contacts, learn the mechanics of the business, and generally keep abreast of developments in your area—in other words, continually hustling.

2. Who you know is sometimes as important as what you know (an old saying, but true). Had I not known Friend #1 and Friend #2 (both successful business-people), I would never have been in a position to earn this kind of referral fee. Obviously, all that I did is put two people together and then get out of the way. But my being in a position to do that was not pure luck. I had earned a reputation in my area for knowing a lot about real estate and when Friend #1 needed the recommendation of a good leasing broker, he called me. He trusted my judgment and integrity.

For my part, although I have never been one of those people who makes decisions about friends and acquaintances on the basis of what someone has to offer me, neither am I a reverse snob. If I like someone and he is a successful whatever, I make a point of learning and understanding what he does and how my particular set of skills or network may be able to help him. In that regard, I'm a big believer in listening. Whenever someone I am with wants to talk, I get real quiet and focus. When Friend #1 called me to speak about his possible need for new space, I knew about the company he ran and what he did. Same with Friend #2. I understood his business and knew that he would do an excellent job for Friend #1.

I like both of these men very much. If either lost his job and had nothing of business interest to me, I would still value and desire their friendship. But once I have a relationship with someone, I'm going to understand his job and his needs and his interests, and if he ever mentions a requirement for real estate, I'm going to offer my services.

Mortgage Brokerage

Another great way to learn about the world of real estate investing and to meet people in the business is mortgage brokerage. Mortgage brokers are individuals who make their living by putting together people in need of debt or equity to acquire or refinance real estate with the people or institutions that want to lend to or invest in real estate.

Today there are countless numbers of institutions and people with money that want to lend to or invest with real estate entrepreneurs. And there is no limit to the number of ways to structure deals between lenders and investors and entrepreneurs. The job of a good mortgage broker is to know where all the money is and who wants to lend/invest what, and in what kind of deals, and with what kind of expectations.

As you might expect, a good mortgage broker needs to understand how lenders value real estate and risk. Again, we're not talking about brain surgery. Many of the principles we have discussed—such as cap rates and discounted cash flow analyses—are the tools of the mortgage lender . . . and thus the mortgage broker needs to understand these analyses as well.

Mortgage brokers earn their money by putting together borrowers and lenders, and like real estate brokers, they receive a fee based on the amount of money loaned (or invested). Generally this fee is paid by the borrower. It declines with the amount of the loan, but most of the time the fee is in the neighborhood of 1 percent of the loan amount. And when you're dealing in large commercial mortgages, you can make a very good living. A friend of mine recently obtained a $65 million mortgage for a client of his. The fee: $500,000. And as he did not sell his time—perhaps he put in 50 hours—he earned $10,000 per hour. By the way, I do, of course, recognize that to be in a position to make larger deals, a real estate broker or mortgage broker needs to invest a lot of "start-up time" learning the business and developing a following, but so do those who sell their time by the hour.

I am giving you numbers of actual deals for one reason and one reason only: I want you to see the POTENTIAL rewards of the real estate brokerage and mortgage brokerage businesses. I want you to see that the rewards are not tied to a certain number of hours invested or capital at risk. But I also do not want you to think that these rewards come easy. All of the most successful players in the real estate and mortgage brokerage businesses are diligent, clever, and tough. They work very hard at being good at their profession. They constantly work at being good at the mechanics of the business, are always networking, are always on the prowl for new accounts (buyers, sellers, tenants, landlords, borrowers, lenders). But as a lawyer, I do the same thing. And my doctor friends work hard too. As do my consultant friends. What is extraordinary about the real estate and mortgage brokerage businesses, in my view, is that the potential rewards are so large. If you play it well, the sky is the limit.

Residential Brokerage

There are a lot of books out there about the residential brokerage business, how to get into it and be successful at it. (A fun and informative read is Barbara Corcoran's

Confessions of a Real Estate Entrepreneur

Use What You've Got, and Other Business Lessons I Learned from My Mom (Penguin, 2003). So I will limit my comments to just a few points:

1. Residential real estate brokers are entrepreneurs too. They have no guaranteed income. They rely on their wits, their hustle, their street smarts, and their work ethic.

2. Residential real estate brokerage is a sleeper business. No one goes to college to become one. It is sort of a default for people who have started in other businesses or endeavors (e.g., raising a family). I think that's a shame because it's a great business. As with commercial real estate brokerage, there's no capital at risk, and commissions are tied to the sales price of a house, not the hours invested. And as with any other entrepreneurial venture, the residential real estate brokers set their own schedule, working the number and type of hours they want. The top brokers are highly competitive (because where there's a lot of money to be made, there are a lot of residential brokers), great sellers, great networkers, and hard workers. But they are rewarded commensurately. The most successful, meaning those working in metropolitan areas selling the most expensive residences, can make serious incomes, upwards of $1 million per year.

3. Residential real estate brokers do not have the reputation of being very businesslike. Many people still think of them as people who sell houses when they're not busy doing other things. But that is no longer true. Because housing prices have risen so much in the last 10 years, potential commission revenue has gone up too. Anytime there is an opportunity to make $500,000 a year or more, essentially running your own business (each residential broker is an independent contractor), people with serious business skills will be attracted. And that is what has happened in the last 10 or so years. Today, the top residential brokers in each community are highly professional, usually very ethical individuals, and in the business for the long term.

Conclusion

As you can probably tell, I love the brokerage business. I love it because it requires no capital, just your time. I love it because it rewards those who hustle the most and who work the hardest. I love it because it is so low tech and really just about people skills. I love it because it is a wonderful point of entry into the world of real estate entrepreneuring. And I love it because it can be so lucrative.

Now it's time for a little more information about basic real estate concepts. As you are going to learn in the next chapter, there are ways to make money with real estate without even having an ownership interest.

14

Leases and Other Property Interests

It's important for the real estate entrepreneur to understand that there is plenty of money to be made even when he does not own real estate. What's almost as important as ownership is control. The best example to demonstrate this principle is leasehold interest. There are times when a player cannot convince a property owner to sell. Perhaps the owner has owned the property for such a long time that a sale will force him to recognize a huge capital gain, which he may not want to do. There are also times when an owner is emotionally attached to his property (perhaps it has been in the family for years) and he cannot psychologically part with the ownership interest. In these situations, a long-term lease may work as well (sometimes better) as an outright purchase of an ownership interest.

Ground Leases

Ground Leases are often the solution to a developer's inability to convince a landowner to sell. Here's an example:

> Remember our friend Joe Entrepreneur from Chapter 4 who has a retailer buddy (Mr. Retailer) wanting a 40,000-square-foot store? You may recall

Confessions of a Real Estate Entrepreneur

that Joe was able to locate a five-acre piece owned by Isaac Newton. But where Joe was able to convince Isaac to sell in Chapter 4, not so in this chapter. In fact, Isaac Newton has changed his mind about selling and decided that since his land has been in the family for 25 years, it is just not right for him to sell it.

As you may recall, Joe Entrepreneur was willing to pay Isaac $3 million for his land. Now, however, Joe has to take a different tack since Isaac won't sell:

JOE: Well, I am of course disappointed that you're not interested in selling your land to me, but perhaps there is another way . . . perhaps we can work out a Ground Lease arrangement.

ISAAC: What is that?

JOE: Well, often when a landowner does not want to part with the ownership of a property, a potential buyer will lease the property instead, signing a lease to occupy the property for 99 years, after which time possession reverts to the owner.

ISAAC: That sounds interesting.

JOE: Yes, and it can work out very well for the property owner because he gets the benefits of a sale . . . without paying Uncle Sam a large capital gains tax, since there is no transfer of title.

ISAAC: How much rent will you pay for the land?

JOE: Well, I would rather be an owner than a tenant . . . I'm sure you can understand that. Before you had decided not to sell, I suggested a price of $3 million. So working off the back of an envelope, I would say that had you sold, you would have paid the federal and state taxes of 20 percent on your gain. Since your family has owned the land for so long, that would be almost $600,000, leaving you $2.4 million. If you invested that today in, say, a long-term safe government instrument, you would earn about 5 percent, or $120,000 per year.

ISAAC: Yes, I follow you.

JOE: So, what if I pay you $120,000 per year, plus the real estate taxes and insurance on the property? We sign a 99-year ground lease and the rent goes up every 10 years by an inflation factor.

ISAAC: Sounds okay.

JOE: Oh, Isaac, one more thing. Since I will not have ownership of the property, I'll need you to agree to subordinate to my bank so that I can get financing to build a store on your land.

Leases and Other Property Interests

ISAAC: Please explain.

JOE: Well, my lenders will want to have a mortgage on your land.

ISAAC: Does that mean the lenders can foreclose on my land if you default on your loans?

JOE: Yes, it does mean that, but there are plenty of protections for you before that can happen. For one, you will see and approve the construction budget. Two, you'll see and approve the Lease Agreement with the tenant to whom I will be leasing the finished building. Three, you'll have the right to step into my shoes and finish the project should I default.

ISAAC: Hmm . . . I need to think about this.

How Isaac responds to Joe's request will dictate the direction this deal takes. Isaac may feel that the Ground Lease is an attractive proposition and so he may be willing to sign the Subordination Agreement as requested. This puts his land at risk, but if he feels that the fundamentals of the deal are sound (the Lease to the retailer and the construction budget), he may go forward since he can step into Joe's position should Joe default on his mortgage.

Or Isaac may feel that he's not a developer, nor does he want to be. He may not care how good Joe's deal looks on paper; he may have no interest in stepping into the deal should Joe default. And he may have no intention of putting his land at risk. If Isaac responds this way, then Joe (never giving up, of course) must try to convince his lender to take a lien not on the fee (ownership) position on the land, but rather, on the leasehold interest created by the Ground Lease.

Joe can argue to his lender that the fundamentals of the deal are sufficiently strong such that should he default, the lender can step into his position as Ground Lessee and operate (or sell) the leasehold interest (remember that the rent from Mr. Retailer will more than cover the proposed Ground Rent of $120,000/year). The lender may or may not go for that. Procedures for foreclosing on a Ground Lease are not nearly as well established as they are for foreclosing on an ownership interest in real estate. If the lender does agree to make a leasehold mortgage, the interest rates and terms on that loan will be higher and tougher than for a standard mortgage. In addition, the lender will want Joe to obtain from Isaac a Non-Disturbance and Attornment Agreement, which says in effect that should Joe default under the Ground Lease, Isaac will give the lender notice of that fact and let the lender step into Joe's shoes as Ground Lessee. Then the lender (or its assignee) can finish or operate the project. (The lender will also want to be sure that the Ground Lease is assignable so that if it does, in fact, have to foreclose on its leasehold position and take over the deal, it can sell the Ground Lease and presumably recoup its loan.)

Fortunately, I make the examples, and so, as instructed by me, Isaac has decided that he likes Joe's proposal for a Ground Lease and does not want to risk losing this deal. What's more, he feels that the fundamentals of the deal are strong, and in the worst case he'll step in and run/own the project. Therefore, he's okay with subordinating (think subjecting) his fee interest to Joe's lender's mortgage.

So Joe and Isaac enter a 99-year Ground Lease. Although Joe may have preferred an ownership interest (and that is not always the case), he has done well for himself. Here's why:

1. He has tied up control of the property for 99 years. And he's done this with almost no outlay of capital. When Joe was buying the land, he had to find $3 million to close. In this chapter, however, Joe has no cash obligation until his first month's rent is due.

2. He has tied up the property for a very long time at what could turn out to be a very favorable rental. In earlier chapters we assumed that Joe could borrow money for about 6 percent. Had he borrowed all $3 million to buy the land, he would have an interest expense of $180,000. Contrast that with his Ground Lease payments, which for the first 10 years of the Lease are only $120,000 per year.

What's more, Joe has tied the ground rent increases to some inflation factor (people usually use the Consumer Price Index, or CPI). This may be very favorable to Joe since, in many instances, inflation has not kept up with the appreciation in value of a well-located piece of land (and, of course, what starts out as a marginal location can turn into a great one).

For example, let's say that inflation in the 10 years following the execution of the Ground Lease will be an average of 2.5 percent per year. Even with compounding, that would mean Joe would be paying an annual ground rent of $153,000 beginning in year 11 of the Ground Lease (2016). But if the land has appreciated faster than inflation, his rental payments have decreased in terms of the percentage of the land value. If the land was worth $3 million in 2005, then Joe's payments of $120,000 per year are 4 percent of land value. Now if the land appreciates at 5 percent per year (compounded), it's worth over $5 million by 2016. Since inflation has been only 2.5 percent, Joe's ground rent payments of $153,000 are now only 3 percent of land value. Although I'm just making up numbers here to illustrate a point, the fact is that well-located land has almost always appreciated at a higher rate than inflation and many smart real estate entrepreneurs have made great Ground Lease deals for themselves when they peg increases to inflation.

It's true that 99 years later Joe does not have anything to show for his effort, since control and possession of the land will revert to Isaac's great-grandchildren.

Leases and Other Property Interests

But Joe and his great-grandchildren have long since paid off their mortgage and have had a great run for 99 years, making tons of money.

The point is: there are times when a Ground Lease is a wonderful tool for the real estate entrepreneur. Here's a pop quiz: What other clause might Joe have put in the Ground Lease that would be beneficial to him? How about a **right of first refusal**? This is a clause that basically states:

> If at any time after the execution of this Ground Lease, the Ground Lessor wishes to sell the Property, then it must allow the Ground Lessee 30 days to match any bona fide, third-party offer that Ground Lessor is prepared to accept. If Ground Lessee desires to match said offer, it must sign a Contract to purchase within 30 days of Ground Lessor's notification, with closing 60 days thereafter. If, however, Ground Lessee does not indicate its desire to match said offer, then Ground Lessor may sell to the third party, so long as the Contract that the Ground Lessor signs is identical in terms to those offered the Ground Lessee.

In other words, the Ground Lessee always has the last crack at buying the property, and these rights of first refusal can be very valuable. Here's why: The existence of a right of first refusal will often put a chill on the sale of a property. Buyers do not want to do a lot of homework and make an offer **knowing that someone else has 30 days to swoop in, match their offer, and get the deal.** As a result, many potential buyers will not pursue a property with a right of first refusal attached to it. Therefore, the Ground Lessee may be in a position to buy the property at below market value (if and when the Ground Lessor or his descendants decide to sell).

Master Leases

Another example of how to make money with leaseholds is to approach the owner of a building and agree to **Master Lease** his entire property. For example, a real estate entrepreneur may lust for a 100,000-square-foot industrial building owned by a person who just won't sell it. However, since the building is empty, the owner will presumably be happy to lease it to the entrepreneur on a long-term basis and allow the entrepreneur to sublease it without restriction.

Let's step into the shoes of an entrepreneur who wants to buy this building:

> He calculates what it will cost him to subdivide the building and sublease it to companies that need 20,000 sf blocks of industrial space. After doing his homework, the entrepreneur enters a lease with the owner for the

entire building for 25 years at a triple net rent of $5/sf (fixed for the entire lease term). The entrepreneur then subdivides the building into four 20,000 sf sections and one 10,000 sf section (the remaining 10,000 sf is core factor, which he will include in his rentable square feet).

Pop quiz: What will be the rentable sf of a 20,000 sf unit? A 10,000 sf unit? Remember our discussion of an Add-On factor?

Let's assume that the entrepreneur's cost to create these five units is $350,000. He borrows the money to do this, and the constant on his loan is 14 percent (assuming a 10-year repayment schedule), so he's paying about $50,000 per year in debt service (principal and interest).

Over the next six months the entrepreneur (master lessee) is able to lease all five spaces at an average rental of $8/sf (nnn—shorthand for triple net). So, how is he doing with this deal?

Revenues (90,000 sf @ $8/sf)	$720,000/yr
Debt Service	($ 50,000/yr)
Master Rent Obligation	($500,000/yr)
Profit	$170,000/yr

Not too bad. And in 10 years the entrepreneur will have paid off his loan and still have 15 years left on his Master Lease. What's more, rents will presumably increase over that period, so the sublease rental income which the entrepreneur receives will go up (whereas the rents payable to the owner of the building are flat for the entire term).

Yes, there is risk. Over the course of a long-term lease there will most certainly be vacancies and retrofit expense and brokers to pay. But a smart entrepreneur will have taken all of this into account when he offered the $5/sf (nnn) in rent. And although the property owner wanted increases in this rent over time, the entrepreneur successfully resisted, arguing that he was taking all of the risk and that the property owner was assured of $500,000 per year (nnn) for 25 years, no matter what.

Other Property Interests

There may be other ways to tie up a piece of real estate and/or split it into sub-interests without having to buy. An example of this is air rights. There are times when the owner of a building in a metropolitan area will not sell you his property but may sell you air rights: the right to develop *above* his building. Perhaps you can go up another 20 stories over the roof of his building, and by owning the air rights to do that, you pull off an excellent real estate deal.

Conclusion

Good real estate entrepreneurs never take no for an answer. When they see a property they want but the owner won't sell, they don't get discouraged. They just think of another way to skin the cat. One such tool is the acquisition of control (albeit not ownership) or some subinterest therein. The type of interest one may acquire in a piece of real estate is only limited by the creativity of the real estate entrepreneur. By now you see a recurring theme in this book:

> The ability to do _____ (fill in the blank) is only limited by the creativity and strength of will of the real estate entrepreneur.

It is often said that one needs money to make money. But that's just not always the case in the real estate entrepreneuring world. If you can create a good deal, you should be able to find the money to make it happen. There's lots and lots of money around seeking good real estate deals, and the next chapter should help you find, borrow, or partner up with "other people's money."

15

Other People's Money

Every successful real estate entrepreneur has learned how to make money with other people's money. Whether it's capital from lenders or investors, unless a real estate player started in the business with a lot of his own money, at some point in his career he used other people's funds to build his own net worth.

There have been many articles and books written about the concept of leverage—the use of another's capital to help you move into a higher position (like the lever that helps you move a heavy rock). I am going to distill for you the whole key to real estate leverage:

If you can get someone else's money to help you consummate a deal:

(a) Without putting the fundamentals of the deal at undue risk; and

(b) While keeping a disproportionate share of the upside, then

Take as much as you can.

Okay, I hear you saying, "What the heck is he talking about?" You will understand as you read through this chapter.

Real Estate Lenders

Real estate lenders are content earning a spread on their money between what they pay for it (either to their depositors or to their lenders) and what they loan it out at. They do not expect to be part of the success (or failure) of a deal. They are not equity players.

Many real estate lenders are banks. Banks have depositors, and banks pay their depositors interest on the money deposited in the bank. Just for purposes of discussion, let's say that interest is 3 percent. Then banks attempt to attract borrowers (such as real estate entrepreneurs) to borrow this money at higher rates, say 7 percent. And banks are quite happy with their 4 percent spread because if they loan millions of dollars, that 4 percent spread adds up.

Banks don't care if you use their money to make yourself millions. They are happy to get their 4 percent spread. And that should be fine with you too. Since banks do not want any part of your upside on a deal, they are our best example of how to use leverage. Take as much of their money as they will give you (so long as the amount of debt does not put the deal in jeopardy). Someday, when you sell or refinance, you will hopefully make a huge profit and owe them no portion of it. You just give them back their money and say "Thanks." Since the bank earns NONE of the upside, even though they're putting up 70 to 80 percent of the money to purchase the deal, this situation fits within our above rule for leverage. (I realize that I have not addressed the risk of a recourse loan, i.e., when the borrower's personal assets are exposed. But, remember my premise: never take so much debt that the deal is at undue risk—in this way you are hopefully okay whether the loan is recourse or nonrecourse.)

Here is an important point for a young real estate entrepreneur to understand: LENDERS NEED YOU. Real estate lenders are not only risk adverse, most of them do not know how to make the kinds of returns that you will pay them, like the 7 percent in our example above. That is why they need to make real estate loans and put their money to work. At some point in your career you will realize that real estate lenders need you as much or more than you need them. I did not get that until one day I was speaking with a very successful developer and he said that at the end of every year his bank bought him a new car. I could not believe that.

"Why?" I asked.

"Well, on average I borrow $100 million from them over the course of the year," the developer told me. "If they can earn a spread of three or four points on that money, they're earning $3 to $4 million per year off my efforts. Shouldn't they show their appreciation at the end of each year?"

"Now I get it," I replied.

There is another important point to understand about real estate lenders: although they all have certain rules and lending policies, the more they want to do business with you, the more they'll work to tailor a loan to your needs. And when

Other People's Money

you deal with enough different real estate lenders who want to do business with you, you'll find that you can usually get the type and terms of loan (so long as you are reasonable) that you need to make a deal. That is why I advocate that young real estate players foster good relationships with several different real estate lenders.

There are innumerable ways to use leverage to improve your position in the real estate game. I'll tell you about one method that worked for my partners and me when we started in the business:

As you know, we were always looking to add value to properties, and that is how we selected the properties we purchased.

One day we come across a run-down building that was being used as an antique store. It was about 8,000 square feet in a good location and with good parking. We contacted the owner and asked if he would consider selling the building. He said that he would but wanted us to know that the rent he was getting from the antique store was not much. The good news, however, was that the antique store did not have a lease, so its occupancy was on a month-to-month basis (and could be terminated with 30-days' prior notice).

The store was paying $8/sf triple net. Therefore, the net operating income from the building was $64,000/year, and using a cap rate of 10 percent, we paid $640,000 for the building. The bank's appraiser valued the building at $600,000 (in other words, he thought we were overpaying), and the bank agreed to lend us 80 percent of $600,000, or $480,000. Therefore, we had to come up with $160,000 (plus some closing costs), which was not easy for us at this time in our career.

Anyway, we closed and immediately asked the antique store to leave. We had done our homework and we knew that the building was structurally sound. We also knew that in order to attract new tenants to the building, we would have to do some significant cosmetic renovations, which we did soon after purchase, to the tune of $100,000. Now we were in the deal for $740,000—$260,000 of which was our own capital. That was a lot of money for us (some of which was borrowed from friends), and we were very uncomfortable with the project at this point since we had essentially all of our liquid assets tied up in one deal.

But then we began to implement our plan. We believed that the highest and best use of the property was as an office building, and so we began to lease out the building to office tenants. Our asking rent was $22/sf gross plus utilities. Operating expenses (including real estate taxes) were $6/sf, and so our net operating income was $16/sf. We completed the leasing of the building in about three months and we asked the real estate brokers who helped us to wait about 30 days for their commissions (about $25,000). We then immediately asked the bank to have its appraiser revalue the property.

The net operating income of the property was now $128,000 ($16/sf × 8,000 sf) with annual increases in rents every year. The bank's appraiser was impressed with the renovations we had done and with the new leases. He was now comfortable using a cap rate of 9 percent and with our new NOI of $128,000, he came up with a valuation of $1.4 million. Now you might say that's crazy when just a year ago the building was worth only $600,000. But I would say you are wrong . . . there is no intrinsic value to real estate. Real estate is worth what the investment community says it is worth. And our new leases said that this building was now worth $1.4 million.

So we go back to our banker with the new appraisal.

BANKER: Wow, that is a nice increase in value. How much did you spend on renovating the building?

ME: Is that relevant? Suppose we spent nothing but were able to re-lease the building in a way that had not been done before.

BANKER (LAUGHING): Well, you're right . . . what I really care about is what the appraisal says . . . but I still want to know how much you spent.

So I told him: $100,000.

But that did not deter him. Based on the fact that the investment community was now saying the value of the property was $1.4 million, he was willing to loan us 75 percent of that amount, or $1,050,000. So about a year after buying the building we refinanced it, and here's what our Closing Statement looked like:

Loan proceeds		$1,050,000
Repay existing first mortgage	$480,000	
Repay cash to purchase	160,000	
Repay cash to renovate	100,000	
Pay real estate brokers	25,000	
Closing costs	10,000	
Total:	$ 775,000	775,000
NET LOAN PROCEEDS:		$ 275,000

What had we accomplished?

Well, by adding value to a piece of real estate, we were able to refinance it within one year of purchase and take out of the deal net proceeds to us of $275,000. Not bad.

Other People's Money

Never confuse actual gain with taxable gain: Even though debt proceeds are not taxable, do not be confused into thinking that the additional loan proceeds will somehow reduce your gain on sale. For example, if we had sold this property for $1.4 million immediately after the refinance, our taxable gain would be calculated as follows:

Sale price		$1,400,000
Purchase price	$640,000	
Renovations	100,000	
Commissions	25,000	
Closing Costs	10,000	
Total	$775,000	775,000
Taxable gain		**$ 625,000**

But our actual gain (with the added debt) would look like:

Sale price	$1,400,000
Loan repayment	1,050,000
Actual gain	**$ 350,000**

What's more, this money was tax free. The government does not consider loan proceeds to be income since you have an obligation to pay the money back.

In other words, although you receive the loan proceeds "tax free," when you sell, the government still gets its share of the actual (taxable) gain.

On the other hand, "tax free" cash in the possession of an entrepreneur can be a beautiful thing, the premise being that an entrepreneur can use that cash to grow and grow. Yes, on sale of the property the entrepreneur will need to pay taxes. But sometimes a real estate player will not sell for years and years and will just keep refinancing a property to take out additional "tax free" cash as and when he can.

In our example, with the $275,000 additional funds to work with, we were excited. Needless to say, we put that $275,000 to good use, levering ourselves up into bigger and bigger deals.

What about risk? Were we taking undue risk using loan proceeds as they were our money? Well, I don't think so. Although these were recourse loans (my partner and I had to sign personally for the money), we were not overly leveraged (75 percent loan-to-value) and the rental income was more than enough to cover the debt service. (One way lenders double-check their loan amount is to do what's called a "debt service coverage analysis." In essence, they make sure there is enough net income to cover the debt service; usually they want the net income to equal at least 1.2 times the debt service.)

Confessions of a Real Estate Entrepreneur

Now, you could argue that without finding a building that had the potential for upside (in the renovation and re-leasing), we would never have been able to pull off this good deal. Well, that's true, of course; FINDING DEALS WHERE YOU CAN ADD VALUE is a critical component of real estate entrepreneuring. And in order to do that, you may need to leave your comfort zone. In other words, a real estate entrepreneur cannot always play it safe. You may need to move from one property type to another (e.g., office to industrial) or to a new geographic area.

You'll recall that I've recently been buying in Miami Beach, even though I'd been buying and selling almost exclusively in Fairfield County, Connecticut, for 20 years. The reason I stopped buying in Connecticut is that the market there became so mature that I had trouble finding ADDED VALUE opportunities. And when one did pop up, all the real estate entrepreneurs in the market would compete for it such that the deals got skinnier and skinnier as all that entrepreneurial air rushed into any vacuum. Still, it was not easy for me to start buying in Miami. Frankly, I was scared. I had had a good 20-year run in Connecticut, and I knew the market intimately. In Miami I was a rookie all over again—learning the market, the people, the customs. Eventually, however, I got comfortable with the area and have had a nice five-year run there. And I am continually looking around for new areas, new deals, new strategies—anyplace where there is an ADDED VALUE opportunity.

Here's the point: If you're going to be a real estate entrepreneur, part of the equation is finding added value opportunities. They're out there, but they will not come to you. And you may have to stretch to find them.

The point in this chapter, and the subplot of my antique-store-to-office-building story, is that when you do find an Added Value Opportunity, real estate lenders will be there to help you. In our case, by renovating and re-leasing the building we added about $600,000 in value in one year—a very short period of time. Although this may sound "too good to be true," I can tell you that my partners and I followed this exact ADDED VALUE model many times during the ensuing years. And lenders were flocking to do business with us.

Keys to Understand

1. Lenders want to make loans. They need to earn money on their money. They particularly like real estate loans because real estate does not move. It is one of the most financeable assets there is.
2. There is no absolute value to real estate . . . if you can add value and get an appraiser to agree with your position as to the new value, you can go back to a lender who only months earlier was limiting you to $X in loan amount and perhaps get a loan that is some multiple of $X.

162

Other People's Money

3. What is great about real estate lenders is that they're *not* looking to participate with you on the upside. Had we sold the building in the above example instead of refinanced it, we would theoretically have made about $600,000, *and yet our banker would not have been expecting any of that money.* The banker would get its loan back ($480,000) and that's it. That's the kind of "partner" you want (more on that later).

A Refresher on Subordination

In Chapter 3 we spoke to the basics of the real estate game. Hopefully you recall the discussion about subordination. It might be worth going back and rereading the example where John Doe purchased property from Albert Einstein, Albert having agreed to subordinate his purchase money mortgage to the lien of a construction lender.

At the end of that example I left you with a question: Where did Albert Einstein err in his negotiation with John Doe? By way of reminder:

After John Doe purchased the land from Albert for $550,000, he got estimates to build an 8,000-square-foot office building on the land. John concluded that it would cost him about $850,000 in "hard costs" (the actual expenses of construction) and another $100,000 for "soft costs" (construction interest, permits, architects, legal, etc). At the same time, John got an appraisal indicating that a completed and leased office building at that location was worth $2 million. John took his budget and appraisal to several construction lenders and asked for a $1 million construction loan (often lenders will loan 100 percent of a construction budget, although they advance the money as the construction proceeds).

BANKER (AFTER REVIEWING JOHN'S BUDGET): Do you have an appraisal for the completed project?

JOHN: Yes, it shows a value of $2 million.

BANKER: Okay, then we will loan you $1 million and make advances to you as the work proceeds. Given your appraised value, we are very comfortable with a $1 million loan, but of course we're going to have to be in first position.

JOHN: Yes, I know that.

So John closes on his $1 million first mortgage with an executed Subordination Agreement from Albert Einstein. Albert's $450,000 second mortgage now being in second position.

Is Albert in a bad position behind $1 million of construction debt? Well, he should be okay since the bank has reviewed the budget and is only advancing money

163

as the work proceeds. What's more, an appraiser has put a value of $2 million on the completed property so there should be enough equity to protect Albert. On the other hand, things can and do go wrong at times. Maybe John Doe's budget is off. Or maybe he cannot lease the building as he (and the appraiser) thought. In that case Albert may rue the day he agreed to subordinate. What's more, even if Albert agreed to subordinate, he could have done a better job protecting himself by defining a maximum dollar amount that he would subordinate to. If, for example, he had limited the maximum he would subordinate to, say $750,000, then John Doe would have to put $250,000 of his own money into the construction and that amount of his own capital would hopefully keep John very focused on completing and leasing the property (remember under the present scenario, John has only $100,000 in the deal).

One last point: John Doe, too, could have done a better job negotiating the Subordination Clause in his mortgage to Albert Einstein. What did he do wrong? Well, most construction lenders are short-term lenders, and as soon as the construction is completed, they want to be refinanced out of the deal with a permanent loan. But John did not provide for this second subordination in the Subordination Clause he negotiated with Albert. Remember the exact language?

> Mortgagee (Albert) agrees that it will subordinate the lien of the herein Mortgage to the lien of a mortgage to be hereafter placed on the Property by Mortgagor (John).

When John approaches Albert to subordinate to a new permanent loan on the property, Albert could argue that he had already subordinated his $450,000 mortgage to "*a mortgage* to be hereafter placed on the Property by the Mortgagor." He subordinated to the mortgage that John Doe obtained from the bank for the construction. And Albert could refuse to subordinate again. That could cause John Doe a headache because now he has to come up with $450,000 to pay off Albert if he wants to place a new permanent *first* mortgage on the property. Maybe Albert Einstein was pretty smart after all? Had John been smarter, he might have drafted the Subordination Clause as follows:

> Mortgagee agrees that it will subordinate the lien of the herein Mortgage to one or more mortgages to be placed on the Property by Mortgagor at a time or times subsequent to the date of the Mortgagee's loan.

This language would have forced Albert to subordinate again, to a new first mortgage, the permanent loan "taking out" the construction loan.

As we proceed with the subordination possibilities, let's assume that John did get language from Albert allowing for more than one subordination event. Now let's look at the situation when the construction of the new building is complete and the building is leased. Given the $2 million appraisal, it is certainly conceivable that John will be able to find a permanent lender who will loan him $1.5 million—so long as that lender is in first position. And since Albert is obligated to subordinate to this loan, his $450,000 second mortgage is still on the property, although now behind $1.5 million. In sum, there is now total debt on the property of $1,950,000 even though the appraised value is only $2,000,000.

Will John's new permanent (first) lender be okay with a total debt on the property of $1,950,000? Maybe yes, maybe no. With an appraisal of $2 million and a first mortgage position of $1.5 million, a permanent lender is well protected (75 percent loan-to-value). Its primary concern will be that John not get into trouble with the property given that there is a lot of debt on it. In our example, John is able to convince the new (permanent) lender not to worry as he highlights the rental increases in all of his leases. What's more, he was savvy enough to include language in his Mortgage Deed to Albert Einstein that requires Albert to notify the first mortgagee if John is not keeping up with payments on the second mortgage. This gives John's permanent lender a "heads up" if John starts running into trouble, and presumably the lender can take certain steps to protect itself.

Deals like the above example happen all the time. Lenders want to make loans. In our example, the lender is comfortable with the $2 million appraisal, and it may also have a personal guarantee from John Doe. John for his part is happy too. Even if he is personally on the hook for $1,950,000 of debt, he is very comfortable with his new building and the tenancies therein and he has put approximately $400,000 of tax-free cash in his pocket to use in new deals. Even Albert Einstein is happy so long as John meets all the terms of the second mortgage. And since I am making up all the examples anyway, I can tell you that John did meet all terms of both mortgages, and in fact, five years later sold the property for $3.5 million, paid off both the first and second mortgages, and everybody lived happily ever after.

Institutional Equity

Another source of "other people's money" is the institutional investor who has millions of dollars under management that it needs to put to use in real estate deals. These companies are looking for real estate operators to help them invest this money. They do not have the time or local expertise to buy and operate properties directly and so they need on-the-ground real estate operators to partner with. Since these investors have huge sums under management, and since they have to get their money working, they can be a very good source of capital for larger deals.

These companies are not bankers, and you need to distinguish them right up front from banks, insurance companies, pension funds, and other traditional real estate lenders. They are not interested in a banklike return on their money. To be contracted with a lender, they want a piece of the upside from a successful deal. On the other hand, these investors are not asking you to sign a Promissory Note. There is no risk that these investors will sue you if they do not receive the return of their funds (contrast a lender). In a deal with an institutional investor: if there is a loss, everyone loses their money, pro rata according to who has what invested.

Institutional investors will advance (invest) a much higher percentage of the cost of the deal (up to 99 percent—see below) than will a lender. And here is the key: once the return to the institutional investor hits its hurdle rate (think of it as a threshold rate or cost of funds), **the institutional investor will allow you to earn a disproportionate amount of any increment (return above their hurdle rate).** Therefore, capital from this type of investor meets my requirement as to the use of other people's money, as you can definitely earn a return that is out of proportion to the percentage of your capital invested to the total invested. This probably sounds like a bit of gibberish; hopefully the following examples will help:

I recently met with two institutional investors to review a property I was interested in buying. Let me give you a synopsis of those meetings so you'll understand how institutional equity investors will work with you.

The property for sale is an old (vacant) apartment building. The asking price is $15 million and it needs a total rehab, with a projected construction budget of $20 million (including all soft costs such as interest and taxes during down time, architectural and engineering expenses, permits, insurance, shortfall on operating income prestabilization, etc.). So this deal requires $35 million, larger than I'm comfortable doing on my own.

Both companies have a similar format. They advance most of the equity. They help procure the debt. They are okay with their operating partner earning arm's-length fees for services provided to the partnership. They want an agreed-to return on their capital (the hurdle rate), which, by the way, the operating partner (you) also earns on his capital. And once they hit their hurdle rate, they are amenable to the operating partner earning a **disproportionate amount of the incremental return.** Let's get specific:

80-20 Going In

As indicated, the cost of this project is $35 million, and let's say that the partnership I form with the institutional investor can procure debt of $25 million. This debt must be nonrecourse (unless I'm willing to guarantee it or obtain some kind of credit enhancement as the investor will not guarantee any debt). So we need $10 million of equity.

One of the companies requires that I (the operator) put in at least 20 percent of the equity, or $2 million. This can be my money or funds from a partnership that I form. And the investor contributes the remaining $8 million of the required equity. The company and I now need to agree on a hurdle rate, that is, the return that has to be earned on all capital invested before any proceeds above this return are split between us. If I were putting in only 1 percent of the equity (see below), I would not have much negotiating power, but here, with 20 percent invested, I do have some say. The investor wants to set the hurdle rate at 10 percent, but I disagree and we settle on 9 percent. Also keep in mind that as the local real estate operator, I presumably control this deal, and if the investor likes the deal and wants in, it will be more amenable to my demands. The agreement regarding the hurdle rate is that once the deal returns a 9 percent per year compounded rate to the capital (including mine), the upside above that return (if any) will be divided on some basis other than pro rata to our capital (80-20).

We've done our spreadsheets and believe that once the building is rehabbed and fully leased (stabilized), we can sell it for $50 million. We estimate it will take us five years to achieve a sale at that level. Compounding $10 million at 9 percent for five years, I see that the equity (including mine) must receive $5,386,000 (over the $10 million) before there any further distributions.

Here is our going-in Pro Forma on this deal:

Sales price	$50,000,000
Sales expense (4 percent)	$ 2,000,000
Net sales proceeds	$48,000,000
Debt repayment	$25,000,000 (an interest-only loan)
Equity repayment	$10,000,000
9 percent compounded return	$ 5,386,000
Additional funds to distribute	$ 7,614,000

Okay, now here's where the interesting part comes in. As indicated, once my investor partner achieves his hurdle rate, he is okay with me earning more than 20 percent of the upside. Let's say I ask for 75 percent of the upside (of the $7,614,000). Will he agree?

Well, what he will do first is identify his target rate. This rate is different from the hurdle rate. This is the return my investor hopes to achieve to be really happy. So, he will say to me: "Randel, if I achieve my target rate of 13 percent, compounded annually, I am okay with your earning a big share of the upside over the hurdle rate."

So, we take another look at the Pro Forma. In order for him to earn 13 percent per year compounded on his $8 million investment, he has to get back a total (including the amount of his investment) of $14,740,000. As you can see from the Pro Forma, if we achieve a net sales price of $48 million, there is enough money for both of us to receive a 9 percent compounded return on our equity ($10,000,000) and there is $7,614,000 remaining to divide between us. I have asked for 75 percent of it, which would leave $1,903,000 for my investor partner. If we add up the total return of capital to him it is:

$ 8,000,000	His share of the initial equity
4,308,000	9 percent compounded return (his hurdle rate) on his $8 million
<u>1,903,000</u>	25 percent of the upside (the $7,614,000)
$14,211,000	TOTAL

As you can see, this is shy of what he wants to achieve ($14,740,000) so he will probably not agree to my receiving 75 percent of the potential upside. So, we agree on 60 percent. I get 60 percent of all upside funds after the return of equity at a compounded 9 percent (hurdle) rate. And if the deal performs, my partner achieves his target rate of 13 percent (actually more).

In my example, I am presuming that the agreement between us regarding the splitting of the upside is done before the deal is completed. More likely, it will be done after the deal is finished and the returns are in, that is, the performance of the deal is clear. The investor, for example, may agree that I receive 60 percent of all upside funds only so long as he hits his targeted rate of 13 percent.

Here is the main point I want to make: my partnership with this investor (so long as the deal performs) gives me a greatly disproportionate return on the upside when compared to my going-in capital of 20 percent of the equity. This is a good thing! Although I invested only 20 percent of the equity, I am walking away with 60 percent of the upside over a return (of 9 percent) to all capital. Here is what I receive:

$2,000,000	Capital back
1,077,250	9 percent compounded return on my capital
<u>4,568,400</u>	60 percent of the upside ($7,614,000)
$7,645,650	TOTAL

What is my return? If you do the math, you will see that my return is over 30 percent per year compounded. Not bad! In addition, this deal warrants and is budgeted for development and management fees and rental commissions (those fees are in the $25 million construction estimate), and my company will earn these fees as well. Why would the institutional investor agree to this deal?

1. They concluded that I'm a credible real estate player with a track record of successful deals.
2. They do not have the manpower or the expertise to find or develop these deals themselves.
3. They like the deal, and I control it (having tied it up with an option or contract).
4. If they earn a 13 percent compounded annual return on their money, they're happy. If I earn 30 percent per year, that does not impact their return.
5. I am prepared to put in $2 million so they can see that I believe in the deal and that I'm taking significant risk. Also, if I'm substantial enough to have $2 million cash to invest, I also likely have a decent-sized organization or

support system behind me, which will improve the likelihood of success with the deal.

Now let's look at my discussion with the other institutional equity investor:

99-1 Going In

The other institutional equity investor, if dealing with an established performer, does not require a minimum investment of 20 percent of the equity. This company will accept much less equity from its partner (the operator). The company's standard line is that it wants its operator partner to put in at least 5 percent of the required equity, but I'm aware of deals it makes with some partners who put in just 1 percent of the equity.

This investor has a different approach to the hurdle rate discussion, however. In our 80-20 example, the institutional investor set a hurdle rate of 9 percent. The 99-1 investor, in contrast, sets the hurdle rate much higher, usually in the range of 12 percent. In other words, this investor will not agree that proceeds be split on a disproportionate basis until it has received a compounded annual return of 12 percent.

The investor's argument has to do with risk-reward. The investor figures that the operator (putting in only 1 percent) does not have a lot to lose. So if the deal starts hitting bumps, the operator may or may not have the perseverance and will to do what it takes to stay the course. Therefore, this institutional investor will require a higher hurdle rate than the 80-20 investor; this investor wants a hurdle rate of 12 percent.

This institutional investor also has a different target rate. Where the 80-20 investor was happy if it earned a 13 percent annual compounded return on its capital, this investor wants to earn a 15 percent Internal Rate of Return (IRR). Do you remember the Internal Rate of Return discussion we had in Chapter 13? For purposes of our discussion here, let's equate IRR with discount rate. So, this investor will only be happy if its capital is returned with enough funds above its investment to earn a 15 percent discount rate on a discounted cash flow analysis.

What this investor will do is prepare a Pro Forma of expected cash flow over the five-year term of the deal. Let's assume there is nothing coming in until the apartment building is sold. So, there are four years of $0 and then $X in the fifth year. This investor then makes certain assumptions about the potential performance of the deal. Its willingness to agree on a disproportionate split of the upside to the operating partner will depend upon its views on the deal's eventual performance. Again, since I make up all the examples anyway, let's assume that this investor believes in the deal and that our Pro Forma above is realistic.

So, it buys into the projection of $23,000,000 in net funds five years after the deal is purchased:

$50,000,000	Sales price
($2,000,000)	Sales expenses
($25,000,000)	Debt repayment
$23,000,000	Net funds

Okay, now let's see what is remaining after the equity ($10,000,000) achieves a 12 percent per year compounded hurdle rate. Ten million dollars compounded annually at 12 percent is $17,623,416. Therefore there is $5,376,584 left to divide between us. I ask for 30 percent of those funds. Will the institutional investor agree?

The investor will do some math. If I get 30 percent of those funds, it gets 70 percent or $3,763,608. Therefore its total funds on sale are:

$ 9,900,000	Capital back
7,447,182	12 percent per year (hurdle rate) on its capital
3,763,608	70 percent of upside funds
$21,110,790	TOTAL

So now the investor asks: What will I invest today in order to receive $21,110,790 in five years (with nothing coming back before that) if I want to achieve a 15 percent IRR? And it makes a spreadsheet, goes to its HP calculator, and does a net present value (NPV) analysis:

2006	2007	2008	2009	2010
$0	$0	$0	$0	$21,110,790

NPV @ 15 percent discount rate = $10,495,793

In other words, a rational investor seeking a 15 percent IRR would invest $10,495,793 today if it knew it was going to receive nothing for four years and then $21,110,790 in the fifth year. Since our institutional investor is only investing $9,900,000, it concludes that it is okay with my receiving 30 percent of the upside.

As with the 80-20 example, the 30 percent split to me will most likely be contingent on the institutional investor actually achieving a 15 percent IRR so the partnership agreement between us might say something like: "Randel gets 30 percent of the upside so long as Institution has achieved not less than a 15 percent IRR on its funds."

Assuming the deal performs as projected, am I happy with my take? Here is what I receive on sale:

$ 100,000	Capital back
76,234	12 percent per year on my capital
1,612,975	30 percent of upside funds
$1,789,209	TOTAL

If you do the math, you will see that the return to me works out to almost 80 percent per year compounded. Not too shabby, and yes, I am quite happy with that. And remember that I have also presumably earned a development fee of some type for five years; whereas this fee is arm's-length and I have had to work for it, I am happy for the cash flow.

But what if the deal does not perform so well? Suppose that in five years we are only able to sell the property for $45 million? After 4 percent selling expenses, we have net sales proceeds of $43.2 million. After repayment of the debt and equity, we have $8.2 million left, and that's only $500,000 more than what we need to pay the hurdle rate of 12 percent, not enough for the institutional investor to achieve the targeted 15 percent IRR. So in that case, there will be none of the disproportionate upside for me. The institutional investor does not achieve its target of a 15 percent IRR, but does at least earn 12 percent per year compounded on its money (plus some upside). Although not ecstatic, it is content with a 12 percent per year compounded return.

What about the real estate operator (me)? Well, I also have earned a compounded 12 percent per year on my money, but I'm probably less happy than the institutional investor since my thinking is not institutional and I haven't done a good job leveraging my time and money into a huge return. (The expectations of the institutional investor and the entrepreneur are very different.)

And that is the mindset that the real estate entrepreneur must bring to the negotiation with the institutional equity investor. If the entrepreneur believes that a sales price of $45 million is more likely than $50 million, he may not want to do the deal with the second investor, who requires that the project hit a 12 percent hurdle rate and an overall 15 percent IRR for the operator to receive a disproportionate return of any upside.

These examples illustrate the factors that must go into the thinking of the entrepreneur partner when negotiating with an institutional equity investor. How much capital is the entrepreneur required to invest? What is the institution's hurdle rate? Target rate? How confident is the entrepreneur in the deal's performance? What kind and amount of fees will the entrepreneur receive during the course of the deal? The entrepreneur must take all of these factors into account.

We have seen that if an entrepreneur finds a good deal and performs, he stands to achieve a very favorable disproportionate return to his capital when his partner is an institutional equity investor. Here is the key to remember: An institutional equity investor can be a great resource for the real estate entrepreneur. These investors have a lot of money to invest and they *have* to put it to work . . . the real estate entrepreneur is therefore very important to them. I have laid out two different ways of forming a partnership with an institutional equity investor and dividing up the prospective proceeds on sale. There are many permutations on these two basic approaches, limited only by (here is that recurring theme again) the creativity of the real estate entrepreneur.

Individual Investors

Individuals are often the source of equity capital for the real estate entrepreneur. Sometimes these individuals are family and friends; sometimes they are just acquaintances. All have money and are seeking diversification and/or high returns. In some respects, dealing with individual investors is preferable to dealing with an institutional investor. Since any one individual investor will presumably be one of many investors in your deal, no one investor has the clout to dictate terms the way an institutional investor often can.

On the other hand, there is a negative to dealing with individual investors: they are people. Therefore, they come to the party with emotions and needs. Some may even become a bother, constantly asking for information and updates and/or panicking if and when the deal hits a bump in the road. What's more, if you take family and friends into your deal and it goes bad, you have a headache that may transcend your real estate life. That is not the case with an institutional investor; these entities are professional investors who understand the ups and downs of real estate investing.

One other point about dealing with individual investors: there are laws about raising money from them. These are called **securities laws** (the interest in a real estate investment being a "security"). I am not going to take space in this book to discuss these laws, but here is my advice: stick with **qualified or accredited investors** (your attorney can give you the definition) . . . basically, rich people. An offering to these individuals is called a **private offering,** and the laws do not require that you register this type of investment with state or federal authorities (the logic being that these investors are sophisticated enough to fend for themselves). That does not mean you can misrepresent anything in your offering materials; all materials describing the prospective deal must be truthful. It just means that you do not need to register or clear your offering in advance if you're only dealing with qualified investors.

Overall, my advancement as a real estate entrepreneur was significantly enhanced by doing deals with individual investors. I must say that I do take my responsibility toward every investor's dollar very seriously, and perhaps that has spurred me to perform at an even higher level than I otherwise would have. In

Other People's Money

any event, I'm very grateful that to date I have never had to call an individual investor and say that a deal lost money. On the other hand, I do know that is always a possibility.

I would like to end this chapter about other people's money by giving you an example of a successful deal that I recently did with individual investor capital.

In 1995, I learned about a 50,000-square-foot office building that was being foreclosed. The lender was in Kentucky, and I hopped on a plane. I offered to buy the building for $4 million immediately after the lender completed the foreclosure. Since everything was happening quickly, I did not have the ability to obtain traditional financing and so asked the lender to take back a $3 million first mortgage at closing. The lender did its homework on me and made several calls to banks and others in Connecticut. They concluded that I was a good risk and so agreed to take back $3 million for two years, giving me time to stabilize the property and then obtain new financing.

Now I needed $1 million to close the deal (plus $150,000 for closing costs and reserves). I used $250,000 of my own money and raised $900,000 from individuals in units as small as $50,000 and as large as $250,000.

My deal with the individual investors was that they had to earn a cumulative preferred annual return of 8 percent before I earned a disproportionate return for creating and operating the deal. A cumulative return means that in any year that I could not pay the 8 percent return, it accumulated, that is, I still owed that return and had to pay it in subsequent years. *Preferred* meant that the 8 percent had to come ahead of any performance rewards that I could earn from the deal.

My deal provided that so long as the investors received the 8 percent per year return, I received a **promote** (this is an important term to the real estate entrepreneur since it describes the situation where the entrepreneur receives something good . . . out of proportion to his investment). In my deal the promote was this: so long as the individuals received the 8 percent per year on their capital for so long as they had capital invested in the deal, I would earn 50 percent of the cash flow generated by the property (if any, above the 8 percent return) and 50 percent of the net proceeds on sale of the property (and, in both cases, the investors would receive the other 50 percent). The investors were comfortable with this format, the $900,000 was raised quickly, and we closed shortly thereafter.

Now I had my work cut out for me. This building was not being run well, and I immediately changed the leasing program. I worked very hard at getting the building rented at higher rents. Within six months the building was fully leased, and at higher average rents than the prior owner had been getting. Within 18 months the building was stabilized and I was able to go to an institutional lender, who did its valuation, concluded that the building was now worth $5.5 million, and loaned me $4.1 million (75 percent loan-to-value). This allowed me to pay back the seller's first mortgage *and* to return all investor capital (in the interim I had been able to make the 8 percent annual payments to them).

So at this point my investors had all their money back, and on a going-forward basis I was entitled to 50 percent of the cash flow and 50 percent of the profits on sale. I continued to operate this property for eight years and sold it for $12 million. Needless to say, I had a nice payday, as did my investors (their return was essentially infinite since at that point they had no money in the deal). In short, everyone was happy.

More Positives Than Negatives

In my view, there are more positives than negatives in working with individual investors. However, be careful to pick your investors carefully. If you see signs that someone is going to be a problem, do not bring them into your deal. The headaches will far outweigh the benefits of their money.

The problem with individual investors is that your growth in the real estate game will be limited by the number of investors you have and the capital they have to invest. As you get into bigger projects, like the apartment building rehab I described above, the need to speak with lots of investors may be outweighed by the benefits of dealing with just one institutional investor. Accordingly, it's likely that at some point you will want to work with institutional equity. But don't forgo the individuals who helped you grow. Bring them in as you can to bigger deals, perhaps by forming a partnership to invest with the institutional investor (remember that the institutional investor is generally okay with your equity coming either from your pocket *or* from a partnership you form).

Here's a pop quiz: Let's say that in the apartment building deal I described above you decide to do a deal with the 80-20 institutional investor, that is, you need to bring $2 million to the party. Let's assume that you invest $500,000 of your own money and raise $1.5 million from individual investors. How might you structure raising that money? What kind of promote will you seek? If the overall deal is successful and sells for $50 million, your partnership will receive an excellent return since, in our example, it is entitled to 60 percent of the upside. Start with this 60 percent return to your partnership and then analyze it in light of the promote you obtained in the partnership that you formed with the individual investors—you'll see in spades what you can do by using other people's money to create a disproportionate return on your capital!

Conclusion

Every good real estate entrepreneur understands how to access and use other people's money to earn disproportionate returns for himself or herself. The best entrepreneurs are particularly good at this. But the reality is that the entrepreneur must first and foremost perform. If the entrepreneur's deals are not successful, that will be the end of the flow of capital from lenders and investors. On the other hand, if the entrepreneur's deals are successful and people are making money with him, then the lenders and investors will stand in line. Here's the point: If your deals are successful, finding the money to do deals will not be a problem for you as you evolve in the real estate game. Always keep in mind that performance is key.

Now on to one of the most important parts of the real estate entrepreneur's challenge: finding deals to which he or she can add value.

16

Finding Deals

Obviously, one of the most important talents a real estate entrepreneur needs to develop is a knack for finding good deals. The only rule that really matters when it comes to deal finding is: WHATEVER WORKS. I have my own thoughts as to what techniques are most likely to produce good opportunities, but you may have better, more productive ideas. What follows are some of the methods that have worked for me.

Brokers

Real estate brokers will be a very fruitful source of deals for you. Real estate brokers are in the information business. They know what is for sale and what may be for sale. If they believe you are a strong buyer, they will call you. One of your goals should be to get calls early: when an owner is about to or has just put his property on the market. In these situations you have a chance to pick up a property without competing against other potential buyers who may be interested. The goal, of course, is to prevent other buyers from pushing up the price.

On the other hand, getting to a seller or potential seller early can, at times, be counterproductive. Some sellers have unrealistic expectations at the start of the marketing process. And brokers are sometimes the reason. Some brokers compete for selling assignments by telling a seller what he wants to hear: that his property is worth $X when in fact it is worth 75 percent of $X. I consider that practice unethical, but it happens.

In these situations you need to move on, so as not to waste too much time and energy—but don't move too far. If a seller is committed to selling, he will eventually come around to a fair asking price. You want to be there when that happens.

One way to ensure you are in the game when the seller gets real is to tell the broker: "Bill, you and I both know that this property is not worth $X. When Sam Seller gets realistic, please call me right away as I like this property a lot. As soon as his asking price drops to $Y, call me and I will act immediately and close quickly." And this can work, BUT you still need to stay in the broker's face. Good brokers are working many deals at once and they may have four or five (or more) buyers they like to call early. You don't want to be in a situation (I have found myself there more than once) when a deal that you were interested in sells for a price that you would have paid, yet you missed it because you left the deal early (when the price was too high) and then neglected to follow up with the broker. Your goal in these situations is to be the first one the broker calls when the seller drops his price to a realistic number.

What Do Brokers Want?

Obviously, brokers want to make sales with a minimum of "muss and fuss." What they really hate are buyers who don't or can't get deals closed. What they really like are buyers who can and will move quickly and aggressively to tie up a property and then get it closed. Needless to say, you need to convince the active brokers in your area that you fall into the second category. When I started out in the real estate entrepreneuring business, I made a point of meeting the most active brokers in Fairfield County, Connecticut. I wanted to convince them that I could get deals done, and quickly. A typical conversation may have gone like this:

ME: Hi, Broker. I have only lived in Connecticut a year or two but I've been learning the real estate market and I'm ready to buy. I have checked around, and people tell me that you're one of the best brokers in the market (a little flattery never hurts). And so I would like to work with you.

BROKER: Well, that's fine . . . what kinds of properties are you interested in?

ME: I am an added value kind of guy . . . I will buy anything that has upside potential.

BROKER: Well, I know that you're an attorney, but have you ever done deals for yourself?

ME: No, not yet . . . but I promise you that within the next couple of years, I will buy five to ten properties, and I hope that you'll be the one making the commission on all of those purchases.

Finding Deals

BROKER: Yes, I would like that too. What is the price range of what you want to buy?

ME: I have the ability to purchase deals up to $2 million. I have investors lined up. I have a bank committed to work with me.

BROKER: Well, you seem like a nice young man, so let me give you some advice: brokers want to work with people who can move quickly to get deals under Contract and then closed. I don't want to waste time with tire kickers or people who can't get a deal closed. When I have a good property to sell, I need to know that the people I bring it to are going to make the deal.

ME: I get all that . . . Try me out and I promise you that you won't be disappointed.

Several of those conversations were fruitful and brokers began to bring me deals, which I bought and closed. Of course, I did not purchase every deal, but I moved quickly when it was a good one. And even if I did not buy, I immediately indicated to the broker when a deal was not for me, so he could bring it to others. In this way, I built good relationships with brokers and ensured myself a constant deal flow.

What's Scary about Working with Brokers?

Well, first, the fact that they are brokers. They want you to buy, and their job is to convince you to buy. Although you want them to bring you deals, you cannot put the decision to buy in their hands. Otherwise you will be buying everything they bring to you, as their point of view is that every deal they are marketing is a good deal. You have to recognize that a broker's motivation is to sell, and that his information on the market, on the history of the property, on the reasons the owner is selling, and on other relevant facts may be colored by a desire to earn a commission. Whereas good, honest brokers can be an enormous help to your entrepreneuring, you still need to do your own homework and double-check what you're being told. Here's an example:

A broker friend of mine is currently selling a sizable office building in Fairfield County. He's a top-flight broker with a great track record. He is very honest, *but*, as instructed by his client the seller, the Pro Forma (projecting NOI from the property for the five years after the close) presented to the buyer community included some assumptions that, in my view, were not reasonable.

His company prepared a Pro Forma just like we discussed in Chapter 13. One of the variables in the software package he used (ARGUS) is the probability of tenant renewals. This is a big, important number because a property owner incurs considerable costs when a tenant leaves a building: downtime, retrofitting of the space, leasing commissions on reletting the space, and legal fees (new lease).

Confessions of a Real Estate Entrepreneur

The seller had instructed the broker to input an 80 percent lease renewal probability factor. The ARGUS program then assumed that in every year in which a lease was expiring, the odds were 80 percent that the tenant would renew, and the costs the owner would incur for brokerage and fit-up were 20 percent of what the expenses would be if the tenant left.

This is a little confusing so let's look at a specific example. Say that you're looking at a Pro Forma for a multi-tenant building you are interested in buying. And let's say that this Pro Forma assumes that any time a tenant leaves the building, the owner will incur $20/sf in retrofit expenditures and $6/sf in brokerage costs in procuring a new tenant. Now many Pro Formas prepared for multi-tenant buildings do not make a case-by-case analysis as to the probability of each tenant renewing. The Pro Forma will simply make a gross assumption: in our example, the Pro Forma assumed that there was an 80 percent probability that every tenant would renew when his or her lease expired. This means that in every year a lease or leases expire, the Pro Forma would input a cost equal to 20 percent of the square footage of the space times $26/sf (retrofit expenditures and brokerage costs).

Now you could argue that in a building where all the tenants were very happy and likely to renew, this program hurt the seller. But in such a building the seller would never prepare a Pro Forma with an 80 percent renewal probability. Rather, in a building with most tenants likely to renew, the seller's renewal probability would be 95 percent.

Now back to the story of the multi-tenant office building for sale. So my broker friend prepares a Pro Forma that makes a gross assumption, to wit: an 80 percent probability that all tenants will renew. *But* there was one large tenant in the building, and if a prospective buyer did his homework, he would have learned that the probability of this particular tenant renewing was about 10 percent—far from 80 percent! And as to this large tenant, if a prospective buyer does the math on retrofit and brokerage expenses and assumes 90 percent of these costs in the year the large tenant's lease expires, he'll find that the adjusted operating income in that year is much, much lower than shown in the seller's Pro Forma.

Did my broker friend do something unethical in preparing a Pro Forma with an 80 percent renewal probability when he had good reason to know that the large tenant would most likely leave the building? Well, you decide. Here were his instructions from the Seller:

SELLER: Look, no one knows *for sure* whether that [large] tenant will stay or go. New management may come in tomorrow and make a decision to stay. The building as a whole has experienced an 80 percent renewal history over the last five years. What's more, anyone analyzing this building for purchase is a sophisticated real estate investor. Let him make his own assumptions and adjust the Pro Forma accordingly if he wants to. If I'm going to sell this building, I want to put my best foot forward, and the numbers look a lot better with an 80 percent renewal probability figure for all the tenants. That's the figure I want to use.

My point: the Broker had prepared a real nice sales package for this property including a well-thought-out Pro Forma. But if a prospective buyer did not double-check all of the broker's assumptions and do his own homework as to the probability of the large tenant staying put, he might have purchased based upon a Pro Forma with a fatal flaw.

A Final Comment about Brokers

As I suggested in Chapter 13, real estate brokerage is a great point of entry into the world of real estate entrepreneuring. As a result, there are some brokers who occasionally dip into the buying world. In other words, they dig up a good deal and pick it off for themselves.

Some buyers won't work with these brokers because they figure that the broker will buy good properties for himself and offer for sale only marginal deals. I don't have that feeling. My sense in general is this: I am only going to buy a property that makes sense to me. If it meets my criteria, then I'm a buyer. If a broker brings me a deal that he passed on and it meets my particular criteria, then so what? Similarly, some people do not believe you can get good deals from brokers because these are the deals that everyone is seeing. Again I say: So what? You are only going to buy a property that works for you. The fact that many others have seen and passed on a deal is not determinative to me.

For example, the deal that put me on the map in Connecticut was the factory outlet shopping center conversion in Norwalk that I related in Chapter 8. This property had been for sale for many months before I ever spoke with the seller, and all the smart real estate entrepreneurs and investors in the area had decided it was overpriced. Perhaps because I was young and had little to lose, I took a run at it and got lucky. But the fact is, one of the most important talents a real estate entrepreneur can develop is the ability to identify opportunity where others cannot see it. And so I will never reject a deal out of hand just because lots of other people have seen it before me.

Your Network

Perhaps the best source of deals for you will be the network you develop in your market area. Here's a list of some of the people in my network who have helped me find deals:

Confessions of a Real Estate Entrepreneur

Accountant

Appraiser

Attorney

Banker

City Hall employee

Consultant

Financial planner

Insurance agent

Mortgage broker

Residential real estate broker

Stockbroker

All of these people speak with individuals who may be thinking about selling real estate. If the people in your network believe in you (that you are honorable, will treat their contact fairly, and can get a deal done), why wouldn't they contact you to suggest you call _____ about a property he or she may be selling?

You can also create an environment where people who do not even know you will call. If you develop a reputation for integrity, creativity, and the ability to close, people call. How do you get the word out about yourself? Well, PR is a component of the real estate game. In other words, let the world know that you are a buyer and that you can get deals done.

Self-promotion is not always comfortable, but if it helps you get good deals, then you may have to bite the bullet and go for it. Whatever you think of Donald Trump, for example, no one can contest that he is a great promoter and worth learning from in that regard. So if you do a successful deal, you might issue a press release. (Or you might do something really wacky like write a book.) You should be in touch with business reporters in your area. You should continually endeavor to get the word out about your real estate activities since you never know who might read or hear about you and decide that you're just the right person to buy his or her property. By way of example:

My partner and I are about to sell a small apartment building in Miami Beach. We want to avoid paying a broker's commission (±$100,000) and so we decided to create a list of everyone who bought a building like ours in the prior 24 months. Obtaining information from the City Clerk's Office and the Multiple Listing Service, we were able to compile a list and we have been calling everyone on it. But since most people buy in an entity form, it is not always easy to get a name and phone number for the individual who runs the buying entity. Still, we are making calls. At the same time we are familiar with one local woman who has been buying and renovating apartment buildings. She is very successful and produces beautiful projects and (on conversion) achieves record-setting sales prices. And she gets (orchestrates?) good press. We have seen this press and so we decided to call her. As it happens, she may end up being our buyer. The point: This woman got the word out about herself, her willingness to buy, and the type of properties she was interested in. As a result, we (a seller) called her, saving ourselves money (the brokerage commission) but also saving her money (since we are not paying a commission, we are more flexible with the price) and giving her a first look at a deal that is of great interest to her.

General Interest Media and Trade Journals

Sometimes you can find a deal from general interest media, which reports on the events in your market area. A company is relocating or being sold. Another company is laying off hundreds of employees. A corporation just got hit with a huge lawsuit. These events can lead to the disposition of real estate. I scour the papers for this kind of information and when I find something interesting, I make a call. I will not pretend that my hit rate is high; most calls are not productive. BUT, it only takes one—and if you find a good deal as a result, it may be well worth all of your effort.

In addition, every area of the country has trade journals—publications about the real estate activities in a particular market. I constantly read these publications for tips about property that I might purchase. I find a particularly fruitful section in these publications to be the listing of recently recorded documents. You may have to do some homework, but I'm sure there is a periodical of some type in your area that will list recorded documents, for example, Deeds, Mortgage Deeds, Releases, Foreclosures, and **Lis Pendens**. I pay particular attention to the recently recorded Lis Pendens.

A Lis Pendens (Latin for "thing pending") is a document that is used by a lender to put the world on notice that a property owner is in default of his mortgage. It usually precedes the commencement of a foreclosure action. It is usually a sign of incipient trouble and therefore important information for a real estate entrepreneur. I learned about one of my best deals by reading the Lis Pendens section of one of the Connecticut real estate trade journals. Unbeknownst to me, and the other real estate entrepreneurs in my area, there was a property owner in trouble with a well-located office building. The lender was frustrated with the owner's late payments on the mortgage and was threatening a foreclosure. In the meantime, the lender's attorney decided to put a Lis Pendens on the Land Records. The trade journal had a service that picked up all recorded documents, and a week after the recording it was published in this periodical.

Fortunately for me, I saw it early the morning of publication and I was in touch with the lender that day. I was surprised to learn about the problem but was quick to communicate to the lender that if it foreclosed, I would be happy to purchase the property (or even the note if it wanted to sell that prior to completing the foreclosure). Shortly afterward we struck a deal: the lender decided to foreclose and take title, and we reached an agreement that upon conclusion of the foreclosure, I would purchase at a preagreed price. Years later I sold that building for a large profit, and as you might expect, I have been a religious reader of the Lis Pendens section in my local trade journals ever since.

City Hall

One thing that some real estate entrepreneurs do is regularly wander around City Hall. They nose around the various offices like Zoning, Building, and Engineering to see if they can pick up any helpful information, almost all of which is available to the public. These entrepreneurs let it be known in these city offices what they're looking to buy. They hope to develop relationships with people in these offices . . . who sometimes learn about potential deals early . . . in an effort to get a call with some helpful information.

These entrepreneurs also spend time in the City Clerk's Office, where documents are recorded. Sometimes they see or hear of something valuable before others. For example, someone who was in the City Clerk's Office the day the Lis Pendens in my story above was recorded on the land records would have learned about it a week before I did, and perhaps beat me to the deal.

Cold Calling/Driving the Area

I have often just driven an area, looking for what I hope are opportunities to buy. In fact, when I began my real estate entrepreneuring, I was always in the car looking for run-down houses (my first foray into real estate) that I could buy, renovate, and resell. One of the contractors I was working with joked that I would buy anything that had boarded-up windows. He was close to right.

Whenever I saw a property that looked like it was not being maintained (financial problems?), I would cold call the owner. Sometimes it worked, sometimes it didn't.

The advantages of this approach are obvious: occasionally you can find a good buy before a broker and/or competing buyers get into the picture. The disadvantage of this approach is that by making the opening gambit to an owner, you may be communicating too much interest, causing him to push his price above market. In other words, by asking the owner whether he wants to sell, you have already positioned yourself as the supplicant and the negotiating power is with the owner. On the other hand, since you will only buy at a price that makes sense to you anyway, what difference does it make? If the seller is willing and accepts an offer from you that works, then you buy. If not, hopefully you have not wasted too much time.

Conclusion

There is no one right way to find deals. I think about looking for deals like I think about the impressive card trick where the magician finds the selected card by throwing the deck against a wall, and (if the trick works) one card sticks to the wall (yes, the chosen card). Hence, the expression, "Throw everything against the wall and see what sticks." And that is my theory with deal finding: try everything and hope something sticks (works).

To find deals, you must be proactive, and that's hard because life is easier when you react than when you proact. That's because, in part, you never know what will work and what won't. But if you don't spend part of your week, every single week, scouting deals, or laying the groundwork for doing so (e.g., networking), you may end up with a lot of real estate skills but no opportunities to apply them. Deal flow is really, really important to the real estate entrepreneur, and you need to be constantly thinking about it.

Up until this point in the book I have spoken mostly about the art of buying. But in order to cash in on the properties which you bought and to which you hopefully added a lot of value, you also need to know how to sell. Let's look at when and how to sell in the next chapter.

17

When You're a Seller

$\mathbf{M}$ost of our discussion to this point in the book has been about trying to acquire property. But a real estate entrepreneur also needs to know when to sell . . . and how.

When to Sell?

There is no one answer to this question, and your particular response will depend on your personal circumstances at a particular moment in time. Some real estate players never want to sell. Others are "merchants," continually buying, creating value, and then selling. Certainly, real estate entrepreneuring, like many business endeavors, is about buying low and selling high. But knowing *when* to sell is not easy.

In writing this book, I have had to think through my own philosophy on selling. In general it would be this: when you have added value to a property to the point where your incremental gains in value will generate returns on your capital in the deal that are "institutional" (i.e., returns that would be satisfactory to big institutions like pension funds, about 5 to 8 percent per year) rather than entrepreneurial, it's time to start thinking about selling. As real estate entrepreneurs, there is a time when we should take advantage of the value we have added, and put our money to use elsewhere—with of course the goal of achieving higher than institutional-type returns.

This is easier said than done. First of all, believe it or not, many of us become emotionally attached to real estate—inanimate though it may be. Especially after working long and hard to make a deal successful, it's hard to sell that deal. Second, it is not easy to put money to use at our targeted, entrepreneurial returns. It's a lot of work to find the opportunities and then execute them. Sometimes it's just easier to leave things alone. There is nothing at all wrong with this decision, by the way. But as a real estate entrepreneur with a goal of earning returns of, say, 20 percent per year or more on our money, one has to eventually get off his duff, sell, and start again.

How to Sell?

When I'm a seller, I believe in using brokers. A good broker will have a large group of potential buyers for your property, and this will ensure that you get the best price on sale. What's more, having the broker between you and the prospective purchaser is a good thing. The broker can sell you and your property in ways that you cannot. Since you are obviously biased, a purchaser will not take everything you say about your property in the same way as if it came from an "independent" third party. Yes, I know what you're thinking: a broker is far from independent. And that is absolutely correct and known by all buyers. But somehow when information comes from a source other than the seller, it just seems to have a little more weight to it.

Notwithstanding my general predilection toward using brokers, I have on several occasions sold property directly, that is, without a broker involved. Since I've been in the game in my area of the country for many years, I know many of the likely candidates to buy my properties. In time you too will learn who is buying what and what he or she will pay for a particular type of deal. Since brokerage commissions on larger transactions can be significant (think 2 to 3 percent of the sales price), there's money to be saved when selling direct.

The critical skills in selling a commercial property are: (1) knowing how to position the property to be attractive to a purchaser and (2) knowing how to negotiate the price and terms of sale. In terms of positioning, you need to think like a buyer. First, the building should be physically attractive. If you have not already done so in your effort to add value, you need to address all obvious cosmetic deficiencies in your property. Even really smart real estate entrepreneurs buy at least in part from their gut, which means that to some degree they are seduced by properties that are physically attractive (even though they know that sometimes the ugliest properties can present the best opportunities to add value).

Second, tee the property up for the most logical buyer. Some sellers who own an apartment building that they believe is a great candidate for a condo conversion will go through the process of filing the condominium paperwork before putting the building on the market. This takes some time and money but may make the property more desirable to a potential condo-converter buyer. On the other hand, the prefiling may backfire if the potential buyer has different thoughts about how to structure the condominium. (By the way, none of this is fatal—a Condo Declaration can always be amended.) Similarly, if you're selling an office building and you know that your likely buyer is an institutional-type investor (think nonentrepreneurial) who will just want to collect rents with a minimum of management headaches, be sure that all your systems (roof, heating/air-conditioning, electrical) are in good condition, with service contracts in place and recent maintenance histories available to the prospective buyer.

Finally, and perhaps most important, think about the rent roll. If you have a lot of leases expiring in the near future, then it may not be the right time to sell. Unless all of your leases are under market (and if so, then perhaps you haven't done your job as a real estate entrepreneur), a buyer will discount the price he offers when there are a lot of leases about to expire. He'll see these expirations as potential headaches and expense, and may assume lower renewal probabilities, longer down time (between tenants), and higher costs to re-lease than are warranted. So prior to putting your property on the market, renew existing leases as best you can and/or lease vacant space so you do not have significant potential tenant turnover in the immediate future. The goal here is to have leases expiring on a staggered basis beginning a few years out; for example, 20 percent of your space expiring in 36 months, another 20 percent in 48 months, and so on. In this situation a buyer will be comfortable with the fact that: (1) He has several years to understand the building before any leases expire, and (2) he won't be facing any single year when a major portion of the building's space becomes available.

Here's the point: An entrepreneur's job is to add every ounce of value to a property that he can. That includes making the building as attractive as possible to the nonentrepreneurs, that is, buyers who will accept lower returns and pay the highest price. One way to get a buyer like that comfortable is to take all the guesswork out of the deal. The nonentrepreneur is more conservative than you are. So even though you may think that leases expiring in your building are a good thing—perhaps an opportunity to kick up rental income—the nonentrepreneur may not think that way and may discount his offer due to the perceived (albeit not actual) risk. You want to present a no-risk, no-brainer deal to your buyers. Try to take all the risk out of the deal, whether it is leasing risk, physical risk (capital improvements), or even legal risk (e.g., filing condo conversion paperwork), BEFORE you put it up for sale—that is the job of the entrepreneur.

The Pro Forma Dance

Once you have an interested buyer, the negotiation over price and terms begins. I sometimes think of this process as a dance. We discussed above how most commercial properties are valued on the basis of a cash flow projected forward in a five- or ten-year Pro Forma. The dance starts when the Seller prepares a Pro Forma showing what he believes the cash flow from the property will look like over the ensuing five or ten years. In preparing the Pro Forma, the Seller makes projections and assumptions that (carrying the dance analogy perhaps a bit too far) "put his best foot forward." The Buyer then reviews the Pro Forma and makes his own assumptions. Some of the major points in question are:

- What percent of gross rents should be deducted to account for vacancy issues?
- Which tenants will renew when their leases expire?
- What will market rents be two, three, and four years out into the future?
- As to leases that expire and tenants who leave, how much time will be required to re-lease the vacated space?
- As to leases that expire and tenants who leave, what kind of fit-up allowance will be necessary to attract new tenants? And, what will brokerage expenses be?
- How will operating expenses and real estate taxes increase in the years following the sale?
- Will the new owner be able to pass these increases on to the tenants? (Take note of the fact that even though a Lease Agreement may allow for passing these expenses on to the tenants, sometimes market conditions take precedent and a Landlord is not always able to bill a tenant for these increases.)
- What kind of reserve should the new owner establish for maintenance issues and/or capital improvements?
- What will be the market cap rate five or ten years from purchase, that is, when the buyer turns around and resells?

Another point in this discussion is the appropriate discount or cap rate that the parties should use in valuing the Pro Forma's projected net income.

It is the discussion of these issues that reminds me of a dance. The Seller makes a point. The Buyer counterpoints. The Seller responds and the Buyer replies. And so on. Eventually all the points are thrashed out and there is some number that the parties agree (or don't) represents the value of the building. The same dance may then occur as the parties make their case for any terms (e.g., closing date or seller financing) that may be part of the deal.

Sooner or later the parties reach a resolution: Either they agree on price and terms or they go their separate ways. If you are a Seller and want to maximize the probability of success with the Pro Forma dance, be prepared for the questions of prospective buyers. Be prepared to justify the assumptions you have made in the Pro Forma. Be prepared to dance: know how you will respond when the Buyer questions your various assumptions.

The Real Estate Contract: The Buyer's Due Diligence

When I'm a Seller, I'm very happy to give the Buyer time to do due diligence. In fact, I want him to do it. So long as the requested time is reasonable, I never dispute a due diligence provision in the Real Estate Contract. And during the due diligence period, I always turn over to the Buyer all the documents or information he wants. In other words, I cooperate 100 percent.

In return, what I want in the Real Estate Contract is the following language in the Due Diligence Clause:

> In the event that the Purchaser does not elect its herein right to terminate this Contract upon the conclusion of the due diligence period, then Purchaser acknowledges: (1) that it has received from the Seller any and all information, documents, or other materials it requested, (2) that it has had unlimited access to the property for the purpose of conducting whatever inspections, studies, or analyses it may have wished to perform, (3) that it is not relying on any information provided by the Seller or any representative or agent of the Seller, and (4) that it is fully satisfied with the condition of the property, with the leases and rental information pertinent to the property, and with all other matters that might be relevant in its decision to purchase.

In other words, I do not want the Buyer ever coming back after the closing and saying that I did not provide him with some piece of information, or misled him, or hindered his due diligence. What I am saying to my buyer is this:

> "Do whatever due diligence you want. If you are not successful with this property, do not blame me. You had all the information that I had. What you do with it is your business."

Second Thoughts?

Notwithstanding the fact that you did everything right with your property prior to the sale, there may be times when your buyer will turn around and sell the property a couple of years later at a price significantly higher than you sold it for. So be it. Sometimes the real estate investment world gets hot for a certain type of property or a specific location . . . or sometimes a buyer comes along who just has to have a certain property. The result may be that the value of the property you sold may increase dramatically in the period immediately subsequent to your sale. Forget about it. You cannot predict such things, so never look back.

Similarly, there may be times when your buyer does not do as well with the property as he (or you) would have liked. Forget about that as well. If I know that I disclosed everything about the property, helped the buyer learn about the building, and gave him unlimited access to the building, then I feel absolved from anything that may occur after the closing.

Some people say that the only good sales are the ones when both parties are unhappy, that is, the seller wanted more money for his building and the buyer wanted to pay less. I do not subscribe to that point of view. To me, both parties should be happy: the seller should feel that he got a good return on his entrepreneurial efforts (presumably buying for X and selling for some multiple thereof), and the buyer should feel that his new acquisition presents him with a good opportunity to earn the kind of returns he's looking for.

Conclusion

Knowing when and how to sell is a critical component of good real estate entrepreneuring. Basically the rule is this: if you have added all the value to the property that is possible, then you've done your entrepreneurial duty and it's time to sell. Position the property for the type of buyer you anticipate will be interested in it. Many times that buyer will be nonentrepreneurial (if he were entrepreneurial, he would not be interested in your building, since all the added value is presumably already out of it). Your buyer will probably favor a predictable, safe return. Give it to him.

Okay, time to switch gears. Heard the latest lawyer joke? There sure are a lot out there. Here's one I heard recently that I thought was kind of funny:

Guy walks into a crowded bar and screams: "All lawyers are jerks."

One guy stands up and says: "Hey, I take offense at that."

Screamer says: "Argh, another lawyer."

Guy says: "No, I'm a jerk."

Well, like it or not, lawyers are critical participants in the real estate game. You need to understand them . . . you need to speak their language. You need to stop telling lawyer jokes.

18

Attorneys

Since I've practiced real estate law for 25 years now, I can't help but include a chapter on how to deal with attorneys. At the risk of upsetting some of my brethren, here goes.

Rule 1: Do Not Rely on Your Attorney to Finalize a Deal

One of the big mistakes I see young real estate entrepreneurs make is assuming that once they shake hands with the other party and call their attorney to "paper" the deal, the deal will get done . . . HUGE MISTAKE. Attorneys are just like any other professional. They have a particular expertise and can be of great assistance to you. But if you turn over the negotiation of the documents or consummation of the deal to your attorney, you may very well be disappointed.

Let's take the best case: Your attorney is very interested in your business and wants to do his very best for you. But he has many other clients that he feels similarly about. You are a valued client. But so are the others.

A good rule to remember with busy lawyers is that "the squeaky wheel gets the grease." In other words, stay in your attorney's face. Do not relinquish matters to him. Without becoming a huge pest, call regularly to check on the status of your documentation, the closing, or whatever else he may be doing for you. Do not assume that all is well if you do not hear anything. Do not adopt the policy that "no news is good news." No news may instead mean that your busy attorney has dropped the ball and nothing is happening. What's more, the fact that nothing is happening may well be working against you; for example, maybe the seller is entertaining another offer while you're relaxing, thinking that your attorney has everything in hand.

There's another reason not to let your attorney take over the negotiation or flow of the deal: many attorneys are just not that good at it (even though they think they are). I know of one real estate attorney in my area with a real big ego. He loves to take over the negotiation of documents and deal points as if he's the principal. He's a big table-pounder and loves screaming, "No way, no how will my client ever agree to that point" even though he is not, in fact, sure whether his client will or will not agree to the point . . . he just likes to create the impression and reputation that he is a "tough" guy. The problem is, he's only tough when he has no skin in the game. In other words, he has nothing to lose. On more than one occasion I've seen him hurt his client's position by antagonizing opposing parties or attorneys.

As the person with the most at stake, you have to keep control of your attorney. He or she has a specific job to do, and that is to get the documents drafted and/or reviewed and signed; or, the deal closed. If you give your attorney too much leeway over the process, you are submitting to his or her personality and style, and that can impact your deal. That is a mistake. So, for several reasons, KEEP CONTROL, KEEP CONTROL, KEEP CONTROL.

Rule 2: Do Not Rely on Your Attorney to Address Potential Business Issues in Important Documents

Nobody is going to care as much as you do about the accuracy of the important deal documents. Your attorney will, of course, try to do a good job and identify all issues. But you cannot put 100 percent reliance on his review. If, for example, your attorney is reviewing a proposed Promissory Note submitted by a lender for your signature, YOU MUST ALSO REVIEW the Note.

Using the Promissory Note as an example, there are many business points that you need to be very clear about: the interest rate and how it adjusts, the amortization schedule, the prepayment and assumption clauses, and the recourse provisions. If you expect that your attorney will identify all business issues in the documents, you are mistaken. He may not be familiar with all the discussions you've had with the lender and/or other parties in the transaction. He may not know (or remember) all the moving parts in a deal. He may just be busy and miss something he should have caught. Finally, he may also be thinking that you'll review the business points in important documents, and therefore he may gloss over them. I learned this point the hard way, once from a client's point of view, and once as the attorney who dropped the ball.

My first story is about a man who was for years a successful developer until he ran into big problems with a deal he was doing in Florida.

He'd ground leased a piece of land on which he wanted to build a major office park. The location was great and he had good tenant interest before he even broke ground. He had financing lined up and was ready to close on the construction loan when the bank's attorney pointed out problems with language in the ground lease, specifically that the ground lessor had not agreed to subordinate its land to the lien of a construction loan. As we learned in earlier chapters, construction lenders usually want a first mortgage on land to be developed, and this particular lender would not accept a leasehold mortgage instead. As a result the deal was stalled because the ground lessor was not willing to subject its property to the developer's lender's mortgage. From here the deal spun out of control and lawsuits ensued, including a lawsuit by the ground lessor against the developer for breach of the covenant to pay rent (the developer had personally guaranteed the ground lease payments). Eventually the developer went belly up.

One day I was having lunch with him. He was a gracious, stand-up guy, not a blamer, and yet when I pressed him as to what had happened, here's what he said:

DEVELOPER: You know, Jim, I'm from the old school. I never went to college and I always viewed attorneys as people with a great education and experience. I knew that the ground lease needed to contain a subordination clause, but it was 30 pages long and I never read it. I figured that the attorney would tell me if there were any problems. He never brought anything up, so I figured it was fine and signed the ground lease when it was presented to me. My mistake . . . and I'm paying the price.

Needless to say, I walked away from that lunch vowing never to assume that an attorney had performed the homework or review that I should do for myself.

The second story happened early in my legal career and is painful to retell, since I was the attorney who blew it.

Confessions of a Real Estate Entrepreneur

I was representing a young entrepreneur who was buying a building to house his company. He was borrowing $2 million from a local bank in order to fund the purchase. The interest rate on the loan, as indicated in the commitment letter from the bank, was "fixed for three years at 8 percent and then adjusted annually to 2.5 points over the then existing prime rate." The prime rate at the time of the loan was 6.5 percent. The language in the Promissory Note prepared by lender's counsel read as follows:

> The loan rate shall be fixed at 8.0 percent for the first three years of the loan and then shall adjust to a rate equal to 2.5 points over the prime rate.

This clause looked okay to me. But it did not look okay to my client. Here's how our conversation went after he took the time to review the Promissory Note:

CLIENT: Jim, what if the prime rate is 7 percent three years from now?

ME: Well, then the Bank will adjust the rate to 9.5 percent.

CLIENT: Okay, I get that . . . but what if the prime rate is 4 percent?

ME: Well, then your rate will be 6.5 percent.

CLIENT: Where does it say that?

ME: Right here (I went to the clause quickly, showing him that I had in fact read the Promissory Note several times) . . . the Note says "2.5 points over the prime rate."

CLIENT: What prime rate?

ME (STARTING TO FUMBLE A BIT): Well, the prime rate as of the time of the adjustment date, three years from the date you sign the Note.

CLIENT: Where does it say that? It seems to me that the Note should say the interest rate will change to 2.5 points over the prime rate that exists *as of the date of the adjustment* [he emphasized the words]. Rates are high right now and I think they are going to go down. While I'm sure the Bank will adjust my rate upward if the prime rate happens to go up, if the prime rate goes down, I want the language very clear that the adjusted interest rate is tied to the prime rate *as exists three years from now.*

ME: Duh.

In fact he was 100 percent correct, and perhaps had I read the Note a few more times I would have picked up his point in advance of our meeting. The reality is that in reviewing the Note, I wasn't thinking like the person who would actually be paying the interest on the loan three years later. I was thinking like a lawyer, looking for legal issues, and not like a principal. Had my client not read the Promissory Note, there could have been a real problem at some point in the future. It's not that I was lazy. I had in fact read the Note several times. It was just that my orientation in doing so was not the same as the person who would actually be writing the interest checks. Yes, I should have picked up the point and I did not—shame on me. But fortunately my client was sharper than I and what better way for me to learn this important lesson: no matter how diligent and well-intentioned your attorney may be, he or she is not going to do as careful or comprehensive a job reviewing deal documents as you will. As I gravitated into the world of entrepreneuring and was more often the principal than the attorney, I learned to never entrust document review to my attorney . . . I always look over his or her shoulder at all times.

Rule 3: Never Be Afraid to Ask Stupid Questions

As I've stated, I believe you need to review all important documents, particularly with respect to the business points. And, although this may surprise you, I also recommend that you attempt to understand even the legal points in the documents. Now I understand that lawyers do not make it easy for nonlawyers to understand legal documents. Half of the wording is mumbo-jumbo, or lawyer-speak. But do not skip over this stuff. When you are unsure about something, ask your attorney what it means and do not quit asking until you have an understanding of what it is that you are committing to.

Attorneys want to do a good job for you. But sometimes they get sloppy, or tired, or busy, or whatever and may even miss legal points. When I'm wearing my lawyer's hat, I try my best to identify all legal issues that the client needs to know about. But even here, in my area of expertise, I sometimes come up short. Time for another embarrassing example:

A client of mine was selling an expensive house and buying a less expensive house. She was nervous about timing these two transactions because she needed to be out of the house she was selling by a certain date (July 1) and was concerned that the person from whom she was buying (the Seller, to her) was not going to keep to the scheduled closing date of the sale to her (also July 1). If that happened, she'd have a big problem. If she did not close her purchase on the same day as she sold, she would have nowhere for her and her family to go upon consummating the sale. So she said to me:

CLIENT: I do not know how you want to write it, but please put some language in the Real Estate Contract of the house I'm buying to indicate that my Seller *must* close on July 1.

Confessions of a Real Estate Entrepreneur

So I added language that said: "Seller agrees that the closing date shall be July 1, 2005, and that as to said date, time is of the essence." Now "time is of the essence" is a defined term in the law. It means that the indicated date is written in stone; there is no wiggle room as to that date. It is powerful language. Her Seller agreed to this language, and my client came to my office to sign the Real Estate Contract. She reviewed the sentence I had added . . . and then asked me:

CLIENT: What does this mean . . . "time is of the essence"?

ME: Well, it means that the closing date has to be July 1, 2005–no matter what. It means that if your Seller is not able to close on July 1, then he will be in default of the Real Estate Contract and you can sue him.

CLIENT (THINKING FOR A MINUTE): I see. Well what happens if the person who is buying my house delays that closing and cannot close on July 1? As you know, I need the sale of my house to go through so that I have the funds to close on my purchase. Does the "time is of the essence" language apply to me as well? Can I be in default of the Contract if I cannot consummate my purchase on July 1?

ME (STARTING TO FEEL A LITTLE QUEASY): Well, yes it does.

CLIENT: Well, then I cannot sign this. As you know, I cannot afford to buy the new house until my sale goes through. If my Purchaser is delayed, then I have to delay the closing on the house I am buying. There must be another way to word what I need to accomplish.

ME: OOPS.

So instead of the "time is of the essence" language, I reached an agreement with the attorney for the Seller to my client that the Seller would pay a per diem for any day after July 1 that he delayed the closing. The per diem was high enough to hold his feet to the fire, that is, to make sure that he would close on July 1. The Seller was okay with this language *(even though it did not go both ways)* because (1) he intended to close on July 1, and (2) he wanted to keep the deal together and give my client assurance that he would not delay the closing. Still, had something happened that could change his plans, the per diem was severe enough to ensure that he did not change his mind or his plans about closing on July 1.

And guess what happened? The person buying my client's house was not able to close on July 1 as scheduled. Therefore, my client was not able to consummate the closing of the house she was purchasing on July 1. Had she not had some wiggle room as to when she could close, she would have been in default of the Contract and could have lost her 10 percent down payment! Thank goodness she asked me what "time is of the essence" meant.

Here's the point: My client did not understand the language I had inserted into the Real Estate Contract. AND SO SHE ASKED ME WHAT IT MEANT. When I explained it, she realized that this language did not work for her; that if she, too, was subject to the "time is of the essence" provision and her buyer delayed, she could be in real trouble. Thankfully my client read the document and asked me about the legal language she did not understand.

Rule 4: Do Not Negotiate Fees or Delay Payment

If you are a successful real estate entrepreneur, you're going to make a lot of money. Perhaps much more than your attorney makes. And this rubs some attorneys (not all) the wrong way. Attorneys go to college (four years), then law school (three hard years), then take a Bar Exam. That's a lot of schooling. Some attorneys think that puts them on some higher level than those with less education. (I myself think that too much schooling can be a bad thing—it can diminish entrepreneurial fervor by making a person too analytical—sometimes you just have to stop number-crunching and get in the game and start swinging.)

I believe that a client should pay his attorney immediately upon receipt of an invoice. Certainly in the course of a deal, you need your attorney to be your friend. If he feels that you don't trust him, if he feels that you don't think he's entitled to a fair payday for his efforts, if he feels that you don't respect the expertise he brings to your team . . . well, then you are not likely to get out of him the type of services you need.

I do not believe that a client should attempt to negotiate a flat fee for a deal in advance of engaging an attorney. I know that people will disagree with me on this. There is something certain and fair, they believe, about agreeing to a fee in advance. But that presumes a deal takes a predictable course, and very few deals do. An attorney may have agreed to do a closing for X, thinking the deal would take Y hours, and then get upset when the deal takes much longer. As a result, the hours you'll get out of him will not be his best and may impact your deal. If you have questions about an attorney's billing practice, speak to others who have used him. Attorneys who are gougers get a reputation. Attorneys who bill fairly also get a reputation. If at the end of a matter you aren't happy with your attorney's billing, then vote with your feet and find someone else to represent you in the future.

Rule 5: Understand How Your Attorney Views Risk–Yours and His

Some real estate entrepreneurs like to ask their attorney what he thinks of a deal. Though that may be okay when you've worked with an attorney for a long time (and know each other well), most of the time it's probably a waste of time. First of all, most attorneys are risk-adverse. They are not entrepreneurial. Unlike an entrepreneur, they have a real job with a predictable income and they like it that way. So how valuable is their assessment of risk? In general, they do not like risk. You, on the other hand, as a real estate entrepreneur, are married to risk . . . your goal is to have a good relationship with it. Asking an attorney what he or she thinks about a risky venture may get you off point; there is nothing wrong with asking people for advice, just look for someone who is not risk-adverse by nature.

Then there are the attorneys who do not mind taking risks, so long as it is with someone else's money. If you ask these attorneys for advice, you'll get it . . . it just won't have any value. These attorneys like to live vicariously—swinging for the fences with other people's funds. I am not suggesting that these attorneys are not well-intentioned; they might not even know what they are doing. It's just that advice from this type of individual is not that valuable either.

Finally, you need to assess the risk quotient of your attorney as it applies to his handling of your matters. Some attorneys are very concerned about giving advice or handling matters that can come back to bite them in the form of client complaints or even malpractice suits. These attorneys can be problematic when they are handling your matters as they may be overly cautious in the preparation and review of legal documents, causing headaches with the other counsel (and perhaps party). And these attorneys can be a challenge to you, the client. By highlighting every little issue (even if the risk identified is one in a thousand) that could possibly cause a problem in the deal, these attorneys can get inside your head and get you off track. The reality is that these attorneys may believe that the likelihood of problems from some of the issues they are raising are minute, yet they feel the need to bring the issues to the forefront so that you can never gripe at a later time.

Certainly you want an attorney who will protect your interests and identify legal issues that you need to consider. But, for me anyway, I want a lawyer who is a deal maker and not a deal breaker. I want him to figure out how to get past potential problems and not just identify them and make mountains out of mole-hills. I want him to point out realistic concerns, not cover his own butt with lots of correspondence and e-mails (so that he has a record of having warned me). I want someone who is complementary to me, helping me assess risk and deal with it. I don't want someone who is (consciously or unconsciously) more concerned about his own potential liability than about getting my deal done.

Conclusion

As indicated, I have practiced real estate law for 25 years. I've learned a tremendous amount from my contemporaries. But I have also seen situations where an attorney did his client a disservice. As I gravitated toward becoming a principal

Attorneys

in deals, I learned that I could not rely on attorneys to take over a deal for me. To watch over all the business points, or even the legal points. To help me assess the risk of a deal. It is only natural for each of us to want to believe that someone is watching out for our best interests . . . but if you put this responsibility entirely in the hands of your attorney, you could be very disappointed.

Wow, have we learned a lot. Now on to some fun stuff: how to persuade someone to your point of view.

19

The Art of Persuasion

I have been looking forward to writing this and the next chapter: about the art of persuasion and the skills a person needs to increase his or her likelihood of success at real estate entrepreneuring. That's because I'm a big believer in the premise that success in the real estate world is more a function of people skills than factors such as superior intelligence, higher education, or even capital.

The concepts of the real estate game are not difficult to understand. This stuff is not high tech. You don't need to be a brain surgeon (or for that matter a surgeon of any type). You don't need to have graduated from college, and in fact I know several very successful (and wealthy) real estate entrepreneurs who never even went to college. In my view, success in this game is much more dependent on your individual, personal talents for understanding and connecting with people. And these are skills that can be learned and honed.

First we're going to speak to what it takes to convince someone across the table to come around to your point of view. I have some definite opinions about this subject, although I acknowledge that there are many paths to get from Point A to Point B and there is no one right way. In the 10 "lessons" in this chapter, I'll outline my views on how to best accomplish a successful persuasion. By no stretch are my ideas meant to be exclusive; they represent themes that I've developed over time, observing others and learning by doing. And by the way, every time I'm about to go into an important business persuasion situation, I mentally review each of these points.

Let me begin by stating what I mean by a persuasion. It could be a phone call, a business meeting, a golf outing. It is any opportunity to sway another person to your point of view. Sometimes you're selling, sometimes buying, sometimes looking for capital. In all cases, your success in the real estate world depends at least in part on your ability to convince people to think the way you would like them to. This art—and it is an art—is what I call the **Art of Persuasion.**

Lesson 1: Prepare, Prepare, Prepare

I think that far too many people go into a persuasion opportunity—where they have a chance to convince somebody of something—without any forethought as to what they're going to say and/or how they are going to respond to what the other party will likely say. This totally amazes me. Unless someone is fantastically good "on his feet" (most of us are not), going into this type of opportunity unprepared is just plain stupid.

Think of something important that you might have written recently. If you went back to reread it, you probably made improvements and corrections. Maybe you did that again and again until you got it just the way you wanted it. The more you considered it, the more you reviewed and revised, the better it got.

This is the same process you should take with an oral presentation, that is, any nonwritten opportunity to persuade someone to your point of view. Think through what you want to say, the high points you want to emphasize. Think through what the other party's responses are likely to be. Then step away and think about it a little more. Perhaps your initial thoughts can be improved upon. Review and revise just as if you were putting your comments in writing.

Take your presentation apart and divide it into pieces: What exactly do I want this person to conclude? What is my most likely strategy for achieving that? What are the points that will best effect my persuasion? How should I initially communicate those points? What should be the tenor of my pitch? Deferential? Aggressive? Passionate? At what point should I attempt to conclude the meeting? What if the meeting veers off in one of three or four possible directions? And so on.

In my judgment, the more you think about your comments, the more likely you'll be successful. Leave as little to chance as possible. One slight sidetrack: I am not suggesting that you try to memorize your presentation, because then your comments may seem stiff and rehearsed. Obviously, you need to come across as natural and sincere. The key is that you should always have some kind of outline in your head that you can revert to as necessary.

Lesson 2: The More They Like You, the Greater the Probability of Success

This point is so basic it's almost embarrassing to write about. And I wouldn't except I can't believe how many people miss out on persuasion opportunities because they forget this most fundamental point: people are most inclined to decide in your favor if they like you.

Great persuaders have what I call "connectibility." They size up people quickly and then connect with them, quickly finding some kind of commonality and then leveraging that into "likability."

I don't believe that people who are good at this are fake. I think they just like people, understand the process by which one person likes another, and put themselves in a position to be liked. From this position, they enhance the probability of success with their presentation.

Why some people are likable and others aren't is the subject of many books and well beyond the scope of this chapter. My goal here is to get you to think about whether you put people at ease or not. Look in the mirror and take an accounting of what tendencies or habits you have that may be off-putting. Then make a conscious effort to change them. I have done that over and over the last 25 years. I don't know if I'm more likable as a result, but I do know that whenever engaged in a business persuasion, I am very conscious of not doing or saying something that might put someone off.

Let me give you an example of someone who forgot to look in the mirror before he went into a business meeting. The individual in question ("Owner") is actually a pretty nice guy who, at times, lets his ego get out of control. Here is how his ego almost cost me $100,000.

Owner had recently purchased a building and needed to lease it, since it was mostly vacant. I was the broker for a decent-sized prospective tenant and I brought my clients to Owner's building.

My clients liked the building, and after an extended period of negotiation, Lease Agreements were ready for signature. I was pleased because I was on the brink of earning a $100,000 commission. Against my wishes (I never, never believe in celebrating anything until it is DONE), Owner decided that we should have a "celebratory" lunch with the three principals of the company that I represented. I hated the idea, but I would have hated it more if I was not there.

When the lunch began, the three principals were very excited about moving into the building. Had the Lease Agreement been ready and in front of us at that time, they would have quickly signed it. Unfortunately, it was still in their attorney's hands for delivery to them the next day.

Confessions of a Real Estate Entrepreneur

At first the lunch went well, although Owner could not resist "holding court," rehashing for the three principals all the wonderful features of his building. He just could not hear the sound of his voice enough.

Anyway, on and on he goes . . . blah, blah, blah . . . even after one of the principals tried to change the subject. I was increasingly uncomfortable, though I was not sure why. I guess it was one of those feelings of impending doom when you don't know what's going to happen, you just know something is and that it won't be good.

I knew that the only concern the three principals had during the Lease negotiations was that Owner's property did not have enough parking. Each of the principals had an expensive car, and none of them wanted to worry about finding a parking space when he came to the building. This subject came up during the Lease negotiations, of course, and Owner had gotten each of them comfortable with the amount of available parking. At the start of the lunch, the issue was no longer in anyone's mind. Until, that is, Owner regaled them with the story of how he had just made a deal for the rest of the vacant space in the building:

OWNER: They wanted all sorts of concessions from me, including reserved parking for their executives, but I told them they were moving into the best building in the County and I WAS NOT WILLING TO MAKE SPECIAL ARRANGEMENTS FOR ANYBODY.

PRINCIPAL #1 OF MY CLIENT (SHOWING A BIT OF CONCERN): Why were they worried? Do they need a lot of parking?

OWNER: Yes, I think so, but I told them they were going to have to catch as catch can, just like everybody else.

PRINCIPAL #2 (STARTING TO SQUIRM IN HIS CHAIR MORE THAN I WAS HAPPY WITH): Do you know how many employees they have?

OWNER (COULD HE BE ANY MORE TONE DEAF?): All I know is that it's a lot . . . but when they considered all the amenities of my building, they figured they'd make do.

At this point, desperately wanting to jump in with "How about those Yankees?" I pretend I am choking on a piece of bread, hoping that will distract everyone. No such luck.

PRINCIPAL #3: But, Owner, as you know, one of the things we've been unsure about is parking. Now you tell us that this large tenant going into your building may create a parking problem for us.

OWNER (FINALLY, FINALLY REALIZING WHAT A BIG MOUTH HE HAD): No, no . . . let me explain.

The Art of Persuasion

And the deal came within inches of crashing. My $100,000 gone in an instant. Fortunately, the deal was resurrected and I got paid. But I made a mental note at the time to write about the incident if I ever wrote a book.

There is so much that the Owner did wrong here that I hesitate to single out just one thing. But for now let's focus on his ego. He was so impressed with himself and with his building that he forgot about likability and let his ego get the best of him. Not only did he almost lose this deal, but I can assure you that his imperious attitude did nothing to ingratiate him to my clients. Fortunately for Owner, the deal was so close to getting made that my clients were reluctant to start looking for new space. Owner also neglected a very basic rule of real estate entrepreneuring: until the deal is done, there is no deal. Therefore, he needed to continue to sell right up to the point of signature. Instead, he was too busy blowing his own horn to hear the drumbeat of concern arising right across the table from him.

Now of course there are a lot of reasons that people are off-putting besides ego, but I think that's a big one. Some successful people tend to let their ego grow in proportion to their bank account. And even truly likable people have off-putting characteristics. You will recall that I suggested doing a constant self-analysis of your likable and not-so-likable traits. What about you do people like? What about you do people tend to pull away from? We all have things that people like about us and that people don't like about us.

Okay, just to emphasize the point, here's an example of a self-analysis I did a few years back:

ME (SPEAKING TO MYSELF): Jim, you can be pedantic. You may have a lot of information and you like to share it, and even if your motivations are good ones, you tend to go on and on. Get over yourself. What you know may help people make money but we are not talking about the Bill of Rights here. And maybe your dissemination of information is not even that righteous. Perhaps what motivates you is the desire to exert power over others, and people can sense stuff like that. That's offensive. CUT IT OUT.

And in time I did. (Unless writing this book counts as being pedantic.)

Now let me divert for a minute. I think that trying *too hard* to be likable can backfire. I have a broker friend who is not a naturally warm person. So he read all the right books and went to the Dale Carnegie course on "How to Win Friends and Influence People." But he still tried too hard at times, and when he went into a meeting it was immediately obvious to the others in the room that his efforts at warmth were mechanical. It was as if his conversation was programmed:

BROKER: So, tell me about your children. What are your interests? What is your view on _____?

And so on. It was clear to all but the most self-absorbed (those who think people actually do have an interest in them) that my buddy was trained to ask the right questions. It's not that he didn't care, it's just that he was so structured that people assumed he was being artificial. With time, however, he got much better at exuding his genuine warmth and is a very successful broker today.

I have no easy answers for how to make yourself more connected—such that people will want to do business with you. All I know is that it requires a lifetime of self-analysis and constant course correction.

Lesson 3: Keep Control of the Discussion

The Owner in the story above (who could not hear his own voice enough) has served this book well because he violated so many of my rules of persuasion that I can use his example as a warning on several counts. Another rule he violated is that he let the discussion at lunch wander into dangerous waters. He knew that parking had been a big concern for my clients. But instead of keeping the discussion away from that subject, so as not to revive concerns that had already been put to bed, he inadvertently steered the boat right into choppy waters. A huge NO-NO.

During law school I learned about always trying to keep control of a discussion. I learned this lesson from the professor who taught a course on Trial Practice. One of the lessons this professor hammered into us again and again was that when you're cross-examining a witness, always know the answer to every question before you ask it (in other words, keep control of the witness). And always stop asking questions on a particular topic if you get the witness to make some kind of definitive, helpful statement.

During the course of a trial you are trying to persuade a judge or jury. Their minds will wander and you only have so many opportunities to convince them of a particular point. What the professor was trying to teach us was that if you're lucky enough to make your point, then SHUT UP.

You may enjoy the true story he used to emphasize his lesson:

Plaintiff was suing Defendant. The two had been in a barroom brawl. Plaintiff was claiming that Defendant bit off his nose (it had been sewn back on) during the fight. Defendant denied that and claimed that the nose was sliced off when the Plaintiff fell back against a mirror and cut himself. (If the Defendant had, in fact, bitten off the nose, then the Plaintiff had a claim for punitive damages due to aggravated assault. So the issue in the trial was how the nose had come off.)

The Art of Persuasion

The attorney for Defendant was cross-examining one of Plaintiff's friends. This friend was testifying for Plaintiff, taking the position that Defendant had bitten off Plaintiff's nose. The attorney for Defendant was trying to establish that this witness was not in a position in the bar to actually see Defendant bite off the Plaintiff's nose.

LAWYER: Now, is it not true that you were in the restroom during the fight?

FRIEND: Yes.

LAWYER: And as you reentered the room, the fight was being stopped . . . correct?

FRIEND: Yes.

LAWYER: So you could not have actually seen Defendant bite off Plaintiff's nose . . . correct?

FRIEND: Yes, that is true.

Now my professor starts jumping up and down and yelling: "Okay, he made his point! The judge and jury have heard Plaintiff's friend—the sole eyewitness to the fight besides Plaintiff and Defendant themselves—admit that he did not see the biting. The lawyer should just smile knowingly at the jury, turn to the judge with a flourish and say smugly, 'No more questions, Your Honor.' But, I am sorry to say, this attorney had not taken my evidence course and he did something very stupid. He asked Plaintiff's friend one more question":

LAWYER: So, then is it not correct that there is no way you could know whether Defendant had bitten off Plaintiff's nose?

FRIEND: No, that is not true . . . I saw him spit it out.

DUH. This story teaches us to make our points and then move on to other topics or just shut up. Of course, had Defendant's lawyer not asked that last (one too many) question, Plaintiff's lawyer could have stood up and reexamined the witness, asking him how he knew that Defendant had bitten off Plaintiff's nose. But there's something oh so meaty (no pun intended) about the Defendant's own lawyer messing up in front of everyone. Thinking he has the case won and then . . . BAM! And for years and years this story has entertained law students and emphasized the point my professor wanted to make: *Keep control of the witness. Keep control of the persuasion.*

Here's a good example of the same point from a real estate negotiation I was involved with:

Purchaser is trying to convince Seller to take back a $500,000 second mortgage, behind a $2 million first mortgage that the Purchaser will be obtaining to buy Seller's property. The sales price they have agreed on

Confessions of a Real Estate Entrepreneur

is $3 million. Purchaser correctly anticipated that Seller would be concerned about the total amount of debt on the property and might therefore resist taking back a $500,000 second mortgage.

In fact Seller was concerned. He did not want to be in a second mortgage position behind $2 million of debt. Although Seller believed that Purchaser would eventually be fine with the property, he believed that the first several years of ownership would be tough, as Purchaser needed to increase the rent roll by leasing vacant space and re-leasing spaces that were presently leased at undermarket rents. Seller worried that until Purchaser was able to do that, Purchaser would be struggling to make ends meet. And if Purchaser got into trouble and the first mortgage lender had to foreclose, Seller would be in a precarious position behind a large first mortgage. He did not want that and so was on the fence as to whether to take back the $500,000 second mortgage as Purchaser had requested.

Purchaser knew all this and asked Seller for a meeting, to try to persuade him to take back the $500,000 second mortgage.

PURCHASER: Mr. Seller, it would help me greatly if you would take back the second mortgage. I can probably raise that money, but frankly that could take a lot of time and distract me from what I need to do to get this deal closed.

SELLER: Yes, I understand . . . but I think you understand my concerns. By the way, what is your interest rate on the first mortgage?

PURCHASER: A fixed five-year rate of 6.5 percent.

SELLER (FEELING BETTER): Well, that is certainly reasonable.

PURCHASER: Yes, and the first mortgagee has agreed to an interest-only loan for the first 24 months to help give me the time I need to get the building leased to a level we both know is achievable.

SELLER (FEELING COMFORTABLE NOW): Well, that sounds very good. Okay, I'll take back the second mortgage.

Now is the time that Purchaser should have been thinking about the story of the lawyer who asked one too many questions. He had what he wanted, an agreement from Seller to take back a second mortgage. Okay, Purchaser, change the subject. Go to the bathroom. Smile, shake hands, say thanks and goodbye. BUT DON'T KEEP BLABBING.

Instead he kept blabbing:

PURCHASER: Thanks very much. I really appreciate it. In the meantime, I will work on my lender to see if I can get them to extend out the amortization schedule after the interest-only period is up.

(WHY, PURCHASER? WHY?)

The Art of Persuasion

SELLER (LITTLE ALARM BELLS GOING OFF): Oh yes, I forgot to ask: what is the amortization schedule of the first mortgage after the interest-only period is up?

PURCHASER (REALIZING HIS HUGE MISTAKE): Well, I'm still working on that, but the first mortgage lender is asking for a 10-year schedule.

SELLER (CONCERNED): Wow, that is very, very quick. That could put you in a very precarious financial position.

Another example of a party losing control of a persuasion. Purchaser had the agreement he wanted from Seller. He should have SHUT UP and changed the subject. But he lost his concentration and kept talking, adding gratuitous information that Seller was not asking about: the accelerated amortization schedule that the first mortgage lender was asking for. This information scared Seller because he felt that if Purchaser did not get to a certain rent roll in the first two years of ownership (the interest-only period), Purchaser might get into trouble once the heavy amortization schedule kicked in. As it turned out, Seller did not take back the second mortgage.

I need to make an important point at this juncture. As with the story of the nose-biting incident and this story of Purchaser who could not stop talking, it is very possible that critical information will come out anyway. For example, Seller may have agreed to take back the second mortgage and then a week later learned about the heavy amortization of the first mortgage and changed his mind. That is part of an ongoing negotiation. But here is the point I want to hammer home:

I believe that in all persuasions, whether in one meeting or over several months, there are critical junctures: times when a concession or agreement elicited from the other party can make for your eventual success, whatever else may happen over the course of the deal.

For example, whereas Seller in our example could have changed his mind if/when he learned that Purchaser's first mortgage had an accelerated amortization schedule, *here are other possibilities of what might happen:*

- Neither Seller nor his attorney ever focuses on the amortization schedule and the issue never comes up.
- Seller learns about it but decides that he had given his word and shook hands . . . therefore, he cannot subsequently change his position.
- The deal moves so far forward that by the time Seller learns about the accelerated amortization he decides that although he is not happy about it, he will live with it since he does not want to start over with a new deal.

- The relationship with Seller and Purchaser grows over time, so that by the time Seller learns about the accelerated amortization, he is comfortable with it as his confidence in Purchaser's integrity and ability is high.

My point is that once you obtain a concession or agreement from the other party, cement it with a handshake and go forward. Of course, things can change and people can change their minds, but people have lots of other things to think about and the issue may never come up. What's more, one of the most powerful forces in nature is *inertia*. Once you get what you want, leave it alone and let the momentum of the deal proceed. You might be surprised at how often a deal stays together *just because* parties hate to reverse course and start over. Let inertia work for you.

I think the reason my Evidence professor got so upset with the Defendant's lawyer for asking one too many questions was that this lawyer also forgot about the drama of the witness's concession. The Defendant's lawyer could have sat down after the witness said he could not have seen the Defendant bite the Plaintiff's nose off. It was a dramatic and powerful moment. Somehow, with all the other things floating around in our minds day after day, some stuff sticks and some does not. That thought was sticky. Jurors would remember it. And even though the Plaintiff's lawyer could then get up and have the witness explain what he saw (nose coming out of Defendant's mouth), the flourish and stickiness of the initial moment might have had some kind of subliminal impact on how the jurors would decide. Once the Plaintiff's lawyer stood up and reexamined (rehabilitated) his witness, it was as if the witness needed help from the lawyer, and the impact of his subsequent testimony would not be as compelling.

Same thing with moments in a negotiation. There are high points and low points. When Purchaser in our example got an agreement from Seller that Seller would take back a second mortgage, that was a high point. Purchaser should have cemented it with a handshake and left the topic. Seller has tons and tons of other thoughts in his head, and even if he later discovers the accelerated amortization and worries about it, the impact of the worries may not rise to the level of the drama of his shaking hands with Purchaser and the two of them leaving the room with a firm deal. As you can see, I think there's real value to obtaining a concession or agreement even if the other party does not have all the facts and may later learn of potentially detrimental information.

Finally, what about ethics? Is Purchaser in our accelerated amortization example obligated to give Seller all information about the first mortgage? One could argue both sides of that question, but I come out on the side of no.

Seller could have always asked about the amortization, and then Purchaser must of course tell the truth. But Seller just did not think about this point and never asked. Is it Purchaser's job to help Seller by raising issues that may be harmful to Purchaser's position? Not to me. Maybe it's because, as an entrepreneur, I'm an optimist. If I was Purchaser, it would never occur to me that I'd put Seller—or any other lender, for that matter—in a position where he might lose his money. I would be thinking that there's no question but that I'd stabilize the building within the first couple of years and meet all of my loan obligations to both the first and second (Seller) mortgage lenders. In my mind I'm not withholding relevant information from Seller . . . he's not going to get into trouble with me. So in the example I would steer clear of offering information that could dissuade Seller from taking back the requested second mortgage.

Lesson 4: Know Your Subject Matter

This is related to the first lesson, Preparation. When you enter a business discussion, you need to be ready to tap dance: changing direction and improvising as needed if and when you meet resistance from the other party. In that regard, I estimate that I have been in hundreds of persuasion opportunities where the first approach I made did not receive a warm reception. But as I became a more experienced real estate entrepreneur, and learned the tools that others in the business have used to overcome resistance to certain ideas, I was able to better respond to these situations of initial negativity.

Part and parcel of knowing when to change direction is knowing your subject. As a real estate entrepreneur, you are often negotiating a deal with a number of different terms and conditions. As you enter a discussion with the other party, you need to be not only conversant with all the terms and conditions at issue, but also with the tools one can use to address the other party's specific concerns. Here's an example:

Let's say you own a building and you're negotiating a lease with a prospective tenant. You'd like to make this deal although you are concerned about the tenant's creditworthiness since it is a young company. The proposed lease is for 20,000 square feet (more than half of your building), and the total expense for brokerage commissions and fit-up allowances is $25/sf, or $500,000, all of which will be expended soon after the Lease is executed. In addition, the prospective tenant has requested six months of free rent, which, when added to the $500,000 up-front expenditure for brokerage and fit-up, makes you nervous: if the tenant gets into financial trouble in month seven, and can't start paying rent, you're out $500,000 and six months of rent.

You have your first meeting with the president of the prospective tenant (let's call him Mr. Tenant) and one of your goals is to establish a good working relationship with him. You realize that he could be offended

Confessions of a Real Estate Entrepreneur

by your verbalizing concerns about the company's creditworthiness. You know the subject needs to be raised, however, and you've spent some time before the meeting considering how to present your concerns to him.

You: Hi, Tenant, my name is Landlord. I'm happy to meet you.

Mr. Tenant: Yes, same here.

You: We are excited by your interest in our building. Your broker has told us about your company and it sounds like you have a great business.

Mr. Tenant: Thanks . . . we think so, and we believe your building can work well for us.

You: My understanding from our respective brokers is that we have agreed on most of the important deal points.

Mr. Tenant: That is my understanding as well.

You: In my mind, there are only two topics remaining to be discussed. I understand that you have requested a six-month free rent period. I'd like to speak to that. And, as you are probably aware, given the amount of our up-front expenditures to consummate your lease, my lender will want to be sure that we receive adequate credit enhancements, given that your company is only two years old.

By the way, I often blame my lender (they don't mind) when this type of discussion comes up. Sometimes a lender actually does have language in the mortgage requiring notification (and consent) prior to executing a lease with any tenant in excess of X square feet. And on occasion the lender may require its consent to any lease transaction where the rent is less than $Y/sf (just in case the lender forecloses on the building, it wants to be sure it's getting market rents). Most of the time, however, the lender lets you do your own thing and is not at all involved in leasing decisions. Still, a lot of businesspeople assume that a real estate owner has to go to his lender for major decisions, and so in order not to offend prospective tenants when I have this type of discussion, I tend to blame my concerns on my lender.

Mr. Tenant: As you know, we're a young company and have no credit history to speak of. That's why I offered through the brokers to give you a two-month security deposit.

You: Yes, I understand that. Unfortunately, given the amount of brokerage commissions we will be paying and the amount of the fit-up allowance we've agreed to, a two-month security deposit does not give us the coverage we need. I was hoping you would be able to increase that to six months. (**Approach #1**)

The Art of Persuasion

MR. TENANT: While I understand your point, I just do not have that kind of cash to leave in a security deposit account for the term of the lease.

YOU: Well, how about we do this: you make an initial deposit equal to six months' rent, and then, assuming everything works out fine, I return one-sixth of the deposit at the end of year two, one-sixth at the end of year three, and so on. (**Approach #2**)

MR. TENANT: No, that won't work for me because it still requires me to write a big check today and we really need to use that cash elsewhere right now.

YOU: Yes, of course, I can understand that. Do you believe your lender or investors would be willing to issue a letter of credit? (**Approach #3**)

Note that I'm not asking Mr. Tenant to tell me whether *he'd* be willing to give me a letter of credit. I want to give him an out . . . allowing him to blame it on others, just as I did with my lender above. I'm asking whether he thinks that *his lender or investors* would be willing. That way if he does not think he can get a letter of credit, the question and his response do not affect our relationship (i.e., *him* telling me no).

MR. TENANT: I had considered that too, but our lender and investors feel that any letters of credit they issue will have to be used for our material suppliers . . . without an uninterrupted and adequate supply of raw materials, we cannot grow the business the way we need to.

YOU (NEVER, NEVER LOSING PATIENCE): Makes sense. Well, I imagine you have some pretty well-heeled investors. Do you think one or more of them would consider personally guaranteeing some amount of your company's rent obligation? (**Approach #4**)

MR. TENANT: I could ask, but I doubt it.

YOU: As I have indicated, our lender's concern is that we are expending a large amount of money up front to pay your broker and to fit-up the space for your needs. These expenditures total about $500,000, and if our lender approves the lease to you, it will be advancing us some of this money, and would feel a lot better with the credit enhancements I've been mentioning. But perhaps we go at this a different way: Do you think you can get your broker to take his commission over time? Instead of getting paid on lease signing, perhaps he will allow us to pay him over the course of the lease. (**Approach #5**)

This is a good tack because it does not take anything away from the prospective tenant. But it holds risks for the owner as many brokers will resent this approach

Confessions of a Real Estate Entrepreneur

in that it puts them in the uncomfortable position of standing in the way of the deal if they refuse. And brokers will remember that you did this to them (and may, in the future, be reluctant to bring tenants to your buildings). On the other hand, when I have to use this approach, I always call and apologize to the broker and explain that without his help (in accepting his commission over time), there would be no deal and hence no commission.

> MR. TENANT: That sounds good to me, and I'm sure that our broker will work with you on this.
>
> YOU: Great, because that's about $75,000 of the $500,000 up-front money. Still, we have to address the $425,000 fit-up allowance. And, of course, we still have not discussed the free rent.
>
> MR. TENANT: That free rent is important to us . . . in any young business, cash flow is critical.
>
> YOU: Yes, I agree, but as you know, we not only have to keep our lender happy, we also have investors who we're responsible to. I can't be in a situation where they second-guess how we handled these matters, and they may do that if I don't adequately protect our position. So please forgive me but I have to play "responsible Landlord." So here's my suggestion: I'll agree to the six months of free rent but I can only give you two months up front, with the remaining four months in the twenty-fourth, thirty-sixth, forty-eighth, and sixtieth months of the lease. **(Approach #6)**

As you can see, what you are doing is trying to push back your up-front expenses until later in the lease. That way, if the tenant does get into financial trouble and you have to evict him, you are not out as much money as you would be if you gave him the free rent in the first six months of the lease.

> MR. TENANT: I can live with that.
>
> YOU: Well, we're really close now . . . somehow I must reduce our up-front exposure with the fit-up money. I have an idea: if you use our construction company to do the fit-up work, we'll reduce our profit on the job by 50 percent . . . based on a budget of ±$400,000, that will shave $40,000 off the cost. **(Approach #7)**
>
> MR. TENANT: As long as the quality of what they do is as good as everyone else, I have no problem with that.
>
> YOU: Well, that reduces our up-front expenditure to about $385,000. I have another suggestion: of that $385,000 we will pay you $200,000

216

immediately upon completion of your work in fitting out the space, but we want to have approval over the modifications that you make. In this way I feel that—and please forgive me for saying this—just in case you get into trouble, the work done to the space will be what a new tenant would want done anyway. (**Approach #8**)

MR. TENANT: Well, we weren't planning on doing anything crazy with the fit-up allowance. I'm told that at least $150,000 is for cosmetics, new carpet and paint, and new lighting. Do you have any problem with that?

YOU (SMILING): No, not so long as the color and carpet selections are not outrageous.

MR. TENANT (SMILING BACK): No problem, we just want a clean, standard look.

YOU (NOW WE'RE FRIENDS): Okay, I didn't think you were a pink and purple kind of guy. So do we have a deal? We'll reimburse you $200,000 as soon as your initial fit-up is completed and you'll agree to replace the carpet in the space, install new lighting, and repaint. Whatever else you do is up to you, and we'll reimburse you up to another $185,000, say at the beginning of year three, so long as your company has met all of the terms and conditions of the Lease Agreement to that point (**Approach #9**). Sound okay?

MR. TENANT: Yes, I can live with that . . . we have a deal.

What this imaginary dialogue shows you is that if you come into a discussion armed with all the tools a landlord has to protect his interest with a noncreditworthy tenant—in this case credit enhancements and devices for pushing back up-front expenditures—you can often bob and weave your way into a deal. When in a similar situation, listen to what the other party is telling you. Do not push him into a corner if you believe he can't give you what you want. Shuck and jive . . . come back at him from another angle and with different ideas. Do not press or embarrass. Listen, listen, listen. And while you're listening, keep rolling through your mental Rolodex of ways to handle the type of situation you are in. That is why I believe it's so important to know your business. The more tools you have in your toolbelt, the more likely it is that you'll make a deal.

Lesson 5: Listen, Listen, Listen

I am convinced that one of the most underrated skills in business is the art of listening. So many people enter a discussion and state their points, but they never

Confessions of a Real Estate Entrepreneur

really hear the opposing party. They miss key signals to what the other party will really do (or not do). And so they may push at the wrong times or ignore an opportunity to close the gap on a deal.

I think you can develop listening skills. Concentrate and stay very focused on what the other person (or people) in the conversation is saying. Don't let your mind drift. Watch for signals. Body language. Eyes shifting. Voice rising. Tempo of speech changing. What is this person telling you?

Listening is also a sign of respect. I don't know about you, but one of the things I hate is when I'm having a discussion with someone who seems to be drifting. What really drives me crazy, for example, is when, during the conversation, I say something like:

"Yes, I have two daughters. One graduated college last year and one is at the University of Wisconsin."

And the other person shortly thereafter asks: "Are your daughters in college?"

He or she might as well just wear a sign on his or her forehead:

I AM HERE WITH YOU IN BODY BUT MY MIND IS ELSEWHERE. YOU CAN KEEP TALKING, BUT JUST SO YOU KNOW, I'M NOT PAYING ATTENTION.

What a really bad way to establish a connection.

I find that I can use listening skills I've developed to win people over (see Lesson 2). When I'm with someone, I listen very, very carefully. And I remember stuff they told me that I can then bring up later. For example, someone may tell me in a conversation that he or she went to elementary school in Midland, Texas. Later in the conversation, sometimes much later or perhaps even in a subsequent meeting, I will refer to Midland and show the other person that I've listened to every word they have ever said to me. That always wins people over. In fact, it always wins me over when someone does it to me. So take advantage of opportunities to position yourself for a successful persuasion by LISTENING.

Lesson 6: Stay Focused

One of my favorite scenes is in *The Hustler,* a movie starring Paul Newman and Jackie Gleason (I realize that I'm dating myself). Paul Newman is the young-up-and-coming-pool-playing stud and Jackie Gleason is the established star (Minnesota Fats). Paul is beating Jackie big-time and keeps winning as the night wears on. But Jackie doesn't tire. At one point he excuses himself and goes to the men's room to freshen up. He washes his face, combs his hair, rubs talcum powder on his hands, and comes back ready to play, whereas Paul is tired (and a bit cocky). Soon afterward the tide turns and Jackie wins back everything he had lost and then cleans Paul out. What is the lesson? Never tire. Never lose focus.

Sometimes it will take you hours to win over someone. Maybe even multiple meetings. But never lose focus or concentration. When you let down, you can lose. You say something stupid. You interrupt your momentum. Your chance to convince the other party passes.

To stay focused, you have to stay alert and strong. Most of us know our body rhythms. I know that I am great before noon and start to get woozy from about 3 p.m. on. So I try to schedule important meetings for the early morning, hoping I will have achieved my goal well before I start to fade. Perhaps you're more of an afternoon/evening person. If so, you should avoid early morning meetings.

There are times, however, when you cannot control the time or duration of a meeting. In these situations, you just need to hang tough. I remember one closing that went from about 2 p.m. to 2 a.m. Needless to say, I was exhausted when I finally got home (as the new owner of an excellent property). But I'm proud to say that I did not lose focus . . . 12 hours of concentration fueled by adrenaline. Wow, did I get a lot of sleep the next few days.

Lesson 7: Establish Your Limits in Advance

As a corollary of Lesson 1 (Preparation), I do not believe you should enter a persuasion opportunity unless you have defined for yourself exactly where your limits are as to open deal points. As an example, you should know in advance what you'll sell for or what you'll buy for. This way you will not fall prey to fatigue or seduction or undue optimism or, I might add, the skills of a very good persuader across the table. In other words, you won't be caught in whatever web the other party is spinning.

I know I'm not that clearheaded when I get excited. Sometimes it's my own presentation and passion that gets me pumped up. Sometimes it's my reaction to the other player's point of view or attitude or condescension. Whatever, when I get revved up, I lose the ability to calculate in a clearheaded fashion.

So I try never to make important decisions during the heat of a meeting. Instead I endeavor to identify my lines in the cool light of day prior to the meeting. This helps me avoid making a commitment that later I'm unable to keep.

Knowing my parameters also helps me with persuasion. I come to the conversation knowing where I can bend and where I cannot. I don't waste time or focus trying to analyze a counterproposal that is outside my boundaries. I don't show weakness by hesitating or wavering, since I respond quickly because I know, from preparation, what I will or won't do.

People can be persuaded by firmness on your part. And firmness comes from knowing exactly where your parameters are. It's when you yourself are unsure that dumb stuff can happen.

Lesson 8: Become the Other Party

There are a lot of elements to this point, but the main thrust of it is that people generally make up their minds about something as much for subconscious reasons as for conscious reasons. My belief is that there is always a lot of subliminal stuff going on when we decide on something. And as a persuader, I feel it's my job to try to connect up with the subliminal side of the person I'm trying to persuade.

Now needless to say, unless I've known someone a long time, I will never really get into his head and know what motivates him. What I'm talking about here are perhaps more superficial levels of connection that are still, in my view, very important.

What I try to do when I'm engaged in persuasion is convince the other party that I am a lot *like them*. That whatever they are (short of criminal or some such thing), I am too. You might think of the chameleon, the animal that can change its color so it blends in with its surroundings so much as to be invisible. My goal is similar: to adapt to the personality of the other party, in tone, manner, speech, and approach, to make him or her very comfortable. I think about doing this in a variety of ways.

One example, of course, is the substance of the conversation. Before we get into the details of a persuasion, I am always searching for common ground that may temper the initial strangeness between any two people who have just met. How many times when you're meeting someone for the first time do you experience an immediate connection once the two of you hit on a subject of mutual interest? You're at a cocktail party and doing the normal small talk and then, voilà, something comes up that's of interest to both parties and the conversation takes off. Well, that's what I try to do right from the start . . . find something of interest to the other person and then go with it. I'm a big reader. I am the ultimate "Jack-of-All-Trades, Master of None" when it comes to subjects that may interest people. I know enough to speak to almost any topic, although not enough to get into any depth. Still, I figure if I can get the conversation to first base and get someone talking about _____ (sports, travel, science, art, etc.), that is, whatever interests them, then there will be an immediate warming of the natural coolness that exists between two strangers.

After I've found some kind of common ground on which to develop our relationship, I pay attention to the vocabulary, syntax, and tempo of the other party's speaking. I want to match it because I want the other party to think that I'm just like him. I obviously would not use multi-syllable SAT words with an unschooled person. And I've used off-color words with people who sprinkle their conversation that way. I'm also a big believer in mirroring the pace of the other party's speaking style. I am pretty good at parroting what I hear. So when I have a fix on the other party's tempo and rhythm of speaking, I slowly begin to match it. Most of the time, for me anyway, this means slowing down. In that regard, I cannot tell you how many times I've reminded myself over the years: "Slow it down, slow it down . . . listen to the pace . . . you're going too fast."

So what do you think about this? Do you think it's deceitful? I don't. I'm not trying to trick someone into doing something they don't want to do. I'm not that good. The people with whom I am engaging are not going to be bamboozled by me, nor am I trying for that. I'm just trying to establish a bond between us that will hopefully lead to a successful persuasion.

In short, people are most comfortable with others who are like them. The normal barriers we have all built up to strangers come down that much more quickly when people sense the person they're speaking with is just like them. All I'm trying to do is accelerate the pace at which that initial strangeness will diminish. And my ultimate hope, of course, is to find a common meeting ground with my new best friend.

Lesson 9: Two Beats before Speaking

Over time I have learned to "listen" to what I'm going to say before I say it. I think everyone can do this if they just concentrate. When I'm engaged in a persuasion, I try to stay in the "zone" by using half of my brain to listen carefully to what the other party is saying and the other half of my brain to play out my response. The goal, of course, is to test-run my next comment before it leaves my mouth.

I cannot say that I can do this all the time, and like everyone, there are times when I desperately wish that I could pull back a comment I had just made. But when my technique works, it can save me from saying something stupid or embarrassing.

What I try to do is consciously create two beats between the thought in my head and the articulation of it through my mouth. I've found that after years of trying to do this, I no longer even know I'm doing it. Over the years I guess I have trained my brain to set off a warning bell if I'm about to say something really dumb. Here's an example that occurred during a simple conversation I was having just last week; I was not trying to persuade anyone of anything, but in this case the business habit I had developed saved me a red face.

I was having lunch with a friend of mine who I knew was going through a divorce. We were discussing a deal and he was complaining about a broker whom he felt was delaying things. My friend was going off on this broker, and I didn't like the guy either and wanted to support my friend's position and say something. I remembered that this broker had been married and divorced three times in five years and a comment popped *into my mind* that was uncomplimentary about his marital success rate. And then I heard myself *in my head* making the comment. Fortunately, however, since my brain was two beats ahead of my mouth, I was able to decide that the comment was inappropriate to a guy going through a divorce. So I shut up and said nothing.

Now I know that I certainly did not invent the two beat policy. The adage "Think before you speak" is ancient and wise advice. I'm just suggesting that when you're engaged in a persuasion, you need to concentrate on your thoughts and try to put a little censor between them and the vocalization of them.

Lesson 10: Don't Push

I think that the most common mistake I see in communication intended to persuade is the PUSH, when one party is trying too hard to persuade another. Like anything, there is subtlety required in good persuasion. You have to find the right balance between energy and commitment on the one hand, and pressure and pushiness on the other.

Start with the proposition that people are smart. That whoever you are trying to persuade can sense when you're anxious. And understand that most people react negatively to pressure. Hard selling is, to me, a waste of time and energy. People will not make a decision in your favor no matter how firm your voice or steely your resolve. They will make a decision in your favor *if* they believe that such a decision will work to *their* favor. That is the most basic principle to understand about persuasion: **people do what they do and decide what they decide because they believe the action or decision they're making is to their advantage**.

If you're going to be a successful persuader, you need to figure out what will convince the other party that your proposal or offer or suggestion to them is *to their advantage*. It's okay that what you propose is obviously good for you. People accept that and are generally comfortable with win-win situations. They might like to believe that what you're suggesting is better for them than for you, but they'll still be okay *if it's good for you too*.

I've seen young entrepreneurs try too hard on many occasions. They may really need a favorable decision from the other party and they just can't help pushing too hard. It is always a mistake. Or they may be very close to a deal they have been working on for a long time, can feel the finish line, and push the pedal to the floor in their anxiety to get the deal done. MISTAKE. Often in the real estate game you can be 99.99 percent of the way to the end line *but* without that last 1/100 of 1 percent, you are nowhere. Without closing the deal, all the work you've done to that point in time is meaningless. In this situation we are all especially vulnerable to pressing for a decision that will get us that last 1/100 of 1 percent. **My advice**: Train yourself to keep your cool until you pass the finish line. NEVER, NEVER LOSE PATIENCE. When I feel myself doing that, I try to go into a meditative kind of state in which I repeat the mantra: DO NOT PRESS . . . DO NOT PRESS.

Even though you're 99.99 percent to the end line, if you press for that last 1/100 of 1 percent, your persuasive skills will be diminished. KEEP YOUR COOL. KEEP YOUR COOL. Recently I was tested in this regard:

> I was acting as a broker for a public company and had worked on negotiating a 50,000 sf long-term lease for them. The potential commission to me if the deal got done was $400,000.
>
> All the major deal points were negotiated, and the lease documents had been prepared and reviewed by the respective attorneys. Everyone had signed off on the deal and the Lease Agreement was on my client's desk for signature. Then, out of the blue, my client's general counsel decided he wanted to take one last look at the Lease Agreement.
>
> Maybe because he was just feeling ornery that day, he came up with two points he wanted in the Lease that were extremely minor in scope and almost silly to ask for. What's more, these points were in fact so insignificant that I feared the Landlord would be offended by the request (especially in the eleventh hour, fifty-ninth minute, and fifty-ninth second). I had two choices: either convince my client's general counsel to drop his requests or convince the Landlord to acquiesce. Since the protocol in this deal (and most deals) was that I speak with the Landlord's broker, I called him up:
>
> ME: I am almost embarrassed to ask you this, but my client has two more small requests.
>
> HIM: Are you kidding . . . these are such minor points, my client will be upset just by the asking.
>
> ME: I know, I know, but please give it a try.
>
> He does and comes back to me.
>
> HIM: Jim, my client got really upset with me for asking. He said "NO" about five times. We have negotiated a good deal for your client over the last several months. We have negotiated the language of the Lease Agreement. Enough is enough. Tell your client to quit messing around.
>
> ME: Okay.
>
> I knew now that somehow I needed to convince the general counsel to drop his requests. This is the kind of persuasion that can get your

Confessions of a Real Estate Entrepreneur

heart beating. If I was successful, we had a deal and I was $400,000 to the good. If I was unsuccessful and he got his back up and stood pat, and the Landlord did the same, no deal and no $400,000. This is an example of being 99.99 percent there but actually nowhere without the last 1/100 of 1 percent.

So I scheduled a phone call with the general counsel. As I prepared for this conversation, I had to resist what every bone in my body was screaming at me to say:

> YOU HAVE TO BE KIDDING. WE'VE GOTTEN ALL OF OUR MAJOR DEAL POINTS, INCLUDING SEVERAL SIZABLE CONCESSIONS FROM THE LANDLORD. THE LEASE AGREEMENT HAS BEEN NEGOTIATED AT LENGTH, WITH A LOT OF TIME INVESTED ON ALL SIDES. THESE LAST TWO POINTS OF YOURS ARE SO MINOR AS TO BE INSIGNICANT. YOU'RE NOT REALLY GOING TO PURSUE THEM, ARE YOU?

But an hour before the conversation was to happen I focused on my mantra and repeated over and over: DO NOT PRESS. DO NOT PRESS. DO NOT PRESS. And I tried to think of ways to convince the general counsel that he did not need what he was asking for. I came up with an approach that helped him feel that he was getting his way: I suggested that some of the other language in the Lease that he had negotiated and persuaded the Landlord to include would, as a practical matter, cover his two new points. I did not want him to feel that he was in a corner. I wanted him to feel that he had raised legitimate points but that in practice he would get what he wanted anyway. Therefore, by dropping his points, he would not lose anything.

Our conversation was calm and measured. I quietly explained to him how other provisions in the Lease Agreement would protect his company. Fortunately, he agreed and decided to drop his points. And the deal got done.

We all get excited and anxious when we're in the heat of the battle, especially when we sense that we're close to a great deal or a good payday. Any of us can lose our heads trying to cross those final inches to the goal line. But just as in football, when you extend your arm and try to reach the ball across the goal line, sometimes it can be swatted out of your hands (I like sports analogies). Hence a fumble. I'm sure you get it.

There is a subset to the DON'T PUSH rule that I subscribe to: Don't Recriminate. In business, people will disappoint you. Over the years, many people have told me they're going to do this or that, and sometimes they just don't do it. Other times people do something harmful to me, even though they said that they would do just the opposite. You know what? That's people . . . we all make mistakes, and often it's not out of malice. Here's my rule when this happens to me: I NEVER PUSH THE PERSON WHO HURT ME INTO A CORNER. I always give them a gracious out. I never, never want to burn a bridge.

A friend of mine has a similar approach but states it in slightly different terms. Whenever one of us would get angry at someone who "did us wrong," my friend would say: "Jim, if you're going to go after the king, you'd better kill him." My friend talks like this . . . he's a little Yodalike, but I think his point is essentially: "Be careful about striking out at someone because they will most likely strike back at you, and before you know it, you have a war on your hands."

In life, you just never know what the future will hold. My rule is that I do not want to ever create animosity with someone who may someday be able to help me. Many years ago I felt that the CFO of a company cheated me out of a $125,000 commission. He had asked me to lease his building, and I had sent him a Commission Agreement for signature. But he stalled returning it to me. In the meantime I had found a tenant for his building and my client liked this space and instructed me to make a deal for it. But I still had no signed Commission Agreement. And, unfortunately for me, I was no longer in a position of control. My client wanted the space and so I had to (and did) do my best to get it for him. Since I never got a signed Commission Agreement, I had no legal basis to get paid. And . . . I got stiffed.

Now, I was very angry, of course. But I knew that the CFO was basically a decent guy and that someone somewhere was forcing him to do what he was doing. So although I was unhappy and told him that, I never went to the next level and threw in his face the fact that he was the front man in what I considered a scam job. In other words, I never pushed him into a corner. I subsequently learned that the CEO of the company the CFO worked for (his boss) had made him withhold the commission to me as the company was in financial trouble and not in a position to make a commission payment. Between me and the company's survival, I was a lot less important. When I learned this, I was happy that I hadn't really struck out at the CFO. I had been able to keep myself in check and did not throw a tantrum. I did not sue anybody. I said to myself, "People do bad things at times, but that does not make them bad people . . . Stay with this guy."

Many years later the CFO and I ran into each other and gave each other a big hug. And he is now running another company and offered to help me with a charity event I sponsor. And, of course, I will soon be pitching him on having my company represent his company in a lease renewal they will be facing. All's well that ends well, and things will usually end well if you're patient.

Conclusion

There are many, many ways to accomplish a successful persuasion. I have tried to identify the rules that I've set for myself. There are of course many others, and perhaps some that will work particularly well for you. There's just one point I need you to take away from this chapter:

> The probability of success in persuading someone to decide in your favor can be greatly increased if you think through the art and the process of persuasion.

In other words, don't just wing it. Don't be like the people who go to a casino and put their chips down and hope for Lady Luck. That may be a fun way to play craps or blackjack or whatever, but it's not the way that is most likely to lead to success at the tables. Learn the rules of the game. Learn the odds. Play smart and with a strategy. Know your limits. The game is to win. Have fun after the win is secured.

20

Success Skills

$\mathbf{O}$ne of the joys of playing at the real estate game for 25 years is that I've met an amazing collection of entrepreneurs. Real estate brokers who make $5 million a year. Developers who take huge risks for multimillion-dollar rewards. Builders who construct enormous buildings in the middle of cities. People who live by their wit and who understand and live with risk, many of whom started with nothing and today have mega-millions.

Okay, so maybe you can tell: I'm an entrepreneur groupie. I love people with high energy, passion, and commitment. I'm fascinated by them and try to learn from them. I watch them and ask a lot of questions. I want to know why they are successful. I try to steal their tricks and assimilate their habits into my life.

This chapter, on Success Skills, is what I have learned over 25 years. Even though 90 percent of the successful entrepreneurs I've been involved with are real estate players, I believe the reasons these people are successful (the theme of this chapter) are applicable to whatever business you may be in or considering. So hopefully this chapter will be helpful to you whether or not you ever venture into the real estate world.

Now let me state my premise right up front: I DO NOT BELIEVE THAT SUCCESS IS AN ACCIDENT. What I do believe is that successful people apply themselves in a way that maximizes the probability of positive outcomes. I also believe that there are commonalities—that successful people in all walks of life do many of the same things to achieve success.

My goal is to identify and discuss the commonalities I have observed. I believe that one can improve his probability of success by watching and emulating successful people. That is why I'm writing this chapter: to give you the insight of what I have seen in the hope that the thoughts herein will help you direct your life energy toward extraordinary business (and personal) reward. So here goes: 13 "Success Skills" presented in no particular order (except the last one).

Success Skill 1: Passion

All of the successful real estate entrepreneurs I have known are passionate about what they do. They really love the game. Many of them are beyond needing money, but they still spend 12-hour days (or more) playing the real estate game for the pure joy and satisfaction it brings.

With passion comes energy. Recently I was shopping to buy a condominium unit in Manhattan. I went to two sales offices for two different new projects. The salesperson in the first office was energetic and attentive. The salesperson in the second office was a notch or two less energized. *But what a difference that notch or two made.* In comparison, the second salesperson seemed flat, and the first condominium project just seemed better to me in some undefined way. My point: a small difference in energy can sometimes be the difference between success and failure.

If you're like the second salesperson, you need to ramp it up if you want great things from the real estate game. If you aren't excited about and energized to be real estate entrepreneuring, then you may fall flat too. My general rule is that if you aren't passionate and energetic and hyped up about what you do, then do something else. The business world has a way of rewarding high energy and punishing anything less.

I'm lucky because I kind of happened into real estate entrepreneuring. I was certainly not one of those kids who knew from an early age what he wanted to be. Upon getting out of law school, I read a book or two about real estate, tried a deal, and I was hooked.

What specifically do I love about the business? I love that it is primarily a people business. As I've stated in this book several times, the real estate game is about basic stuff. You don't need to be a techie to succeed. You don't need years of specialized training. You don't need the skills of a scientist, or a linguist, or a mathematician. You don't even need to start with much (or any) capital. You just need to be good with people.

I love that success comes by living off your wits. There is no one path between Point A and Point B. There is no road map. I get up every morning with

Success Skills

no prescribed route to get what I want (more money coming in than going out). There is something very exciting and energizing about that. At times it can be scary too. Perhaps like people who seek out the scariest rides in an amusement park, entrepreneurs thrive on that feeling of half fear, half excitement that comes from not knowing how they will earn their next dollar. I know that I get a high from uncovering a good opportunity, concluding a successful persuasion, meeting an interesting player, learning a new concept or technique, brokering or closing a great deal, and, of course, consummating a successful project.

People who are passionate about what they do, do not need an alarm clock. Most of the time they cannot wait to get at the game. The challenge, excitement, risk, and reward . . . it all just waits for them every morning. If this is not how you feel about what you're doing every day, then perhaps it's time to make a change.

I learned about passion for what one does when I was a teenager. I grew up in Perkins Township, Ohio. At the time, it was a very small town with not much there except a large armory for the Ohio National Guard. The armory was a cavernous building that the National Guard used for periodic meeting and marching. On occasion there would be other events held there, and in the winter of 1965 it was the site of a scheduled concert.

A group of up-and-coming musicians was traveling across the United States by bus. Every day they would stop in a different town, perform, and leave. One night in February 1965 they were scheduled to stop at the Perkins Armory. I lived very close to the armory so I watched as it was set up for the performers. A small stage was erected and about 500 bridge chairs were set out, since the organizers expected a big crowd from the neighboring towns of Sandusky, Huron, Milan, and others. Large amplifiers were set up throughout the building.

The bus of musicians arrived about 5 p.m., and about that same time Mother Nature also made an appearance: it started to snow . . . really hard. By 7 p.m. the roads were very bad and it was clear that people were not going to be able to get to the armory for the 8 p.m. concert. Since all the musicians were already there, the organizers decided that the concert would go forward. As I lived nearby (within walking distance), I was able to go to the armory. There were about nine other people there.

The musicians came on the stage one by one. Needless to say, it was incredibly awkward, for each singer was performing in front of only 10 people. Given this situation, each performer just went through *the motions* of his or her performance, getting off the stage as quickly as possible. That is, until the final performer. His name was Tom Jones and he was a young Welsh singer. He had recently recorded a song called "What's New Pussycat?" Here's what happened when he took the stage:

JONES (IN A HEAVY WELSH ACCENT): I am very disappointed to see so few of you. But I want to sincerely thank those of you who could get here. I have a new song that I would like to sing for you, and I hope you will enjoy it.

And he belts out "What's New Pussycat?" like he was performing for 10,000 people at Caesar's Palace. Given that there was no one in the room, the amplifiers shook the place. When he was done, I could not catch my breath. His singing had been so powerful that the 10 of us in the audience for this "private" performance were stunned. Tom Jones smiled, bowed (standing ovation), waved, and left the stage.

As I walked home that night, I thought about what had happened. Jones (who went on to have a very successful career, for those of you who do not know of him) did not care that there were only 10 people there that evening. He wanted to be sure that each of those 10 remembered him (and needless to say, I have). He had an enormous passion and energy for performing. And even if the audience was only a couple of farmers who lived near the Perkins Township Armory, he was going to give them 100 percent. And he did!

Perhaps something clicked inside of me that night. Perhaps I recognized something important, about which I am now writing. If you're going to do something, do it to the best of your ability. Give it 100 percent all the time. And if you don't have a passion for what you do, find something else to do. Those who are successful at the real estate game love what they're doing. They are passionate about the process. I don't think you can learn passion. **I think, rather, the goal in life is to find and pursue exactly what it is that you are passionate about.** If it's not real estate, it's still not too late to toss this book out the window.

Success Skill 2: Work Ethic

I have never thought that I am the smartest guy around. But I can be the hardest worker. Almost all of the successful real estate entrepreneurs I know are prodigious workers. They know that "the devil is in the details," and they do not want to let a successful deal slip by because they were not paying attention to the details.

Work can be defined in many ways. Work is not just sitting at your desk and reading documents or making phone calls. Work can be driving around looking for opportunities. Work can be going to social functions attended by people you want to meet. Work can be scanning the newspaper or trade journals, looking for ideas. Work can be speaking with other entrepreneurs about new ideas and concepts.

Many of the super-successful real estate entrepreneurs I know are always "working." Their minds always racing with things to do, ideas to consider, and people to meet. Except when I'm asleep (and there are many nights when I wake up with an idea), my mind is always on, even if in low gear. Often I will be watching television, or reading the newspaper, or taking a shower, and *out of nowhere* a thought pops into my head. I did not even know that my mind was engaged when, WHOOSH . . . some business idea whisks into my consciousness. How that happens, I have no idea.

Success Skills

Obviously there is a time to shut down and reprogram. "All work makes Jack a dull boy" and all that. And I do shut down at times. Certainly I know that life is not about making money. But remember, to me, real estate entrepreneuring is fun. And maybe that explains the work ethic of successful entrepreneurs. To them, there's no line between work and play. They like what they do and so when they are working, they're having fun.

I have been accused of being a workaholic because I spend a lot of time doing business. I realize that this comment is not meant in a complimentary way, but if *workaholic* means someone who wants to be the best he can at his chosen profession, I'm fine with it. In other endeavors, such as sports, people speak admiringly of an athlete who has an "incredible work ethic." Such an athlete works very hard at being the best that he can be. If my spending time reading, writing, or looking at deals is my way of being the best I can be at my profession, why is that any different? So here's my answer to those who accuse me—pejoratively—of being a workaholic:

> I love what I do. I am trying to be the best real estate entrepreneur that I can be. Sometimes the difference between excellence and mediocrity is not that great. I want to do everything I can to make sure I end up in the excellence category . . . So go pound sand.

I do not mean to suggest that I never stray from my program or get lazy at times. But I have developed some kind of built-in control mechanism. Whenever I feel myself getting lazy and taking a shortcut, I try to immediately think about the difference between success and failure . . . and remind myself what a small difference there can be. I say to myself "Don't be a jerk . . . do you want success or failure?" And then, before I know it, I am usually back doing things the right (not lazy) way. At least that's the plan.

Finally, I do recognize that passion and a prodigious work ethic can get in the way of other parts of one's life. Entrepreneurs make sacrifices. They may not spend the time raising their children that others do, or read as many great novels as nonentrepreneurs, or just relax as much as others do. Each of us has to make a choice as to how we want to live. I grew up without much. I always wanted more. For me, the real estate game has been my way to spend time enjoying my days on earth and realizing some of my childhood dreams. I've tried to find a balance in my personal and business lives. Finding that balance is not always easy, of course. Anyway, here's what I want you to take from this lesson:

> If you're not willing to work hard at the real estate game, do not come out of the dugout.

Success Skill 3: Physicality

I've watched top real estate players over 25 years. Most of them are very physically active people. I have my own theory on exercise (I work out a lot), and since this is my book, I'm going to espouse it:

> To be successful in business, you have to be physically active.

Physically active people are, in my view, disciplined in their approach to life. They think more clearly and for longer periods of time. They have higher energy levels. In short, they are more effective. There, I said it. Perhaps I'll get some hate mail from super-successful couch potatoes. You know what . . . don't bother. I know that my views do not apply to everyone in the world. I'm telling you what *I believe* is most likely to lead to your personal success.

I've built up my own workout schedule over many years. I used to be much less active and would skip days and weeks at a time. But, little by little, I found that the more I exercised, the more I enjoyed life and the better I did at it. In the last 20 years or so I have been pretty religious about exercise: Every day I either run, swim, lift weights, or do some other kind of aerobic activity. I also do yoga once or twice a week (terrific for core strength and flexibility). Those are just my personal preferences. Obviously, there are many ways to achieve the goal of being physically active.

Success Skill 4: No Sense of Entitlement

The entrepreneurs I know all seem to have one attitude in common. They do not feel that they're entitled to anything . . . they feel that they have to work for everything they get.

There's a scene in the movie *Kramer vs. Kramer* that helps me explain my sentiment. Dustin Hoffman is a divorced father (Meryl Streep walked out on him) who will lose joint custody of his son if he does not get a job. The problem is that it's the holiday season and everyone in the business world is partying; consequently he's having a very hard time trying to find someone who is even willing to interview him.

Fortunately, he gets a job interview at an ad agency in New York City. Unfortunately, the appointment is scheduled for the afternoon of that agency's holiday party. He shows up in his best outfit, well-groomed and nervous. When he gets there, everyone is partying, drinking, carousing, and not at all interested in interviewing a new hire. He finally finds someone to help him locate the person he's supposed to meet. The interviewer steps out of the party, with a drink in one hand and a beautiful woman on his arm, and tells Dustin to wait in the lobby. So here's the scene: Dustin Hoffman is sitting by himself. It's the holiday season. Everyone else in the world is happily partying. He just wants a job so he does not lose custody of his son. If he does not get that job by the first business day in January, the court will take his son from him. Dustin's face tells it all.

Do you ever get the feeling that Dustin had? That the whole world is at a party and you have to scratch for everything you get? Well, the opposite of that feeling is a sense of entitlement. People who feel entitled think the world owes them a living. They think they're entitled to a paycheck, a bonus, and a certain number of sick and vacation days—a good life with lots of trimmings.

The very successful entrepreneurs I know are more like Dustin Hoffman sitting in the anteroom. They do not expect anything to be handed to them. They want to get into the party big-time but they know they have to scratch and crawl to get there. Even when they have all the money they could possibly spend, they still feel the need to fight their way into whatever party (level of achievement) they have identified as being important. They take nothing for granted.

In my view, an attitude of NON-entitlement will eventually lead to success. Those people who expect that good things should just happen to them most often die waiting. Good things do happen, I believe . . . and not-so-good things. But feeling entitled to the good ones and feeling picked upon when the not-so-good things happen is, in my view, the wrong approach to life.

You want good things to happen? THEN GET OFF YOUR BUTT AND MAKE THEM HAPPEN. Forgive the bromide, but I do believe that success is 99 percent perspiration and 1 percent inspiration. Yes, I do believe that luck can be a factor. But I do not want to depend on it. As Branch Rickey (baseball executive) said: "Luck is the residue of design."

What I believe in most is hard work, drive, determination, and perseverance. I believe that success (both material and metaphysical) will eventually come to those who feel that nobody owes them anything, who feel that they should try their best every single hour of every single day, who feel grateful for what they have and what they acquire, and who do not moan about what else they might have.

Success Skill 5: Discipline

Martha Stewart is reputed to have said, "I can bend steel with my mind." What I believe she meant is that she had the ability to control her thoughts and to focus with heat-like intensity when necessary. That is mental discipline.

I think discipline is critically important for the entrepreneur. Mental and physical discipline. Exercising, eating right, taking care of oneself (making sure the machine is always working). Reading, networking, studying . . . doing what-

Confessions of a Real Estate Entrepreneur

ever one can do to improve his or her knowledge and thereby the prospect of success. Discipline in one's business life: Taking controlled risks. Never getting lazy. Never taking shortcuts or doing less due diligence than is appropriate.

Successful real estate entrepreneurs have learned the benefits of discipline in both their work and their personal lives. There are always exceptions, of course, but the super-successful real estate entrepreneurs I know live a controlled existence. They take care of their bodies. They pay attention to their appearance. They read several newspapers and periodicals a week so they're up on the latest news. They have "to do" lists. They are usually organized, or anxious when they're not. They are disciplined in their approach to deal-making. In that regard, they do not rush headlong into a deal whose numbers are not compelling. They take on risk, of course (part of the game), but they try to minimize and quantify it as best they can. They do not jump at office deals when their expertise is retail or visa versa. And so on.

One of the reasons there were significant real estate problems in the early 1990s (rents and prices dropped as much as 50 percent in some areas of the country) was because everyone and their brother was buying or financing real estate. Many of these people had no knowledge, experience, or business model. They just wanted to be in the game, and their approach was haphazard. And a lack of discipline by both lenders and buyers pushed prices beyond reasonable levels, leading to and exacerbating an eventual crash in value.

I'm not saying that real estate players are conservative. Far from it. Real estate entrepreneurs have to live with risk if they're going to earn entrepreneurial-level returns. Rather, they are disciplined in their approach to buying and financing. And in adhering to the rules they apply to their business practices. This is not conservative; this is smart.

Finally, discipline is needed to deal with the disappointments that inevitably occur in the life of any entrepreneur. Each entrepreneur handles setbacks differently, but those who can put the disappointments behind them quickly will be in the best position to find success around the corner.

Here is a regimen of mine that has stood me in good stead over 25 years of entrepreneuring: I know there will be good days and bad days in the deal-making world. No matter how hard I try, there will be times when I cannot control all aspects of a deal and things will, at times, spin out of control. When I have those days, I try to "steel" my mind to the disappointment. When I get up the next day, I try to perform my usual routine: exercise, read the newspapers, make "to do" lists, and so on—in other words, follow the same pattern I've followed every day before that. I do not let my mind wander to the negatives of the previous day. Instead, I try to think of any possible way that I can reverse the problem I am having with the deal. And if that's not within my control, I start thinking about the next deal. I get up off the ground and go forward, with no concession to the problems or difficulties. Yes, I hear you thinking: "Easier said than done." And of course you're right. But you must try.

Sometimes it takes enormous discipline to follow my regimen. But there is something safe in the regularity of it all. I know there will be good days to follow. I know that if I just keep doing all the right things, there will be a reward for my efforts, maybe not right away, but eventually.

Success Skill 6: Networking

Great real estate entrepreneurs are almost always great networkers, and I know many who started in business with absolutely nothing—no money, no contacts, no fancy education—and worked and networked their way to millions of dollars. These entrepreneurs know some important things about business:

People Are the Key

I can't speak to all businesses, but I do know that in the real estate world people skills are paramount. In short, if you can win over people who can help you on your way up the ladder, you're going to do very well.

My sense is that great networkers are sincere and interested in people. Not all of their friends are rich and powerful. Not all of their friends have the ability to help them. But great networkers understand that the more friends and contacts they have, the greater their chance of success. It's almost a mathematical certainty.

Networking Should Be Part of Your Business Model

As a young lawyer I was very stupid about networking. I thought if I could learn everything about real estate law, read all the articles on important legal issues, and do an extraordinary job for my clients, I would be a very successful lawyer. Contrast me with another lawyer I knew. He was as smart as I (or smarter). But instead of spending hours studying the law, he spent his days networking. Like me, he was new in town and had no idea who could help him. He just had a strategy: meet everyone in town, tell them what you do for a living, give them your business card, and learn a little bit about what they do. And you know what? His approach to business was more successful than mine. While I waited for the phone to ring, his was ringing. While I would give 100 percent focus to my clients' matters, he would give 90 percent of his attention and almost always do just as good a job (and the clients never knew the difference). The fact is, in the first years of our parallel business lives, he was more successful than I was.

I have since learned that networking (and marketing oneself) needs to be part of every entrepreneur's business model. So start now . . . whether you're a 20-year-old or a 60-year-old. You are going to meet people every single day. Learn about what they do. Tell them what you do. Set a goal to meet people who can help you in specific areas of your business. Call them. Ask them for advice. You'll be surprised at the number of positive responses you will get.

When my kids got old enough to understand business, I told each of them to keep a notebook and make a notation in it for every person they meet. I suggested they write down whatever they learned about this individual . . . both business and personal. Then keep referring to the notebook every six months or so . . . update as possible, and attempt to stay in touch with anyone who might be helpful to them. And, of course, when a specific need or opportunity arises, I suggested they contact their new "acquaintance." Someday, I told them, they would look back at this notebook and be shocked at how it had helped them achieve whatever targets they had set for themselves.

Since everyone you meet is a candidate to help you, here is a good rule (a variation of the Golden Rule):

Treat everyone you meet in life with grace and courtesy.

Here's an example that illustrates the point. It's also one of my favorite stories. It's about a good friend of mine who is now the head of a national commercial real estate brokerage company, and who started in business with no money or contacts and worked (and networked) his way to the top of the pyramid. He often tells young brokers about his first deal:

> My friend was 20 years old. As the youngest broker in his firm, he got the least interesting (and potentially least lucrative) assignments. One day he was working the phone handling cold calls (sometimes referred to as "floor duty"), and he got a call from a young lawyer who had decided to go into practice for himself.
>
> LAWYER: Hi, my name is Joe Lawyer and I need someone who can help me find a single office for myself. I know that's not much of an assignment so maybe someone could just give me advice as to how to do that.
>
> MY FRIEND: Well, I'm just starting out myself so I'm happy to help you. I'll get a list of tenants who have a single office to sublease and we can go looking.
>
> LAWYER: I really appreciate that.
>
> And so the young lawyer goes looking with my friend, who is spending a lot of time with no prospect of a big reward. Eventually my friend finds an office that works for the young lawyer and makes a $500 commission. Considering all the work necessary to find this space, this sum was not much of a return on my friend's time.
>
> Now fast-forward two years. My friend gets a call from the young lawyer.
>
> MY FRIEND: So how is your law business working out? I'm sorry I lost touch with you. I called a few times and you were out. I should have left a message.
>
> LAWYER: No problem. Well, to tell you the truth, it didn't work out. In my specialty I learned that a single practitioner just can't make it. The good news is that I attracted the attention of a big law firm, with whom I am now associated.
>
> MY FRIEND: That's great.
>
> LAWYER: And there is a reason I'm calling. Our law firm is moving and I've been asked to head the search committee, and I'd like to hire you to represent us. Would you be willing to do that?
>
> MY FRIEND: Happily.
>
> And the young lawyer's law firm moved and used my friend to represent them. It was a big firm and a big deal. My friend's commission: $1 million. Not bad for a 22-year-old just starting out in the business!

Confessions of a Real Estate Entrepreneur

The Little Things You Do Can Make a Big Difference

I'm always impressed when I meet someone who met me, say, a year or two earlier and he will refer to a conversation we had in our first meeting. We might have spoken about a trip I was about to take. Or some workout program I was trying. Or some book I was reading. Yet the individual will remember our discussion and ask me about it. How can I not be impressed? How can I not feel that this person had a real interest in me and my doings? How could I not consider helping this person if and when an opportunity arose?

> I deal with some top executives in the business world, and I'm constantly taken by their graciousness, even though I'm not someone who can be of great help to them. Years ago I represented (as an attorney) the CEO of a huge company on his personal real estate closing. He paid me a nice fee. This is an important and powerful guy, and everyone in the business world wanted to get to him. Anyway, after his matter was resolved, I (always networking) invited him and his wife to dinner with my wife and me. The four of us had a very nice time, and since I had extended the invitation, I picked up the check. Two days later I got a thank you note from him:

> Dear Jim:

> Just a short note to tell you what a nice time Donna and I had with you and Carol. It was fun to hear about your growing up in a farm town in Ohio . . . it brought back memories of my own childhood. I hope to see you again soon.

> Warm regards,

He didn't have to write me this note. He had already thanked me for picking up the check. But in a way, he couldn't help himself. He had made his way to the top of a major corporation by networking, part of which was a gracious expression of thanks to anyone who had shown him a courtesy. He knew there was little chance that I could ever do something for his company (or for him), but he did what he'd always done: He took the time to write a note. He showed his appreciation, demonstrated that he had paid attention to our conversation, and indicated that he would like to see more of me (which may or may not have been true, but it's a great way to close a thank you note).

Here's what I need you to take from my book:

If becoming a good networker is not part of your business model, then get a new business model.

Success Skill 7: Visualization

I remember when I started out in business. I had an office the size of a large closet. I had a small desk, an old phone, and one tiny window. I had no assistant. What was most humiliating, however, was that the office was located within the space of another company and all day long people visiting that company (no one was visiting me in those days) would walk by my closet-sized office and probably think: "Wow, I wonder what that guy is being punished for."

Yet even though I had no money, no contacts, and no reason to think what I was thinking, I always had a visual image of myself 20 years later with a beautiful office, a phone with all sorts of extensions, and a top-flight assistant. And today I have those things.

Visualization is like a self-fulfilling prophecy. Many successful entrepreneurs start their business life with a picture of their future, even if they have no basis for it. Yet somehow the picture seems real to them, and many feel that it's only a matter of time before they will be living the image. And, in truth, the imaginary picture can spur them on through difficult times.

It's like when I'm working out. At the tail end of a long, exhausting session on the treadmill, when my mind starts to think about slowing down (as Vince Lombardi said, "Fatigue makes cowards of us all"), I switch the channel in my brain to the shower I'll be taking in 10 minutes. I create the feeling in my brain of the hot water invigorating my tired body and the feeling of elation I'll have walking out of the gym. Most of the time that works (although not always).

That's how it is with visualization in the business environment. You may be sitting in a tiny office today, worrying about paying your credit card bills. But if you believe, and *can see yourself* years into the future, your dream can be fulfilled by your effort and determination. Living hand to mouth is only a temporary situation for the entrepreneur. It's a necessary stopping point on the way to success. But it's only temporary. Entrepreneuring is not easy. You'll get discouraged at times. The future may seem bleak. You will get tired of your tiny office and no one to answer your phone. But *never* let the image fade: the picture of you sitting in a fantastic office with sweeping views of the city, your car and driver waiting for you at the end of the day to whisk you to your beautiful country home—or whatever your particular dream may be. That picture, in and of itself, is what can keep your dreams alive.

Success Skill 8: Grit and Perseverance

The successful real estate entrepreneurs I've been close to all have great persistence. These men and women are tough, determined individuals. They understand

and appreciate the importance of grit and perseverance. As a young entrepreneur (in whatever business you may enter), *there are going to be setbacks*. And then more setbacks. And then a few more. If you do not have the stomach for failure and a heart to keep fighting, you may not make it as an entrepreneur, because if you want success you can NEVER, NEVER, NEVER QUIT.

Sometimes being in the business world is like a boxing match. You get knocked down. You get back up. You get knocked down again. You keep getting back up. Sooner or later you get in a punch. Or whoever or whatever is knocking you down gets tired of the fact that you keep bouncing up and stops hitting you. Sometimes the "winner" is the last person standing.

Many of the successful entrepreneurs I know have experienced tough times. In the late 1980s, for example, there were bank failures and overdevelopment and tax law changes, and as a result, in the early 1990s commercial real estate values fell—by as much as 50 percent in some areas of the country! One day you owned a building that you thought was worth $2 million with what you assumed was a conservative mortgage of $1.2 million, and then WHAM, your building was worth $1 million and you were underwater (when your property is worth less than the outstanding debt). Many of the top real estate entrepreneurs today are people who hung in there with these problems, working every day to do what they could to deal with valuation and cash flow problems, and lack of available financing.

During these years my real estate player friends and I would often quote Goethe: "What does not kill me makes me stronger." And I do believe that we got stronger. We toughened up. We continued to deal with the problems, not giving in. Today many of the people with whom I experienced these difficult times (and who, in some cases, were in real financial duress) are very wealthy. They showed true grit and perseverance.

I've thought a lot about perseverance, about the absolute refusal to give in to negative circumstances. I have no "magic bullet" advice for how to persevere in the face of a storm, but when I'm dealing with tough days or weeks, I develop a mantra that I say to myself every morning: "If I keep doing all the right things, don't change my patterns, and stay focused, the situation has to improve." And I go about my day, finding comfort in the familiarity of my routine—even when the rest of the world seems to be spinning against me. And, thank goodness, sooner or later things improve. Maybe this will work for you as well.

Success Skill 9: Running Scared

I just quoted the German philosopher, Johann Goethe. Maybe you can tell that I'm a big reader. I read everything I can, especially books or articles by or about successful people, thinking that just maybe I'll learn something that can help me be a better real estate entrepreneur.

Though I'm not sure why, I believe that many successful entrepreneurs lead their business lives running a little scared. Perhaps when you start life with little and then make a lot, you always carry with you a fear that someone or something is going to come along and take back all the cool stuff you've got. Perhaps you feel somehow unworthy. Perhaps this feeling of running scared is the residue of the disciplines struggling entrepreneurs live by.

In the many years I struggled, I set rules for myself. NEVER, NEVER, NEVER BE LAZY was one of the big ones. I would always try to go the extra mile in an effort to maximize the probability of my success. I was afraid that the one little thing that perhaps I did not do would be the difference between having a successful deal and an unsuccessful one. So I ingrained in myself the feeling that I needed to do everything possible, every single minute of every single day, to ensure my success.

Now, some people would say that today I'm past the point of having to run scared. But you know what? I don't feel that way. I still feel that I have to fight and struggle every single minute of the day. Perhaps this is healthy and perhaps not. At this point in my life I realize that it's just part of who I am and there's little that I can do about it.

My sense is that there are many wealthy entrepreneurs who have a similar attitude about business. Maybe that's how they stay wealthy or get even wealthier. All I know is that I know many rich people who are still running as hard as they can even though they have long since accumulated more money than they can spend in a lifetime.

Now I want to clarify something: I do not mean to suggest that running scared means becoming risk adverse or overly analytical to the point of indecision. A good entrepreneur has to be decisive: accumulating all the facts about a situation and then, looking into his or her gut, making a firm decision. Successful entrepreneurs realize that one can never identify all the twists and turns a deal will take, and that to attempt to do so is both a waste of time and a stumbling block to decisiveness. Rather, a good entrepreneur will have the confidence to know that he can deal with the inevitable curveballs almost any deal will throw at him. Since I quoted the German philosopher Goethe above, in the interest of balance, I will now quote two currently famous businessmen:

Mark Burnett came to the United States in 1982 with $600 in his pocket. Today he is a hugely successful television producer (*Survivor*, *The Apprentice*), and in his book *Jump In!* (Random House, 2005) he makes a good point about decisiveness: the "embodiment of a [my] business philosophy," he writes, "[is what] I simply call 'Jump In'":

It's about taking action. Nothing will ever be perfect, and nothing can be totally planned. The best you can hope for is to be half certain of your plan and know that you and the team you've assembled are willing to work hard enough to overcome the inevitable problems as they arrive . . . If you're passionate, committed, and willing to believe in yourself, anything is possible. It all starts when you take that half certainty, mix it with intuition, and Jump In.

Now words from Donald Trump (certainly one of the most visibly successful real estate businesspeople in the world today): *How to Get Rich* (Random House, 2004). I have never met Mr. Trump so I have no idea what he's like as a person, but I admire the deals he has done and the buildings he's built. Anyway, I read his books (looking for ideas), and the book referenced above includes some good advice for the real estate entrepreneur.

Trump says: "Every day is a reminder to me of how much I don't know . . . so every day becomes a new challenge . . . If I end the day without knowing more than I did when I woke up, it makes me wonder: What did I miss out on today?"

I think Trump's words are an important comment on decisiveness. Here's a guy who has been through a lot. He has bought and sold a ton of properties. He's built offices and residential buildings. He's faced bankruptcy. He has done just about everything in the real estate business. But somehow he learns new things all the time. And here's what that says to me: Although you can and must do a lot of homework before every deal, there will be events and issues that arise *that you did not anticipate*. BUT (and here's the key part) YOU CAN DEAL WITH THEM. Do not let the fear of the unexpected prevent you from going forward when you've prepared as much as possible and, based on all the facts you know, the investment appears fundamentally sound.

On the Subject of Risk

Before we leave the topic of "running scared" I want to spend a little time addressing risk. Obviously, any real estate entrepreneur must develop skills to analyze and live with risk. It is, pure and simple, part of the game. My observation is that young entrepreneurs can at times be overwhelmed by risk analysis. That's because risk analysis is part art and part science. The reality is, there's *no precise way* to quantify what can go wrong (or right). Once an entrepreneur has done all the homework he can, he must make a decision. Then not look back.

In performing risk analysis, we all (of course) try to analyze the probability of bad things happening. We tend not to think as much about unexpected good things that can happen. But as the following story highlights (you read about this deal in Chapter 10), sometimes everything just goes right.

Success Skills

My partner and I bought a building in Milford, Connecticut, that we parlayed into a nice profit. We were successful, in part, because we were able to buy wholesale and sell retail. But the story of this deal also illustrates something about risk: *Sometimes everything just goes right.*

The 200,000-square-foot distribution center we bought in Milford was owned by an institution. If you recall, we argued that the asking price of $7 million was too high because there were very few large tenants in the market. And we did some homework into the institution's reason for selling. We learned that it wanted to boost its second quarter figures and "book" a sale of this building by June 30. Since it was already May by the time the building got to the market, we knew the seller was under tremendous pressure to sell quickly.

As we always do, we did a lot of homework relative to the market (which, by the way, if you're diligent, you can do in about two weeks). We learned that there was no tenant demand in the 200,000 sf size range. But if the building were split into two 100,000 sf spaces, there was adequate tenant demand to justify our purchase.

There was an existing 200,000 sf tenant in the building with two years left on its lease. This tenant was paying a rent of $3.50/sf, or $700,000/year nnn (triple net). The tenant had made it clear that it would be leaving the building at the end of its Lease Term.

The asking price of $7 million for the building was essentially a 10 percent cap rate on the net income. We told the Seller that we would close by the end of June but would only pay $6.6 million. The Seller agreed.

At this point, having done many deals with local banks, we had a good reputation and were able to procure a 95 percent mortgage ($6.3 million). Although this loan had to be personally guaranteed (not all entrepreneurs would have done that—we certainly increased our risk by making that decision), we were able to buy this valuable property with only $300,000 in cash, and we closed on June 29.

We knew that the existing 200,000 sf tenant would be leaving in two years. We also knew that it was highly unlikely that we could find another tenant of this size and so we investigated breaking the building into two spaces (no genius IQ required to make that decision). We learned that at a cost of about $250,000 we could create a demising wall in the building, dividing it into two 100,000-square-foot units.

Hearing that the existing tenant might be interested in leaving the building early, I went to meet with the tenant's CFO and asked whether the tenant might want to buy out of the remaining two years of its Lease. After some conversation, here is the deal that was struck:

1. Tenant would vacate the entire building within 60 days but would continue paying half of the scheduled rent, so $350,000 per year.
2. Tenant would pay us $100,000 as a termination fee.
3. In the event that we leased all 200,000 square feet within the remaining lease term, we would terminate the remaining obligation on the Lease, the $350,000 per year.

And, as agreed, the tenant left the entire building and paid us $100,000. We immediately attempted to find a new tenant, and as we anticipated, there was interest from 100,000 sf users. A toy company was willing to pay $4.50/sf (nnn), but since we had not as yet demised the building into two sections, the rent was reduced to $4.10/sf (nnn) since this new tenant contended (and rightly so) that they would be heating all 200,000 sf of our building. Once the demising wall was in, however, the rent bumped up to $4.50/sf (nnn). So:

1. We now had a 100,000 sf tenant in a 200,000 sf building, paying us $4.10/sf (nnn) on 100,000 square feet.
2. The original tenant had vacated the entire building but was still paying us rent of $350,000 per year.
3. We started looking for a second 100,000 sf tenant, and we found one in a couple of months. They were willing to pay us $4/sf (nnn).
4. We signed a new lease with this second 100,000 sf user and the original tenant was now off the hook.
5. We completed the demising wall; it took us about 60 days and cost $250,000. Once this wall was completed, the rent our first tenant paid us increased to $4.50/sf (nnn).
6. The building was now once again fully leased and occupied (both Leases being 10-year terms) at an annual rent of $850,000 (nnn).
7. We decided to put the building on the market, and we closed about six months later for $10.2 million . . . a profit of $3.6 million in little more than a year.

What does this deal illustrate? Well, sometimes you just get lucky. As my partner said, "Everything went absolutely perfectly on this deal . . . this property was the baby that never cried." Could it have gone the other way? Absolutely. But here's how we analyzed the risk when we decided to buy:

1. We had done our homework; we knew there was tenant demand for 100,000 sf at rents of $3.50/sf (nnn) or higher.
2. We had two years to find tenants; the existing tenant was a good credit and it had two years to go on its Lease.
3. We suspected that the existing tenant wanted out immediately. This gave us the flexibility to look for tenants who wanted immediate occupancy.

4. The rental income from the existing tenant, $700,000/year (nnn), was much more than we needed to cover our debt service. Even at 95 percent financing, after debt service the rental income was yielding us $14,000/month of cash flow, or $168,000. We knew that we had two years of this income and therefore had a cash buffer of about $340,000 ($168,000 × 2).

5. We had staying power. We knew that if everything went wrong and we could not find a tenant, or tenants, for say two years after the existing tenant left the building (a total of four years!), we would still not be in financial distress. True, if the building stayed empty for another year or so after that, we were in trouble. But that seemed to us a very acceptable risk.

As you can see, everything worked out well for us on this deal. We were able to negotiate a favorable buyout with the existing tenant. We were able to find new tenants quickly. We were able to get a demising wall in place for our budgeted amount and to sell the building at a favorable cap rate. My point is that although you must always analyze your downside (i.e., your risk of loss), you cannot forget that just as bad things can happen, good things can too. In our Milford deal, at all the critical turning points good things happened and we were rewarded. That can happen to you as well.

Success Skill 10: Self-Improvement

I am a big believer in self-improvement. My belief is that each of us was born with certain talents and limitations. In my view, the goal in business (life?) is to maximize your talents and minimize your limitations. Before there can be self-improvement, however, there has to be self-analysis.

I'm not talking about in-depth psychoanalysis where a trained professional can perhaps help you get to the root of who you are. That is beyond my expertise. Rather, I'm referring to a periodic process of taking stock, looking hard into the mirror. What about you is holding you back? What is causing you to stumble and underperform? What is causing you to be less successful than you might be, given your particular talents?

At the risk of overexposure, I'll share with you a self-analysis I did years ago. It was the beginning of a new calendar year, and I made an assessment of my performance as a real estate entrepreneur in the previous year. Moves that I had taken and should not have. Moves that I did not make and should have. I found that the mistakes I'd made almost all fell into two categories:

- I acted *impulsively* in certain situations, moving too quickly on deals that needed more thought.
- In other situations, when a deal had a lot of moving parts, I was sluggish in pursuing it *because I was deterred by the complexity*.

Impulsiveness

For whatever reason, I tend to be impulsive, and in my self-analysis I thought of several instances in the prior year when a broker was walking me through a building that on first blush had all the elements of a good deal, and I shot from the hip.

Here's a typical dialogue:

ME: I like it. You'll have my offer in a couple of hours.

BROKER: Jim, I know this seller. If you're not close to the asking price, you're wasting your time.

ME: Don't worry . . . I will be at or very close to the asking price.

A stupid comment on my part. I could just as easily have said: "Well, give me the time to analyze the numbers." But in part because I was impulsive and in part because I did not want the broker calling another purchaser (I was trying to "freeze" the deal), I often committed to a super-quick turnaround and to a price that I had not yet analyzed.

Then, when I was reviewing the numbers of the property later in the day, I'd realize that it was overpriced or had some fundamental economic issue. I would then either retract my promise to make an offer or, equally bad, I would make an offer substantially below the asking price. That activity, repeated over a period of time, gave some brokers the impression that I was just a tire kicker, not really a purchaser . . . or that I was unpredictable and not reliable. I did not want either reputation, because one of the keys to success in the real estate game is to have brokers bringing you deals. (What you always want is "deal flow.")

And so when I gave myself my annual (introspective) physical, I had this conversation with myself:

Jim, you angered one or two good brokers last year. You told them you were going to make quick offers at or about the asking price and then you backed off that representation. You can't be doing that . . . you are too impulsive and it's hurting you. There's nothing wrong with telling people that you can't make an offer until you do your homework. If you're worried about someone else getting into the deal ahead of you, then (a) ask the broker if you can have 24 hours before he shows the deal to anyone else, and/or (b) do your homework quickly. But in any event, *stop acting impulsively!*

Fortunately, I had a receptive patient (me) and I worked to change my impulsiveness and in time was able to keep it in check. Today I am more deliberative and cool-headed in my approach to buying.

Deterred by the Complicated

Through self-analysis I also found that I was missing some good deals because my initial impression of the deal was that it was too complex. When I was looking at a deal that had too many moving parts, I was instinctively shying away, even though the deal might hold great potential if I had just been willing to wade in and take on the challenge of putting all the pieces of the puzzle together. That was a mistake I vowed to change. So I wrote myself a prescription:

> Okay, Jim, when you're facing a deal that seems very complicated, do not just run. Train your mind to analyze each piece of the deal. Force yourself to think the deal through, step by step. The journey of a thousand miles begins with a first step. Take a couple of steps into the deal and analyze what rewards it may hold. Stay with it . . . force yourself to keep an open mind.

And with time I learned that even the most complicated deal becomes much easier to understand and grapple with when broken into its basic pieces. That does not, of course, mean that the deal is necessarily worth doing. Each deal has to be analyzed on its own merits. But I had to (and I believe I have) overcome my knee-jerk reaction to shy from a deal that seemed too complicated for my mind to grasp on the first try.

We Are All a Work in Progress

You can do this same kind of self-analysis. Analyze deals you could have done and did not. Why? Were you too conservative? Too deliberative? Too slow to react? And analyze deals you did and should not have done. Why did you do what you did? Are there patterns? What can you do to make yourself more effective? Self-analysis is not an easy process. Sometimes the answer is obvious and sometimes not. But I believe that the process itself is important. It causes you to take stock. To examine YOU, INC. and see how its bottom line can be improved. That can't be a bad thing!

A top real estate broker in our area has an expression, "Beat yesterday." By that he means always keep trying to move forward and improve over what you did the day before. Each day is a building block for "YOU, INC." Do everything in your power to make "YOU, INC." the most effective, productive, and successful entity you can. And that means constant, unrelenting self-improvement.

Success Skill 11: Grace and Balance

I am about to get into some "touchy-feely" stuff. About personal qualities that I believe are important contributors to one's business and personal success. This section is about Grace and Balance. The following sections are about Karma and then about Integrity.

I struggle a bit to write about topics that are so subjective. Here is an analogy: Athletes make their living with their bodies and know that balance is a critical component of success in sports. We in the business world make our living predominantly with our minds, and yet, in my opinion, we too need to find a balance, a grace . . . a peacefulness. We need to find a place in the infinite levels of business where we are comfortable with ourselves.

On one level, Grace and Balance are easy to address. Here, I'm speaking about how you deal with and treat others in your business. Let me give you a few examples.

Be Respectful of Others' Time

One of my pet peeves is when other people in the deal process do not respect my time. Sometimes it occurs when I'm the lawyer, sometimes when I'm the principal. As an example, one thing that sets me off when I am lawyering a deal is when an overanxious broker will call me for an update on the signing of contracts. Here's the scenario:

> I'm in the middle of a fast-paced deal trying to consummate a long and involved contract negotiation and I am doing my best to get the contract signed. Lawyers are calling lawyers. Investors and lenders are lining up (or not). Documents are being e-mailed back and forth. The cell phone is constantly ringing with calls from someone needing some vital piece of information . . . and then the broker calls:
>
> BROKER: Hey, Jim, how you doing?
>
> ME: Fine, Joe, what's up?
>
> BROKER: Nothing, really, just kind of scoping around for an update on the deal.
>
> ME: Joe, everyone is doing the best they can to get it done . . . I'll let you know when there's some progress.
>
> BROKER: Well, what do you think? Can you give me any timing on when contracts will be signed?
>
> ME (GETTING ANGRY): No I can't, Joe. I'll call you with news when I have it.
>
> BROKER: Yes, I would appreciate that. But if you were to rate the likelihood of contracts getting signed on a scale of 1 to 10 . . .
>
> ME (ANGRY): Joe, it's obvious you have nothing to add at this point. I'm juggling 10 balls trying to get this deal done and I have no time to waste with you. [Hang up.]

Success Skills

Joe was not very smart. People are particularly busy and stressed in the middle of a deal negotiation, and as a broker, you should only call the lawyer or principal when you have some information that may be helpful. *Never* call just because you are curious or overanxious. Respect other people's time, and if you're bored or anxious, go for a walk. P.S.: Speaking of grace and balance, I could have been a little more gracious to the broker . . . but I forgot to tell you that this was the third time he had called in the last five days.

Everybody Has to Make Money

Sometimes entrepreneurs are portrayed as hard-charging, voracious individuals who leave no meat on the bone for anyone but themselves. That has not been my experience in the real estate world. Most of my successful entrepreneur friends understand a very important point: everyone has to eat.

One of the skills in the real estate world, in fact, is knowing how everyone earns their money, and then working to see that others have a payday, just as you want yours. Here's an example of how a client of mine (exemplifying grace and balance) won me over forever:

> I was acting as a broker for an out-of-state company that indicated it wanted to move into Fairfield County, Connecticut. It retained me to help with that move, and because the company seemed so clear on moving (and even exactly where in the county it wanted to move), I did not raise the issue of a "no go" fee (remember Chapter 13?). Silly me.
>
> Anyway, in the ensuing weeks I spent a lot of time showing executives of the company prospective spaces to lease. Then one day, to my surprise, the president of the company called me to indicate that he had changed his mind about moving:
>
> CLIENT: Jim, I'm really sorry to tell you this but as we were in the final stages of negotiating the Lease Agreement, we did a 180-degree turn and just decided not to move. It was not you or the landlord or the space, everything was as we had hoped. We just decided that a move was not the best thing for our business right now.
>
> ME (*TO MYSELF*): OUCH, why in the world didn't you ask for a "no go" fee?
>
> ME (*TO MY CLIENT*): Wow, Bill, I'm sorry to hear that, but that's how things go sometimes.
>
> Although I was of course upset and very disappointed, I stood by my rule to never burn a bridge and kept myself from saying anything accusatory. Little did I know that this principle would be rewarded so quickly:

249

Confessions of a Real Estate Entrepreneur

CLIENT: Jim, as you know, we are not real estate people and we certainly want to work with you in the future. We did not know the protocol for these situations and so we called another real estate brokerage company to get a better understanding of how you might be compensated for your efforts. We learned that there is something called a "no go" fee that you never asked us for. Perhaps that's because we were so certain about moving. Anyway, there's a check in the mail to you. We hope you will find it satisfactory.

ME: Thank you very much.

The president of the company showed graciousness. He knew I'd worked hard to find his company good space and to negotiate a favorable deal on his company's behalf. He appreciated my effort and expertise. He checked with another real estate brokerage company and confirmed what he thought: that with no lease, I would have no payday. Discovering that there was something called a "no go" fee, he decided to pay me one even though I had never brought it up. Needless to say, this individual has won me over forever, and I will double my efforts for them if or when they ever call again.

I try to operate in the same way my client did. When I'm in the middle of a deal, I try to understand how all the people in the deal get paid. I try not to overreach when I have the leverage. I try to see that everyone walking out of the closing room is happy and feels that they have been treated fairly by me. Sometimes it's impossible, but I try.

Play at the Risk Level Comfortable to You

One of my worries about this book is that I'll scare off individuals who want to invest in commercial real estate but who do not want to be thinking in terms of millions of dollars. People who are happy making an extra $20,000 or $30,000 a year doing real estate investing or brokering, for example. If you're one of those people, please know that this book is for you too.

Each of us has a particular risk quotient, that point beyond which risk— even if well thought out and quantified—is just not comfortable. This is not about whether you have a lot of money or not. It's more a factor of how much of what you do have you're willing to put on the line.

Some people can live with enormous risk, always playing at the edge, and if they lose it all, they figure they'll just start all over. I had that attitude early in my career since I had little to lose and I always figured I could somehow make a living. But as I started to accumulate stuff, I was less and less willing to "risk it all." I continued to take calculated risks, of course, but, over time, the percentage of my net worth that I was willing to put on the line in any one deal decreased.

There is no right and wrong when it comes to risk. You have to find your own comfort zone. If you're comfortable risking, say, up to 20 percent of your net worth on a potentially lucrative deal, that's great. Ten percent is great too. Or 5 percent. It's all about what you need to do to sleep at night.

Grace and Balance are all about how you want to play the game. There is no one right way. As an entrepreneur, you can find a place in the game that is right for you.

Success Skill 12: Karma

Karma may seem like a crazy topic to include in a discussion on the qualities needed for business success. But in my mind it's an important part of the process by which one achieves unusual success. Many successful entrepreneurs have struggled. Many started with little or no capital and not much of a safety net under them. And some may have scrimped to make ends meet, living from hand to mouth. Long hours and sleepness nights can give one a great sense of humility and an appreciation of the randomness of life.

An individual who has struggled his or her way to success appreciates what a beautiful gift life is. The opportunity to improve one's situation, based on hard work, is a blessing. Living in the United States, where any person can achieve great wealth and power, is a gift. Most entrepreneurs are very grateful for the lives they lead.

Any super-successful entrepreneur who has had long and difficult struggles, at times unsure of his ability to keep all the balls in the air, knows that life can take strange twists, and that but for a little bit of luck going his way, his life could have turned out much differently. These people realize that there can be a fine line between those who make it big and those who never make it at all. And so, many successful entrepreneurs feel an obligation to improve the lives of those less fortunate.

Hence, Karma—an individual's feeling that what one gets from life, one should give back to life. Treating people of all levels with courtesy and respect. Allocating a certain amount of one's time to charitable or civic causes. Giving constant thanks for all the blessings in one's life. In general, doing one's best to lead a good and generous life.

Here's what I believe:

Those who give to life, get back from life.

Call it Karma or whatever, but I have found that those who have a generosity of spirit in their approach to their fellow human beings are often rewarded many times over. I'm not suggesting that someone up above is keeping track and that if you do one good thing for another person, then the all-powerful will do something good for you. Though I do believe in Karma ("What goes around comes around"), I think that good things flow from the state of mind you bring to life. If you're thankful for all the good turns your life has taken . . . if you realize that things could have gone the other way . . . if you do your best to bring goodness to others, then I believe you will succeed because you have a successful state of mind. You are humble and lack any sense of entitlement. You work to achieve but you also work to be a good person. It may take time (years?), but sooner or later the world recognizes your goodness, people seek you out, and positive energy comes your way. This process is a huge component of business success and, of course, personal gratification.

Success Skill 13: Integrity

I know that some people believe that real estate players are unscrupulous wheeler-dealers. And some are. But I have observed this business for 25 years now, and in my judgment those who survive over the long term are, for the most part, highly honorable people. For those of you who are new to the business world, let me tell you now that "the world can be a very small place." If you act unethically toward another person, that action or inaction can come back to bite you many times over, and in ways you may never anticipate. If you think you're immune to payback, you are not. If you think that the person you hurt is too small to ever make your life miserable, you're wrong.

But Integrity is about more than avoiding trouble from people you may hurt. It is about more than being honorable, so you have a reputation for Integrity (though such a reputation will in fact help you in business). It is about doing and being righteous for the sake of righteousness. Fifteen years ago I made a big mistake in this regard:

> My company was handling properties, both management and brokerage, for lending institutions that had foreclosed and taken over properties they had no expertise to handle. One day a broker called to let me know about an opportunity to work for a company that had just foreclosed on a building in Fairfield, Connecticut. He said he wanted to recommend my company to manage the building (collect the rents, handle the book-keeping, pay the expenses, and deal with tenant complaints) but that he wanted to get the brokerage assignment if and when the insurance company decided to put the building on the market. Our conversation went like this:

BROKER: Jim, I have a relationship with the people at this insurance company and I would like to recommend you for the management, but since you also do brokerage, I want your word that you will not solicit the brokerage assignment should the insurance company decide at some point in the future to sell the building.

ME: You have my word.

And the broker did his part and our company got the management assignment. Over time, as usually happens if you're doing a good job for someone, my company's relationship with the insurance company grew and the person in charge of this account approached me and asked me to handle the sale of the building. I said that I could not do that since I'd gotten this business because of a referral from another broker. I indicated that they should hire him.

The representative from the insurance company got upset with me. She said that business shouldn't work that way and that she should have the right to hire anyone she wanted, and what's more, that there were synergies with the management company also handling the sale.

I relented, sold the building, and made a nice commission. I went to the broker who had gotten me the assignment and offered him a part of the commission, telling him that I had no choice in doing what I'd done since otherwise we might have lost the account. He did not want to hear it. He reminded me that I had given him my word (and I had) and then broke it. For many years our relationship was never the same, though I have worked hard at trying to rehabilitate it. Finally, I feel we're back to where it was.

Here's the point: I screwed up. Once you give your word, whatever the circumstances may be at a later date, honor it. It might surprise you to know that even as I write this book, 15 years after the above incident, I wince when I think of what I did. In part because I want to have a sterling reputation for always keeping my word. But mostly because I feel personally lousy about breaking a promise. The commission I made on the sale of the building has long since been spent and forgotten. But I will never forget the look on the broker's face when I told him that I'd sold the building.

From that date to this minute I have observed a firm rule: no matter what, once I give my word, I'm going to keep it. And by the way, I have made some pretty stupid mistakes since then—making promises or commitments that I should not have—but at least I always kept my word. As one of my friends says, "You have to cash the checks you write with your mouth."

I believe that most successful entrepreneurs live by the credo that there is "no right way to do the wrong thing." Not that entrepreneurs are saints by any stretch.

Confessions of a Real Estate Entrepreneur

I just think that most entrepreneurs who have made it big have a strong sense of right and wrong. They realize that the value of money diminishes with each incremental dollar you make. They realize that your reputation is paramount. They understand that how you feel about yourself is as (more?) important than additional material wealth. Maybe I'm wrong about this—maybe most real estate entrepreneurs are not such lofty individuals—but this is what I choose to believe.

In conclusion, I think there is such a thing as right and wrong, that some areas are clearly black or white. People who don't want to live in the white area always seem to define everything as gray, and I think that's wrong. Lying is wrong. Cheating is wrong. Breaking your word is wrong. And so on.

Business is just a subset of life. If you have an attitude that leads you to always strive to do the right thing, you find good in situations and in people. Your creative juices will not be stymied by negativism or thoughts of wrongdoing. Your optimism about life and its opportunities will be heightened by your own sense of fairness. You will succeed in life because you see life in its purest form: a venue for growth and purity. Successful entrepreneurs are generally upbeat, optimistic people . . . seeing good in the world when at times it is very cloudy. This spirit of goodness leads them to take on risk when more negative people might not. So for what it's worth, in my view:

> The people who succeed in life have a strong sense of right and wrong and always do their best to travel on the right side of the road.

Conclusion

I do not believe that success is an accident. Nor do I believe that success is a set equation where you can put in a little of this and a pinch of that and, BA-BOOM, big money. What I do believe is that there are commonalities among successful people. Of course, there are no guarantees in life, but my premise is that if you lead your business life according to certain precepts, you greatly increase the probability of achieving a successful result.

Each of us has certain talents that can lead us to financial success. We need to maximize the use of those talents. Each of us can also be better at some things. We need to identify those weaknesses and work on them. This chapter on Success Skills is just one person's attempt at identifying and writing about what I have seen work. There are other books you can read. You can watch what successful people do. No reason to reinvent the wheel: watch and emulate.

</>

21

Conclusion

Real estate entrepreneuring has been great to me. Yes, there have been days when I would rather have had a real job with a steady paycheck, but in truth, over the last 25 years I've had very few of those days. Most of the time the business has been exciting, challenging, invigorating, and rewarding. The money is nice, of course, but that's only part of the fun. Dealing with people of all types, income levels, educations, and differing commitments to integrity has been a daily challenge. Figuring out how to acquire a property and add value to it, and then *actually* making it happen as you planned . . . wow, that's really great.

I hope that I've inspired you to consider trying your hand at real estate entrepreneuring. If you do decide to get involved, you should of course have your eyes open. Don't assume that the people you'll be dealing with are any less smart or knowledgeable than you are. In fact, it's better to assume that they're smarter. And don't assume that if you're honorable, all the other players in the game are similarly honorable. As I friend of mine once said: "People have to be careful not to confuse the familiar with the universal." In other words, some of the players you meet may not have read my section on Integrity.

Don't take risk lightly . . . but don't be afraid of risk either. Work hard to understand the risks of the deals you're considering and how you can quantify and minimize them. Don't be impatient . . . all good things are worth waiting for, and one way to get into trouble in the real estate game is by rushing headlong into a deal just to be in a deal. Take your time, do your homework. Always ask yourself: "Is the risk worth the potential reward?"

Don't take your successes for granted. Continue to work at your profession at all times. Network with everyone you can. Read and learn as much as you can about successful deals and entrepreneurs. Somebody smart is always thinking up new concepts and approaches to making money with real estate. If you're clever, you don't need to come up with the idea . . . look at what someone else did and copy it.

Don't ever get a big head and think you are too smart, or clever, or well-capitalized to get hurt. Wake up every morning with the mindset that you'll do everything in your power to move your business life forward because if you're not moving forward, you're moving backward. As a successful entrepreneur I know (who has more money than he could ever spend) says: "I wake up every day thinking that I have zero in the bank and that I'd better figure out a way to make some money that day or I may not eat."

Finally, treat your profession with respect and grace. I believe that those of us in the real estate world who have done well should help others get started and improve their business lives. Offer to help those working their way up the ladder. Bring a generosity of spirit to your life and do what you can to honor our profession by sharing your knowledge and rewards with those less fortunate.

So off you go . . . Here's hoping for your great success. Hopefully, I'll hear from some of you about your successful deals, and maybe in another 20 years I'll write another book about what we learned together.

Index

Index

Index

Index

Index

Index

About the Author

James A. Randel is a real estate attorney, broker, and investor. He has more than 25 years of experience investing in both residential and commercial real estate. He has been a featured commentator on television and has spoken at national real estate conferences around the United States. He is a longtime advocate of the "Added Value" theory of investing.